ONE WORLD, MANY WORLDS

Explorations in Peace and Justice:
New Perspectives on World Order

GENERAL EDITORS

Elise Boulding
Richard Falk
Samuel S. Kim
Saul H. Mendlovitz
R. B. J. Walker

ONE WORLD, MANY WORLDS
STRUGGLES FOR A JUST WORLD PEACE

R. B. J. WALKER

LYNNE RIENNER PUBLISHERS • BOULDER, COLORADO
ZED BOOKS LIMITED • LONDON, ENGLAND

Published in the United States of America in 1988 by
Lynne Rienner Publishers, Inc.
948 North Street, Boulder, Colorado 80302

Published in the United Kingdom in 1988 by
Zed Books Limited
57 Caledonian Road
London N1 9BU England

Library of Congress Cataloging-in-Publication Data
 Walker, R. B. J.
  One world, many worlds: struggles for a just world peace / by
 R. B. J. Walker.
   p. cm. — (Explorations in peace and justice)
  Bibliography: p.
  ISBN 1-55587-108-9 (lib. bdg.)   ISBN 1-55587-109-7 (pbk.)
  1. Peace. 2. Peace—Societies, etc. I. Title. II. Series.
JX1952.W245 1988   87-30414
327.1′72—dc19   CIP

British Library Cataloguing in Publication Data
 Walker, R. B. J.
  One world, many worlds: struggles for a just world peace.
  1. Special Movements
  I. Title
  303.4′84

  ISBN 0-86232-774-1
  ISBN 0-86232-775-X   Pbk

Printed and bound in the United States of America

The paper used in this publication meets
the requirements of the American National
Standard for Permanence of Paper for
Printed Library Materials Z39.48-1984.

Contents

Foreword

We seem to be entering a twilight zone in the history of human consciousness—marked both by accelerating threats to human diversity and survival, and by new assertions of the human spirit from a variety of vantage points. Theoretical assumptions and categories through which human reality has been comprehended and shaped with such confidence have not only become obsolete, but have become stumbling blocks in any attempt to restructure our world. The project of history making on a global scale through a universalist theory of human evolution has come to an end. There is no longer any great optimism about our future prospects.

Against this scenario of the end of universalist history, deep stirrings of people's awareness, assertions of diverse cultures, struggles for justice and dignity, and movements for peace, human rights, and alternative development are making themselves felt in a variety of local and regional settings. This book has grown out of an exploration by the Committee for a Just World Peace of the hopes and potential that are now visible in these different circumstances. But, as the book carefully points out, these stirrings, struggles, and movements neither emanate from nor add up to a coherent alternative in the form of a new historical project toward a more acceptable and desirable future—and meanwhile, the old guard is refining its armory of control and domination. It is showing rare sophistication in hijacking the language and rhetoric—sustainable development, people's participation, empowering the grassroots—and the specific demands and organizational forms—decentralization, alternative technologies, an increasing role for nongovernmental organizations—that have become associated with voices of dissent and challenge. Through all these attempts at cooptation, as well as the use of state repression and militarized terror, the status quo is mounting a substantial backlash on its own behalf and for continuing its old project.

Expressed bluntly, this old project involves integrating the world's political and economic elites in a framework of interdependence, by excluding all those that do not "fit," treating them (several hundred million people) as unwanted and dispensable—indeed, as standing in the way of a prosperous and secure world order. These "misfits" include not just the traditional poor and marginal populations but also a growing number of women of all classes, ethnic communities, and people displaced and rendered shelterless and illiterate by the rapacious march of modern technology.

This *generalized* project of exclusion, dispensability, and triage has led me for some time now to conceptualize the age we are moving into in terms of a fundamental dualism in the human condition, of a growing convergence between various divides, of the rise of not one, not many, but two worlds. This is manifest in a variety of dimensions: the economic dimension, in which the effort to integrate the whole world into a single market excludes large masses of human beings from the productive process; the social dimension, in which the homogenizing thrust of building national and international "security" leaves out a large number of minorities and ethnic communities; and the dimensions of gender and age, in which women and children of all classes are being marginalized by the sweep of modern technology. Moreover, two components of any humanist vision—nature and future, both of which have for long been thought critical—are now increasingly exploited in the interests of fulfilling the here-and-now needs of personal consumption, economic competition, military security, and cultural hegemony by increasingly exclusivist elites. These elites have themselves become nonproductive, insecure, and increasingly reliant on technological fixes to deal with what are at bottom political problems. Ecocide, ethnocide, militarization of cultural life, and a sharp decline in the naturalist-feminist values of nurturance and concern for the whole and for the future are all manifestations of a world that is increasingly divided between those with access to history and those thrown in its dustbin.

Such a system, built on hegemonic drives and exclusivist structures, though motivated by growing concerns at various levels for ensuring stability and security—in place of earlier concerns for progress and prosperity—is turning out to be unstable and unworkable. Responses tend to be ad hoc and driven by panic. We see growing state repression in diverse social settings; chauvinistic appeals directed not only against an external "enemy," but against internal minorities, the poorer classes, and the intellectuals; militarist notions not just of national security, but the security of ruling coteries, and even single individuals; and economic structures living on borrowed time and resources.

It is against this undesirable and unworkable structure of interests, confrontations, exclusions, and annihilations that what this book calls *critical social movements* are struggling. They are struggling against very heavy odds. They do encompass large segments of the human population—the peasantry, the poor, the ethnics, the women—but this is not a game of numbers. Indeed, the numbers game is conducted in ways (electoral machines, the information juggernaut, the ideology of threats against the state) that are pitched against the human majority.

There is a powerful logic to the dualist paradigm of contemporary world development. To challenge it calls not for an alternative paradigm, as suggested in all the talk of a "paradigm shift," but for a rejection of universalist paradigms as a way of comprehending and managing human affairs.

This understanding—that the reality of two worlds is a direct consequence of the paradigm of "one world"—is only beginning to register in the more sensitive minds that (while fully identifying themselves with critical social movements) refuse to be numbed or outsmarted by the confusions, enticements, and doublespeak mounted by the global thinktanks.

This book makes it clear that only by furthering this understanding and by exercising extreme vigilance against exclusion, privilege, and dispensability can the potential optimism visible in the struggles of critical social movements—sketched here so well through a wealth of analytical categories and heuristic concepts—make sense. Without such care and circumspection, and determined interventions based on them, even attempts such as this to identify some of the most hopeful practices of the present could relapse into yet another form of utopian theorizing.

Rajni Kothari

Preface

The main themes that have guided this book have emerged directly from meetings of the Committee for a Just World Peace as a whole in Lisbon, Paris, Frankfurt, and Yokohama from the spring of 1985 to the winter of 1986. They have been refined through more informal meetings, conversations, and correspondences. As rapporteur of the committee, my primary debts are to those who have participated in its deliberations.

Working with the committee has been an enormously stimulating experience. It has also made it especially clear to me just how difficult it is to write about peace, justice, and political practice in a manner that responds to dynamics under way in all parts of the world at the same time. So much is going on in the modern world. The committee's discussions have been correspondingly rich and comprehensive. They have also made me increasingly wary of introducing prematurely rigid classifications of different types of social movements, let alone of trying to root the analysis in any single theoretical tradition. Anyone working in the area of rethinking political life outside of the conventional state boundaries is necessarily caught up in the tension between the rich vocabularies available to discuss life within particular communities and the near silence that is heard once one tries to ask questions about how to respond to problems of peace and justice in an increasingly interconnected world.

Rather than offer a complete report of the committee's work, this book has been written as an interpretation of the committee's overall understanding of the potential of critical social movements at this historical juncture. I have tried to express the committee's sense of the often latent cultural and political discontent in many parts of the world that, although largely ignored by the more entrenched political actors, is now being touched by critical social movements. An indication of some of the thinking behind this interpretation is contained in a previously published volume of essays presented to the committee, *Towards a Just World Peace: Perspectives from Social Movements,* edited by Saul Mendlovitz and myself.

This book inevitably reflects my own judgments about how the different positions expressed within the committee fit together. Inevitably, some themes and perspectives have been stressed more than others. Thus the work is intended to be part, and only part, of an ongoing process through which the committee has been trying both to clarify for itself the practices and aspirations that can now be pursued with reasonable conviction by those active within critical social movements and to affirm its support for others struggling elsewhere. Group discussion suggested new questions and new formulations, and the book was constructed through a sequence of drafts developing a number of themes and formulations for discussion and clarification by the committee. It is thus the product of a long process, a conversation aimed at clarifying what, from all those ideas now circulating about issues of peace and justice, makes sense from the point of view of the experiences of those on the committee.

Those who are familiar with the earlier work of the World Order Models Project (WOMP) of the 1970s will find many of its concerns reappearing here in a new way. In fact, the essay may be read in part as an ongoing dialogue with Saul Mendlovitz and, particularly, with his insistence on the need to think in terms of an emerging global civilization. The continuing influences of Richard Falk and Rajni Kothari are also easily visible throughout.

Despite many critics' complaint that WOMP was merely a utopian project closely allied to Western universalist notions about world federalism or world government, its real force involved an ongoing dialogue about the relationship between universalist-globalist and pluralist-nationalist responses to international problems. This dialogue occurred at a time when discussion of politics in general and international affairs in particular was dominated by the inflated methodological pretensions of U.S. social science and influenced by the way scholars sought to become policy advisers to princes. In this context, groups like WOMP, journals like *Alternatives,* as well as the work of peace researchers and alternative development groups, provided some of the few spaces in which fundamental questions about the interconnected and global character of contemporary human life could be raised in a critical manner at all.

Many of the directions taken in this book reflect the current state of debates that have emerged from this growing transnational research community over the past two decades. These debates have challenged entrenched assumptions guiding conventional thinking about international law and institutions. They show that although political thought and action has for so long been restricted to questions of state, any serious politics must now engage with the determinations and opportunities that arise from emerging global processes. The world is changing rapidly. Neither nostalgia for a world of autonomous states nor models of a centralized world order nurtured by cold war and the ambitions of superpowers and corporations are likely to provide the necessary vision for the world coming into being. To engage in a serious politics now is to discover the need to go beyond the categories beloved by self-proclaimed realists and utopians alike.

Much broader influences are also at work in the way the committee's discussions are reflected here. Many of the ideas expressed are very much in the air, so to speak. They can be found in the broad literatures on concrete problems of peace and development. They infuse some of the most abstract theoretical debate in contemporary sociopolitical theory and philosophy. Many of these ideas will already be well known to people active in critical social movements. I have simply tried to put them together in one place in an accessible, and perhaps provocative, manner. In doing so, I have drawn on my own specialized research both on the political theory of international relations and on contemporary theories of culture and ideology. I have also drawn on the judgments of friends outside the committee who have been actively concerned with social movements. I am particularly indebted to Lester Ruiz and D. L. Sheth of *Alternatives,* to Bradley Klein, and to those individuals with whom I have worked in the Committee on Alternatives for British Columbia, especially Warren Magnusson.

Many of the issues raised in this book are clearly subject to different evaluations, whether on the basis of urgent political interventions or more speculative generalizations. My intention has not been to close off such different evaluations. On the contrary, I have tried to develop the work in a way that creates additional space in which to engage with some exceptionally difficult and urgent problems and in which to encourage serious political practices rooted in the conviction that transformation is already occurring.

This book is thus conceived as a stage of a conversation still very much in process, a preface to work still under way. It should be read as a rather long question about the extent to which this way of interpreting the possibilities of the present does or does not resonate with what people think they are doing in sharply divergent situations. It is offered now in the hope that the conversation might be taken up by those who, whatever their different experiences, share similar commitments and aspirations.

R. B. J. Walker

CHAPTER ONE

Introduction

BOTH DANGERS AND OPPORTUNITIES

This is widely seen as a time of great danger, of looming cataclysms and barbaric injustices. For all the achievements and resources of the modern world, many people feel powerless in the face of huge forces beyond their control. These forces bring violence into the everyday lives of millions.

Some speak of crisis, using the language of apocalypse. Some speak of readjustment, using the language of moderation. A few—the powerful and privileged—still claim to have everything under control. Encouraging signs of optimism are visible in some regions and with respect to some major problems, but people in most societies seem to share a deep uncertainty about the future. For some, uncertainty has become a guiding star.

Such a sense of generalized crisis is obviously not new. Human experience has always been difficult, for some more than for others, for individuals and for societies. Yet, despite the temptation to exaggerate the importance or novelty of our own age, it is impossible to ignore the contemporary feelings of flux and uncertainty. Trajectories are unclear, even confused and contradictory. Ingrained expectations constantly give way to anxious premonitions. A sense of danger merges with a consciousness that we are all living through a period of profound change. For many, the problems are immediate and desperate.

It is easy enough to be overwhelmed by the demands of our contemporary predicament. Even large societies and states now find they have very little room in which to maneuver. Existing institutions seem overburdened with intractable problems. They seem particularly helpless in the face of a general drift toward militarization, environmental degradation, and a widening gulf between rich and poor. The great progressive and revolutionary doctrines of liberalism, socialism, and nationalism, which have had such an impact on what we have now become, have lost much of their vitality. The dreams of past eras, now translated into languages of expertise, power, and common sense, throw only a deceptive light on the possibilities ahead. Meanwhile, much of the space available for creative rethinking is blocked by fundamentalist self-righteousness and terrorist attempts to force a violent breakthrough. Skepticism about the future finds ample supporting evidence. Individuals may feel utterly powerless.

Skepticism is certainly understandable. In an era of rapid change, it is especially important to exercise a controlled suspicion of inherited traditions and grandiose predictions. It is unwise to trust those who proclaim a clear view of the way ahead. But skepticism often slides into cynicism, into resigned acquiescence or the pursuit of shameless self-interest.

Cynicism, despair, and disillusionment are not the only options we have, in spite of all the evident grounds for skepticism. Such responses only serve to amplify existing dangers. Our age remains one of unparalleled opportunities. In fact, more hopeful processes are already under way. Individuals have discovered they can make a difference. Movements of people have been able to resist the worst abuses and articulate new directions. Creative energies remain alive in the modern world.

This book has grown out of an exploration and interpretation of these energies by the Committee for a Just World Peace. Recognizing both the plausibility of skepticism and the dangers of despair, the committee seeks to identify and encourage the processes and initiatives that now seem to offer grounds for optimism. Its particular concern is to examine our contemporary trajectories from the point of view of critical social movements. Whereas most analyses of the challenges of the modern age examine what might be done by the most powerful established actors—by states, political parties, government policy makers, revolutionary mass movements, and international institutions—the committee has been more interested in the practices and visions emerging from such movements in response to immediate problems.

Whatever else is going on in the modern world, the most pressing problems on the political agenda arise from or are intensified by the increasingly global scale of the processes that now shape human activity everywhere. And whatever else is going on among states, political parties, policy makers, mass movements, or international institutions, some of the most interesting and hopeful political processes are now to be found among these critical social movements. These movements are difficult to analyze in a rigorous manner. They defy many of our conventional understandings of what politics is about. It is even more difficult to judge their long-term potential. But at this historical juncture, critical social movements have undoubtedly become vital centers of political creativity. In this book, I argue that these movements are now particularly important sources of insight into the nature and possibilities of a just world peace.

THE COMMITTEE FOR A JUST WORLD PEACE

The Committee for a Just World Peace is only one of many groups trying to make sense of the opportunities and practices that can be expected to encourage less violent and more cooperative ways of organizing human affairs in a world of global structures and responsibilities. It is made up of concerned individuals who have been engaged in specific struggles for peace and justice in different regions, responding to different pressures and aspirations.

Some have brought to the committee their experiences of the political practices in which they are engaged on an almost full-time basis. Some have had the opportunity of being in contact with many different struggles as a result of their participation in both formal international nongovernmental organizations and more informal networks. Some have brought a more academic background to bear on questions about contemporary political practice. Drawing on different experiences and analytical perspectives, the committee is motivated by the conviction that it is now essential to engage in dialogue with people who, although sharing a general concern for the achievement of less violence and greater justice everywhere, understand what a just world peace might mean in the context of different concrete settings.

At the center of the committee's concerns has been the way more and more people, particularly those who are active in critical social movements, are developing a clearer idea of where, amid all the struggles and setbacks, new openings may be discovered and created. In circumstances that seem far removed from each other, sometimes quietly and sometimes in ways that attract world headlines, people act in these openings and find new ways of acting together.

Although difficult to define, critical social movements movements are distinguishable in part by their capacity to recognize and act creatively upon connections among structures, processes, and peoples that do not enter significantly into the calculations of conventional political actors or that are denied by movements of a more reactionary character. Recognizing connections, critical social movements are able to engage not only in struggles around specific problems but also in struggles that recognize the emancipatory potential inherent in certain kinds of connections and solidarities. Acting on such connections and forging new solidarities, critical social movements have the capacity to extend the horizons of our political imagination. Reacting to the intolerable, they extend the boundaries of the possible.

On this basis, people have been able to articulate new understandings of what it means to work for a world free from excesses of violence, poverty, and repression, despite the injustices of the present. They have found new creative energies on the basis of both highly specific forms of social and political struggle and more abstract, even spiritual, explorations. They have engaged in new forms of solidarity between peoples despite very real differences between them. They have begun to envision the broad outlines of what a just world peace might mean in an age that is conscious both of the structural dynamics that link so many people together and the diversity of experiences and interests of people living in sharply contrasting predicaments.

The Committee for a Just World Peace has been particularly interested in the way the term "peace" means quite different things to people living in different circumstances. Indeed, it is becoming increasingly apparent that the search for a less violent and less unjust world must be accompanied by a greater sensitivity to the difficulty of defining peace at all.

Peace is neither a technical policy problem nor an easy utopian aspiration. It is not something to be negotiated between diplomats or between superpowers. It is not the same as just stopping the development of especially nasty weapons. It is certainly not to be confused with the imposition of "order" on those who scream at intolerable conditions. A just world peace must be a project of major historical transformations. It is a challenge both to prevailing structures of power and to our understanding of how people ought to live together. Nor is it a project within the grasp of any single society. Global structures and responsibilities are now inescapable facts of modern life. They impose the broad conditions under which struggles for a just world peace are possible.

Far from being a marginal activity pursued by pacifists and utopians, or something that can safely be left to national leaders and strategists, thinking about peace must now engage some of our most fundamental assumptions about what it means to be human and how we ought to act toward each other. It must involve a serious rethinking of what is meant, for example, by "security," "development," and "democracy." Above all, the process of working toward a just world peace involves a struggle to articulate new conceptions of what it can now mean to have solidarity with other human beings.

We all live on the basis of solidarities with particular groups of people—family, friends, neighborhood, class, gender, ethnic groups, and so on. The character of most of these solidarities varies from society to society. But the primary form of political solidarity almost everywhere is now the state. It is a form that has been established on the basis of complex historical processes, not to mention considerable human misery. As an historically specific political form, the state is characterized, above all, by the celebration of solidarities within territorial boundaries and the minimization of solidarities beyond them. Despite the way solidarity within states is undermined in practice by regional, cultural, and class conflict, as well as by the way particular state institutions are organized, contemporary political life is informed by deeply entrenched patterns of territorial inclusion and exclusion, of community within and anarchy without. Our dominant understandings of what it means to live together—of society, community, and polity—refer to particular groups of people, not to people as inhabitants of one fragile biosphere.

Many philosophical and ethical traditions have postulated ideas about universal species identity and solidarity in the abstract. The gulf between such abstractions and contemporary political practices is obviously very large, not least because conceptions of universality emerging from the most powerful societies find great resistance among societies reluctant to live by the rules of the most powerful. Whatever it may come to mean to say that one has solidarity with all human beings as such, such solidarity will be something that will have to be achieved through concrete human practices, not something formulated abstractly.

These practices will have to involve connections between the experiences of people living in different circumstances. They will have to explore richer understandings of what it means to be secure, or to develop as human beings, or to participate in public life. They will have to respond to forces at least as complex as those that have put the state at the center of contemporary political life. They will have to struggle for a just world peace as an ongoing process, not as a condition that can be specified clearly in advance.

Reflecting these concerns, this book begins by stressing the diversity of historical experiences on the basis of which different peoples interpret and respond to emerging global structures and processes. If global struggles are inescapable, and if a just world peace must therefore be a struggle for One World, it must also be remembered that both present structures and future aspirations are encountered and articulated on the basis of many different experiences, many different histories. The pursuit of a just world peace and new forms of solidarity must be rooted in an equal respect for the claims of both diversity and unity. One World must also be Many Worlds.

On this basis the book will proceed to look briefly at the most significant modern global structures and processes and to examine the way that critical social movements respond to a world that is increasingly interconnected. Attention then shifts to an examination of such movements and the way they have begun to generate new and potentially very creative forms of political action.

Acting in specific situations of suffering and injustice, yet also finding themselves engaged in struggles of connection and imagination, critical social movements are forced to rethink what it now means to engage in political practice in a world of rapid and confusing transformations. Although critical social movements are easily interpreted as marginal and weak, this capacity to engage simultaneously in specific struggles but also to connect with other struggles and to envision alternative possibilities makes such movements especially important for thinking about the future. It enables them to challenge the constitutive principles of the existing order, to struggle for new forms of human community, and to articulate new visions of peace and justice.

It is not that social movements are about to seize power. Indeed, in this book I argue that to think in such terms at all is to try to force contemporary transformations into the ossified images of old revolutions. Movements are significant not because of their overt power in the present but because they carry the seeds of new understandings of what it means to be secure, to develop as a person or community, to participate together in a democratic fashion. Only with a clearer sense of what it means to have security for all people rather than the national security that now renders everyone increasingly insecure; only with an empowering development for all rather than the maldevelopment of both rich and poor; only with more effective processes of democratization everywhere rather than self-perpetuating structures of domination, bureaucratization, and exclusion; and only with a clearer sense of how all these fit together, can a just world peace cease to be a utopian dream and become an ongoing process to which ordinary people with the most meager resources may contribute wherever they are.

INTERPRETATION AND POLITICAL PRACTICE

I am less concerned with giving a full descriptive account of particular critical social movements than with drawing out what they share in common. Different readers will be familiar with different movements and situations and should be able to assess and add to what is being said here in the light of their own specific experiences. The degree of abstraction necessary to an exploration of this kind does not lessen the appreciation of the struggles of very real people in often appalling situations.

Partly because the Committee for a Just World Peace has been concerned with understanding the different conceptions of peace and justice held by movements in various parts of the world, and partly because it is concerned with political practices that are still being shaped and invented, I also adopt in this book a primarily interpretive stance, one less concerned with the causal explanation of the processes that bring violence into the lives of millions of people than with the interpretation of the way people respond to these processes.

Enquiry into human affairs, like all scientific enquiry, depends on a capacity to ask the right questions. This is sometimes forgotten by those who equate scientific analysis with the mechanical application of supposedly objective research techniques. I suggest that many of the most crucial questions are being asked and explored by critical social movements. To try to understand these questions is necessarily to follow an alternative critical logic.

Moreover, enquiry into human affairs, unlike enquiry in the sciences of inert matter on which our dominant images of legitimate knowledge have come to be based, depends in large part on a capacity to interpret the meanings, values, and aspirations that guide the way people act. Historical change is both reflected in and affected by the way people grope for new meanings, new languages, new ways of interpreting their place in the world. A clearer articulation of the most pressing questions of the age can arise from listening carefully to the meanings, values, and aspirations that guide contemporary movements struggling to reconstruct the world in which they live. In this sense, critical social movements discover in practice what many scholars and academics discover more theoretically: The conventional categories of understanding seem out of joint with the times. For scholars and activists alike, it has become necessary to refuse received conceptual boundaries, to search for new forms of understanding, and to develop a clearer sense of the complex relationships between theory and practice, knowing and being.

I do not claim in this book to give a conclusive insight into the major problems of the age. Nor do I have any straightforward answers to the perennial question, "What is to be done?" Indeed, I argue that answers to this question formulated as blueprints for the future, are inherently undesirable. A just world peace must grow out of the ongoing practices of people everywhere, not be molded by those who claim to have a god's-eye view of what is going on. It is sometimes important to resist the inevitable demand for hard-nosed, concrete solutions to particular problems. Credibility in contemporary political debate too often depends on a willingness to present policy options that might be carried out by existing governments and institutions.

It is not that policy options are unavailable. On the contrary, whether about more-sensible arms control procedures, removing the burden of international debt, restructuring international trade or commodity pricing arrangements, and so on, policies that would undoubtedly improve the lot of millions of people are regularly aired in reports, international gatherings, and the more-serious news media. Although many such proposals deserve widespread support, the transformations necessary for a just world peace cannot come from government policies alone, no matter how enlightened these governments may be.

Under present circumstances the question "What is to be done?" invites a degree of arrogance that is all too visible in the behavior of the dominant political forces of our time. It is an arrogance that is inconsistent with the kind of empirical evidence we have before us. This evidence requires a willingness to face up to the uncertainties of the age, not with the demand for instant solutions, but with a more modest openness to the potentials inherent in what is already going on.

The most pressing questions of the age call not only for concrete policy options to be offered to existing elites and institutions but also, and more crucially, for a serious rethinking of the ways in which it is possible for human beings to live together. The call for a just world peace must be also a call for the reconstruction of political life. In this book I suggest that important insights into this deeper process are emerging from practices that are now under way. These insights make it possible to formulate responses to questions about what must be done without capitulating to the illusion—so often dressed up in the pretentious and dangerous claim to realism—that our future lies in the hands of existing elites alone.

I do not presume to tell movements what they should be doing. Nor do I presume to speak on their behalf. I would, rather, affirm the importance of critical social movements at this historical juncture.

Critical social movements may be more or less invisible to those trained in the conventional categories of social analysis or mesmerized by the dominant mass media. They may appear to be only marginal and relatively powerless actors. I argue that it is more plausible to understand them as part of a transformative assault on our inherited notions of authority, legitimacy, and power. They can be understood as part of a broad process of social invention that carries the possibility of reconstructing the conditions for a decent life from the bottom up, without waiting for elites to become enlightened or replaced by still more elites. Critical social movements are important not because they have the immediate capacity to induce existing elites to pursue more enlightened policies but because they participate in a more far-reaching reinvention of political life.

To affirm this view of critical social movements is to assume that six things are possible in a book of this kind:

To begin with, it is possible to show how specific social movements participate in broader patterns of struggle on a worldwide basis. It is certainly important to understand the concrete reality of people suffering in specific traps. Movements act out of immediate necessity. People's experiences in particular situations are quite different. To generalize about them is possibly to violate the integrity of the experiences themselves. But the traps people find themselves in are very often linked to wider menaces, such as militarization or international debt. Although particular movements may act in highly specific locations, they in fact respond to processes that are anything but highly specific. So it is also important to show that no matter how isolated they may feel, particular movements are not alone.

Second, it is possible to reflect on the similarities between the way movements act in different circumstances in order to understand the possibilities that are now being articulated by critical social movements in general. This theme is pursued in terms of the way movements act within new political spaces, discover new ways of acting politically, extend the horizons of what we think it is possible to be as human beings, and establish connections with each other.

Third, it is possible to pursue some of the implications of the ongoing practices of movements for thinking creatively about emerging forms of human solidarity. The traditional statist principle of inclusion and exclusion, of friend and foe, of national community and international anarchy is less and less plausible, despite the rhetoric of those who depend on an enemy "other" to legitimize their own claims to power. Moreover, a solidarity based on the capacity of the workers of the world to unite against capitalism has so far failed to materialize. This does remain a world of both particular political communities and class conflicts. But it is certainly not clear that images of human solidarity rooted in historically and culturally specific experiences of state and class are helpful guides for the future. The practices of critical social movements suggest alternative possibilities.

Fourth, it is possible to extend this analysis to the reconceptualization of a number of important ideas that have come to be considered central to thinking about peace, particularly the dominant concepts of security, development, and democracy. To do so is to take the symbolic function of movements very seriously indeed. Movements act in a world that is moving faster than our concepts and language can adequately comprehend. Peace, for example, is conventionally understood as the opposite of war. Critical social movements increasingly see peace as the opposite of injustice. On the one hand, such movements are able to clarify what remains hidden behind the jargon and clichés of official rhetoric and everyday discourse. On the other, they point to new ways of understanding and expressing the changing dynamics of a world in transition. They demonstrate the necessity and potential of enhancing processes of democratization everywhere.

Fifth, it is possible to express a solidarity not only with those with whom members of the Committee for a Just World Peace are directly involved as individuals but also with those who struggle for similar things under different circumstances.

Sixth, it is possible to speculate in general terms on the concrete practices of critical social movements that might further enhance the prospects for a just world peace.

These possibilities may not add up to a resounding manifesto addressed to the waiting masses, nor to a policy agenda addressed to those closest to state power, nor even to a glorious utopian scheme addressed to the nascent visionary in all of us—some may judge this a sign of weakness. But it is increasingly apparent that such images of the relationship between political analysis and political practice are deeply at odds with the understandings of politics that are emerging from critical social movements themselves. These new understandings are important. What seems inevitable turns out to be merely contingent. What seems strong and unapproachable is, in fact, quite brittle. People discover that they are not powerless in the face of daunting problems but are capable of making enormous advances in the immediate situation in which they live, work, love, and play.

Taken together, these six possibilities amount to different ways of trying to make space for movements. They reflect a willingness to listen, to interpret what is heard, and to recommend—tentatively—on the basis of the interpretation. They suggest ways in which ordinary people can participate in the process of working toward a just world peace in their own everyday lives. They give an emerging sense of coherence to the forces now struggling for expression. They lead to different ways of asking questions about what can and ought to be done.

In short, this book participates in an ongoing politics of interpretation. It grows out of a recognition that the categories and languages in which it is now possible to speak about global problems and political practices incorporate historically specific interests. Although there is no shortage of information about the state of the modern world, it is exceptionally difficult to turn this information into liberating human practices. Information is created largely by elites and for elites. Dominant forms of knowledge and information presume some things are important whereas others are less so. Knowledge and power are intimately associated.

Emerging social and political forces have always had to challenge prevailing categories and interpretations. Such challenges have become especially important in the modern world. Dominant categories are constantly reinforced, not only through overt propaganda and the mass media, but also through pervasive myths about science and progress and sophisticated claims to expertise and legitimacy. It is extremely difficult for emerging social and political forces to put what they are doing into any clear perspective or to see themselves as participating in anything of wider significance.

My concern, therefore, is to sketch an interpretation of processes that seem most important from the perspectives of critical social movements. I seek to affirm that what *people* are doing, often in extreme difficulty and with little clear understanding of how what they are doing resonates with what is going on elsewhere, constitutes a source of considerable hope in the modern world. This is not to say that states, or elites, or political parties, or other more-established political actors are not also doing interesting and hopeful things. But their interpretations of contemporary trajectories are already deeply instilled in us all. There are other voices to be heard. These voices are nurtured in uncertainty and danger. But they aspire to an openness and vision that is blocked by the dominant forces of our time. To engage in struggles for a just world peace in the late twentieth century is to understand that these voices are becoming more and more insistent, more and more aware of how to break through the routines and dogmas that keep us as we are.

CHAPTER TWO

Histories

TRANSFORMATIONS

Some five hundred years ago, great civilizations flourished in China, India, Latin America, Africa, the Islamic world, and elsewhere. At that time, most societies considered themselves to be at the center of the universe. Very few people knew that the earth was a sphere or that other complex societies were spread throughout its apparently vast space. Solidarity and common identity were confined to one's own group, either in a familial, clan, or blood line and/or in a territorially organized polity. Since that time, the world population has increased eightfold, and by the end of this century—barring any major catastrophe—it will have increased twelvefold, to about 6 billion people. This population remains divided in many ways—by state, class, ethnicity, race, gender, and ideology. But it is involved in material and communications processes that are organized on a worldwide basis.

The origins of these processes are conventionally traced back to the transition from feudalism to capitalism and to the emergence of the states system in early modern Europe. This transition has had such profound consequences almost everywhere that it almost monopolizes our modern historical consciousness. It can easily appear as the only point of origin, the beginning of all modern chronologies, the ground on which to demarcate between ancient and modern, primitive and civilized, developing and developed. From other points of view, of course, the transition is only a brief episode in a longer story and part of one story among many. Even so, it remains a crucial episode, one that we have all heard in some version no matter how much it is possible to quarrel with the editing and credits.

The accelerations of the past half-century have led many people to speculate that current transformations are comparable in their significance with that earlier transition. There is even some reason to believe the development of complex global structures implies changes as profound as those that occurred when hunting bands moved into agricultural and urban settings some five to ten thousand years ago. To the extent that such historical analogies are helpful in understanding where we are now, it is important to remember just how little we still know about why or how such major transformations occurred. But it is still useful to think about the way new opportunities were opened up by wholesale changes in the fundamental conditions of human existence.

11

Perhaps the most familiar accounts of the transformations of the modern age focus on spectacular innovations in technology. The conditions of human existence—the way we produce, distribute, and consume things; communicate with one another; alter our biological systems; construct systems of social, political, and even psychological control; or threaten to exterminate ourselves—are all undergoing fundamental changes involving new technologies.

New technologies do not appear out of thin air. They arise from complex social processes. Technological changes may be the most spectacular indicator of contemporary trends, but they arise from and contribute to even more fundamental transformations in economic, political, and cultural life.

Contemporary innovations make it clearer than ever that the world in which we struggle is not simply given—by God or by Nature—but is made by people. It may be that in the end the world must be understood as somehow natural, whether in a secular or a sacred manner. It may even be that the categories of nature and history, nature and nurture, matter and spirit, are not so mutually exclusive as the modern world has come to suppose. We nevertheless live in ways that depend on the accumulated achievements of human beings who have now been engaged in remaking the world for a fairly long time.

Although a sense of the historical significance of the present moment may be common among intellectuals and privileged elites, for many, if not most, people everyday life goes on in a rather familiar fashion. Not everyone is consciously touched by modern technologies. Contemporary global structures often involve connections between the elites of particular societies rather than between those societies as a whole. Messages and currencies flash between the world's capitals and economic centers, but millions remain oblivious to anything beyond the immediate place where they were born.

Furthermore, although it is easy enough to see some of the objective factors that tie so many parts of the world together—trade, communications satellites, wide-bodied jets in international terminals, and grey men from international banks—there is scarcely any real sense of what these things mean for people's loyalties or aspirations. We undoubtedly live in a global "system"; but few people feel or act as if they live in a global "community." Indeed, it is not at all clear what a global community could or should look like.

The transformative quality of the modern world is at once evident to many people in many places and also maddeningly elusive. We can be certain only that things will not remain the same. The status quo cannot hold, despite the claims of those who now benefit from it.

CHALLENGES

The uncertainties of this age of rapid change are experienced initially in the form of concrete problems: poverty and inequality, war and violence, environmental degradation and technological disasters, cultures of alienation and routines of abuse. They are documented in the nearest newspaper or the latest commission report. For mainstream political actors everywhere, these concrete problems appear as short-term projects to be managed or avoided. For others, such problems appear as symptoms of more far-reaching processes, as evidence of a world both in need of and in the process of long-term transformation.

A crisis of manageability is now evident in most societies. Serious doubts are expressed even from conservative quarters about the capacity of existing authorities and institutions to cope with the stresses and strains visible in the major structures that shape the modern world.

Despite signs of considerable progress toward the reduction of nuclear weapons in Europe, the militarization of all aspects of human affairs continues apace. Progress on managing the weapons of war may even mask the insidious insertion of military production into everyday processes of "peace." In economic life, powerful states have found it difficult to exercise control over their own economies, given the changing configuration of the world market and the international division of labor. The scale and mobility of capital and of transnational corporations make claims to economic sovereignty increasingly hollow, especially for smaller states. By virtue of their participation in global economic structures, states are more and more likely to enhance rather than reduce inequality and violence within their borders. In cultural affairs, too, it is no longer clear that the convergence of nationalist aspirations with the territorial instrumentalities of the state is an adequate way of articulating the great variety of cultural identities—religious, ethnic, local, and regional—now struggling for expression. Moreover, whether in terms of political, economic, or cultural problems, necessities of management are invoked to legitimize even more authoritarian and manipulative forms of government.

Concerns about the management of the existing order merge with concerns about the consequences of new forces remaking the world in unforeseen ways. It is in this context that new technologies are invoked most insistently. Whether as weapons or as communications satellites and microchips, many new technologies have the capacity to fundamentally alter the nature of human interaction. With the increasingly capital-intensive nature of modern production processes and the global flexibility of capital flows, economic life is being transformed more rapidly than most economists, let alone ordinary people, can properly comprehend. With the manipulation of genetic codes, people have the capacity to intervene in their own biological, evolution. With new weapons—nuclear, biological, and chemical—as well as more effective means of delivery, people have the capacity to put an end to evolution once and for all.

These new technologies express very complex social forces. They are especially significant for the way they enter into structures and processes that are organized on a global basis rather than within a territorial state. It is not possible to make much sense of the processes that now bring war, poverty, repression, environmental decay, rapid population growth, and so on, without a grasp of how they are structured globally. These processes certainly create problems of manageability for existing political structures. But more significant, it is not at all clear just how far these processes are compatible with existing political practices and jurisdictions. In a world in which political life is dominated by the state, yet many of the most important forces that affect peoples lives are often effectively beyond state control, problems of management can seem less important than the need for new categories of political analysis, new forms of social community, new forms of human solidarity and group identity.

Problems of management and the emergence of new forces converge to create a widespread sense of the bankruptcy of prevailing ideas about what is to be done. The extraordinary appeal of fundamentalisms of one kind or another is particularly telling in this context. Change brings uncertainty, and uncertainty invites a leap into the known or, at least, what is assumed to be known—a religious text, a romanticized dream of an earlier and simpler age, a source of authority that can justify the assertion of order, not to mention the iron fist. The specific character and causes of fundamentalism undoubtedly vary from society to society, but its presence across different societies is striking. It is paralleled by widespread skepticism about the great ideologies that arose in nineteenth-century Europe and have subsequently informed political life almost everywhere. There is even widespread skepticism about the value of any imaginative or utopian aspirations for the future.

There is obviously no shortage of people who, following their fundamentalist convictions or assuming that what has worked before will work again, know exactly where they are going and are all too likely to insist that everyone follow them. For those who remain unconvinced about the "magic of the market," the reliability of space-based defense systems, or the blueprints for "development" imposed by international financial institutions, the contemporary human predicament appears increasingly precarious. Insecurity and survival have become pressing issues even in societies that have become used to material comfort and political stability. The extent to which poverty and abuse continue in a world of plenty, and particularly in a world that prides itself on its advanced civilizational values, is a moral scandal of the very highest order. Fundamentalists and technocrats aside, few people are clear about what is to be done.

The challenges before us may be framed in terms of short-term problems requiring action by existing political authorities as well as of deeper patterns of historical and structural transformation. These challenges lead to another concern: To whom or what does this "us" refer? Who can and ought to respond to these challenges? To draw attention to concrete problems is also to raise very difficult questions about the nature of political life in a world of global structures and fading ideologies.

The state itself is especially problematic in this respect. The state, it must be remembered, is an historical creation. Forms of state vary enormously. In some parts of the world, state institutions continue to monopolize political life. In others, it is necessary to understand the relationship between state and civil society. The formal sovereignty of some states masks the reality of control by other states or transnational enterprises. In others, it masks the complexity of cultural and ethnic divisions. Such variations make it especially difficult to generalize about political life in the modern world on a comparative basis.

Even so, as complex historical creations, all states are subject to continuing change. The conditions under which the state became the primary focus of political life in Europe some centuries ago have been transformed. So have the conditions under which so many states attained formal sovereignty through decolonization in the middle of this century.

Since the 1970s, many analysts have spoken of an emerging crisis in the legitimacy of the state. Some examine the way that so many governments are caught between the extravagance of the claims necessary to maintain legitimacy and the limited options available for their realization. Others are led to observe that states are extremely reluctant to do much about environmental degradation or mass poverty beyond—and often within—their borders. Still others point to the way states claim to be able to ensure security for their citizens while becoming ever more deeply entrenched in worldwide patterns of militarization that induce greater and greater insecurity for everyone.

None of this analysis suggests that the state is in the process of withering away. Most conventional analysts still expect the state to adapt fairly well to new conditions. States engage in a search for better forms of accommodation and agreement. They advocate more effective arms control procedures and the nonproliferation of nuclear weapons. They push for new trade agreements, attempt to prevent the collapse of international financial institutions, look for a more effective niche within the new international division of labor, and promote ways of exercising control over the worldwide flows of capital. There are also indications that states have become stronger, more forceful in asserting their sovereignty, often more forthright in exercising their monopoly over the legitimate use of violence. Even so, the resort to force is often an indication of weakness rather than of strength. It is not always true that where there is a will there is a way.

In any case, the real concern is less the capacity of states to manage the world's problems than the kind of societies that are now possible within states. States do have some capacity to manage, but this capacity often comes at enormous cost. Most states invoke the name of democracy, but most states are characterized by the assertion of authority from above, whether through overt physical force or through cultural and social processes that encourage the manufacture of consent. In materially affluent societies, democracy is often reduced to a commercial pageant. In societies that act in the name of the universal proletariat, democracy has been largely reduced to bureaucracy and state planning. In societies in which the state has been the agent of postcolonial emancipation, the state has frequently been the instrument of middle-class corruption and of violence toward its own people. The universal appeal to democracy occurs in a world of military dictatorships, apartheid, bureaucracies, image consultants, and effective rule by more powerful states. Ordinary people everywhere are left frustrated, isolated, and helpless. In practice, democracy has often become less a process of participation than a systematic structure of exclusion.

Skepticism is most intense toward the state simply because of the historical legacy of the state's claim to the legitimate exercise of power and violence. But the forms taken by most modern social and political institutions—political parties, trade unions, churches, military organizations—are also increasingly subject to intense criticism for being out of touch with rapidly changing circumstances.

Again, this criticism can focus on short-term instrumental concerns about manageability. Here the voices of reaction are often very loud. Trade unions, for example, are everywhere subject to intense attack from entrenched elites and international capital as hindrances to more effective "national" participation in the world economy. The more important forms of critique, however, focus less on problems of instrumental management or efficiency as defined by elites than on the way existing institutions participate in reproducing structures of violence and injustice. The lack of democracy in the modern world is certainly not restricted to the institutions of state. It is no less characteristic of cultural, educational, social, and economic processes.

Confronted with the challenges of the modern age, many people and institutions work very hard to clarify the alternatives. The reports issued under the names of Willy Brandt, Olaf Palme, and Gro Harlem Brundtland are indicative of a wide range of efforts to suggest sensible responses to problems that are obviously beyond the capacity of individual governments. The ignored calls for a New International Economic Order in the mid-1970s exemplify attempts by the most disadvantaged societies to improve their positions through very modest changes in the prevailing economic structures. International organizations both within and outside the United Nations system have created an indispensable source of knowledge about human affairs on a comparative international basis. Whether in terms of human rights, depletion of the ozone layer, destruction of the world's forests, the plight of the world's children, famine in Sub-Saharan Africa, or the oppression of particular peoples, the modern intellectual landscape is full of attempts to articulate more coherent policy directions on the basis of some kind of broad global perspective.

From what has been said so far, however, it should be clear that the demand for more coherent policy proposals is not enough. The challenges before us require more radical changes in the way human affairs are conducted. Some people argue that the state itself is obsolete. Some point their fingers at the states system or global capitalism. They seek ways of abolishing these in favor of economic and political forms that are more rational and humane, forms designed to grow out of more cooperative capabilities rather than reinforce nastier competitive instincts. Others call for modes of knowledge and consciousness that avoid the parochial, atomistic, and instrumental assumptions that have become so influential everywhere.

More coherent policies are certainly needed. So are fundamental changes in the political, economic, and cultural structures in which we live. But beyond the strengths and weaknesses of any particular set of recommendations lie some difficult matters of judgment. For it is far from clear on what grounds it is now possible even to think about either policies or more radical change.

We have become used to expecting state elites to put better policies into effect; but, in fact, they don't, either because they cannot or because they have little wish to. It may be possible to introduce greater coherence into the states system or the world economy; but if our major problems arise directly from these very large structures, a mere tinkering with them seems insufficient.

On the other hand, there are no alternative authorities to which it is possible to appeal. Multinational corporations may have both an international perspective and a global reach, but they can hardly be said to be acting in the interests of everyone living on the planet. International organizations remain very weak, and those that have some power are largely the captives of states. Cosmopolitan philosophies, religions, and ideologies have emerged from many different cultures, but none has yet been able to translate its cosmopolitan pretense into unchallenged legitimacy everywhere. Indeed, cosmopolitan pretense is more likely to be interpreted as imperialist intent.

In fact, it is no longer clear to whom ideas about short term policy and particularly about long-term political and economic changes ought to be addressed. A clearer account of how to respond to the challenges before us, or even what these challenges are exactly, requires a clearer sense of the relationship between concrete problems, the forces that are transforming the conditions of modern human existence, the fading of dominant ideologies, and the emergence of new political energies. This uncertainty about who ought to be doing what ought to be done is what now makes questions about history so important. And questions about history cannot be separated from questions about where we think we are going.

EMERGING SCENARIOS

Looking very selectively, some people now claim to see emerging signs of a sense of renewed optimism about the future. Some have begun to suggest that the dangers that loomed so ominously over the past decade or so are now receding. The world economy, it is said, has achieved a certain buoyancy, despite the collapse of stock markets and worries about the U.S. deficit. Some national economies, or, more accurately, some sectors of those economies, are even thriving. There is occasional talk about the eventual resolution of the debt crisis. Brutal dictatorships have been challenged, especially in Latin America, the Philippines, and South Korea. Some countries have begun to curb their worst environmental abuses. There are even occasional glimpses of sensible behavior in superpower relations, although only rarely on the part of both at the same time. The openings initiated by Gorbachev have been especially encouraging as a sign that significant breakthroughs are possible on some of the most pressing issues of our time.

There are obviously also many reasons to remain skeptical. To look at the nearest newspaper or commission report is to understand that any claims about the present potential for optimism—even where these claims have considerable substance—must be highly qualified. This is so whether we reflect on, for example, arms control, international debt, or environmental abuse. It is perhaps even more so if one takes into account the way that many of the greatest achievements of the modern world have come at very high cost.

Moreover, we are going through a period in which some of these achievements are being rolled back. The onslaught against the social structures of the welfare state in Western Europe and North America is a case in point. The ideologues of the so-called New Right, who have been able to take the political offensive in these societies during the present phase of the transformation of the world economy, have succeeded in resurrecting "survival of the fittest" as a respectable social ethic. Similarly, the great achievements of national independence have been undermined in some places by intensifying relations of dependency and geopolitical penetration.

It is especially important to think very carefully and critically about the grounds on which any renewed sense of optimism should be based. It is not simply that, by measuring selectively, it may be shown that conditions have improved, at least for some. People have also been raising the standards against which human achievements are to be judged. To the extent that we have "progressed," we are able to expect more of the structures that have been created and to be more critical of the barbarities that remain.

In this context, it is instructive to consider the extent to which thinking about the future has come to depend on a particular set of geographical or spatial categories. Over the past twenty-five years, we have become used to thinking in terms of First World, Second World, and Third World. The directions of the compass—East and West, North and South—now serve as a complex analytical framework, distinguishing the presumed fate of those "out there," somewhere else, from those in one's own part of the world. These divisions have become an essential part both of "common sense" and popular rhetoric as well as of more sophisticated renderings of how the world is currently ordered and what it might become.

However, an alternative rendering of the primary divisions of modern political life is now emerging from the reflections of a great number of social movements. This rendering focuses less on the directions of the compass than on the forces experienced by people as inhabitants of a single planet, as well as on the forces that are now creating new patterns of economic, social, cultural, and territorial inclusion and exclusion. These forces are increasingly obscured by the conventional geographical categories.

On the one hand, there are forecasts of general global catastrophe. In its most popular form, this "No World" scenario stresses the likelihood of a general nuclear war. Variations on the theme point to fundamental social forces that, whether through a reliance on ecologically destructive practices or through the encouragement of militarization and institutionalized violence, threaten to bring about a general civilizational collapse.

On the other hand, there are forecasts of an intensification of insecurity for some people in particular. This can be called the "Two Worlds" scenario. It predicts solutions to the problems of our age—but only for some people. It comes with a widely advertised tale of progress and an unadvertised tale of woe. This scenario promises greater international order through better management of the states system; but "order" is then interpreted by the dominant powers and has little to do with changing the underlying social, economic, political, and cultural processes that are leading to a greater resort to military force. In this sense, order is not the same as peace, still less as justice. It simply implies a different kind of violence.

It promises economic recovery and technological miracles; but only for those who are able to participate in the world economy—not for the redundant, the unemployed, the marginalized; and especially not for those premodern indigenous peoples who seem to be the most profound casualties of new technologies. Economic recovery is not the same as better economic times ahead for all; it implies the emergence of two worlds on one planet.

It promises better management of environmental resources, but not beyond limits prescribed by profitability. Those who depend on a close symbiosis with their environment will still be vulnerable to the conflict between profit and conservation, and the broader pleas for a greater ecological sensitivity will be unheard.

It promises a reduction in the abuse of human rights, but only as defined in the narrowest terms. In any case, it also implies the elaboration of new forms of social injustice, as with the extension of the category of "terrorist" to cover the protests of the excluded.

It promises a happier, more meaningful existence for all, but only through the commodification of desire.

This scenario has a less dramatic edge than the first, but is perhaps more plausible. There is no doubt that it is possible to read a number of current trends as signs of improvement and progress, but there are few who would claim that these signs apply generally rather than to particular groups.

Each of these two scenarios comes in stronger and weaker versions. The Two World scenario may appear as an account of intensifying inequalities between people and of the "disappearing middle class"; or it may appear as an account of the way in which some people are effectively becoming dispensable. The archetype of inequality is the relationship between master and slave. But at least the master needed the slave. Now, in some parts of the world, increasing numbers of people seem to be irrelevant to the societies in which they live. Botshabelo, for example, is the second largest black settlement in South Africa after Soweto, with a population of half a million people largely forced off the land by the mechanization of agriculture, but it doesn't even appear on the tour maps. Like the underside of cities, like the unemployed, like whole regions, indeed, in the case of Africa, like whole continents, the marginalized and vulnerable are becoming invisible, superfluous, dispensable. The specific case of South African apartheid, like the plight of the Palestinians, has become a generalized symbol of the world in which we all live.

Similarly, the No World scenario may appear as the obliteration of life on earth or just the disappearance of life as recognizably human. Thus, in addition to predictions of nuclear war or ecological collapse, some analyses portray a generalized drift toward authoritarian forms of politics everywhere, as states struggle to maintain control of the uncontrollable. Analysts point to the further reduction of human existence to instrumental means turned into ends, to processes of cultural homogenization, and to the channeling of fundamental economic and political conflicts into ethnic and racial violence. They stress how we all increasingly feel the pressure of insecurities that used to be felt mainly by specific classes and groups: the extension of instrumental rationality; the authoritarian state; the dispersed nature of power so that powerlessness cannot be attributed to any fundamental causal mechanism; the tendency for social or economic conflicts to shift onto new dimensions of privilege and deprivation creating vulnerabilities in new social sectors with great rapidity. Political manipulation enters ever more insidiously into the general production of cultural meaning through new technologies, especially those of the mass media, medicine, psychiatry, and so on.

These may be only scenarios, but they are by no means easily dismissed. They capture the worries of many scholarly analysts and political activists. And they certainly seem to capture the empirical dynamics of the modern world more accurately than the simplistic spatial distinctions between East and West, North and South. They recognize, for example, that the south exists in the north as well as the other way around.

It is particularly troubling that the conventional political imagination is limited largely to the terrain defined by these two scenarios. The No World scenario has become the broad context in which major problems are specified. It lurks in the background, informing the rhetoric of even the most hardened politician. The Two World scenario, on the other hand, has come to infuse the formulation of solutions. Mainstream politics claims that major improvements can be made or that a certain degree of sanity can be restored to major global structures. But the unwritten context of such claims is a tacit and cynical acceptance that such solutions are available only to some and not to others, "trickle-down" theories notwithstanding.

In fact, the choice between No World and Two Worlds is, for the overwhelming majority of humanity, no choice at all.

HISTORY AND HISTORIES

Even for those who are acutely sensitive to the dynamic quality of the modern world, it is not easy to see where we are or where we are going. To gain perspective, we may try to stand back from the swirl of current events, to fix them within the broader patterns of human endeavor painstakingly sketched by historians. History may encourage more sober reflection. It can turn vertigo into the commonplace. It can provide meanings, a sense of origin, direction, possibilities, purpose. Drawing on the language of necessity, it can even show us what must be done. But drawing on the language of accident and contingency, it may also answer questions about where we are now with a resounding silence.

The flows of history are always difficult to grasp, not least because history is something that people make, not something we can stand back from and observe with clinical detachment. Furthermore, periods of rapid change always induce apprehension. And apprehension not only encourages attempts to maintain order, permanence, and privilege amid impending chaos, but also attempts to capture the rush of events within familiar categories.

It has now become particularly difficult to understand the flux of the contemporary world through a quick glance at what we are leaving behind. Our received histories have themselves begun to absorb the uncertainties of the modern age. Historians still teach, but they are ever more reluctant to give lessons. We may have much to learn from the past, but the past seems to reflect back to us many of our contemporary anxieties. Two grand themes are particularly important in this respect: the wholesale challenge to the vision of progress and development that, explicitly or implicitly, guides so much of the modern historical imagination; and the simple but crucial question "Whose history?"

The exhilarating dream of progress and freedom bequeathed by eighteenth- and nineteenth-century Europe is certainly still alive in some places. Many of the most optimistic visions of that era have been realized—at least for some people. Measuring according to statistics from the World Bank or the United Nations, we may become convinced of the unprecedented accumulation of material wealth, increased longevity, or higher rates of literacy in the world as a whole. Measuring in units of technological innovation, we become aware of the ingenuity of human endeavor and the speed of modern social transformations.

Such dreams can still provide a cocoon from which to view the modern world, to judge its successes and failures, to prescribe its future possibilities. Yet only those who have lost all critical judgment or speak from isolated privilege still confuse such dreams, or even their corroborating evidence, with present realities.

The history of this century cannot be written as a simple tale of progress. Through wars and exterminations, by *dictat* and administration, in poverty and in alienation, this has also been an age of dark shadows. Measured by the excluded, the marginalized, and the oppressed, the dream of progress is a cruel jest. Far from seeing the final transition from barbarism to reason, those living in this century have been witnesses to the capacity of human beings to engage in barbarism in the name of reason itself.

The question "Whose history?" is even more pressing but raises similar difficulties. Once there were histories. Societies claimed origins, articulated myths and lineages, understood themselves as continuous in time. Histories were local, plural, integral to the experience of particular cultures.

With the rise of capitalism in Europe came History: History as a powerful myth obscuring a very complex array of social transformations. Although it is true that the consequences of these transformations have now been felt almost everywhere, the dominant accounts of them have been written by those who gained the most.

The emergence of capitalism remains central to an understanding of where we are now. Historians and social theorists still seek explanations of the specific factors that led to the rapid development of feudalism and then capitalism in Europe, the consequent expansion of capitalism to the global arena, and the relations that were then established between Europe and other economic, political, and cultural systems.

This experience has dominated modern historical scholarship and informs most of our theories of politics, economy, and society. Different explanations have referred to the presumed drives of rational economic man, the expansion of productive forces bursting through outmoded social relations, and the march of increasing rationalization in all realms of social existence. Students of this experience have remained divided about the relative importance of factors arising within particular states—such as the expansion of market relations and urban centers, the disintegration of feudal structures, the development of wage labor, and so on—and from the relationships established between states, both within Europe and as a result of mercantilist and colonialist expansion elsewhere.

Differences among these competing explanations are in some respects less significant than the common search for an underlying logic that would tie the many facets of this transition together. This is partly what has made the work of Karl Marx and Max Weber so influential. Their insights into the universalizing character of capitalism, whether rooted in an account of capitalism as a specific mode of production or in a less economistically conceived process of rationalization, remain indispensable.

Yet alongside this search for an underlying logic to the rise of capitalism, and sometimes converging dangerously with it, has been a simpler tale of "progress," an ethnocentric celebration of both the power and the civilizational pretensions of the West. With its echoes of Judeo-Christian ideas about time, and an ethnocentric arrogance absorbed from nineteenth-century evolutionism, this History continues to impose its unilinear view of where we have come from and where we are going. Societies are envisaged on a grand trek from barbarism and primitive tradition to civilization and modernity. "Development" and "modernization" have become states of national desire.

In some ways, this History has been no more arrogant or ethnocentric than histories constructed by other powerful cultures. It has always aroused suspicion in terms of its empirical accuracy. Even on its home ground, the claim that the future could be projected from an accelerating curve of inevitable progress seemed at odds with observable extremes of poverty and violence. Both Marx and Weber exhibit a deep ambivalence about a progress that comes at the cost of massive brutalization, alienation, or a bureau-cratized world devoid of meaning. Yet, to consult the developmental economists, or the wizards of technological advance, to engage in debates about foreign aid and "trickle-down," to look at school textbooks or Holly-wood movies is to know that the myth of History remains alive and well. It informs the language and common sense in which the complex trajectories of the modern world are most easily fixed in the imagination and subjected to government policies. For most of humanity, however, even for many in the West, this History remains alien. As a view from the center, it exudes power.

In fact, the more it is studied, the more even the rise of/domination by the West refuses to fit into any easy progressive patterns of History. The in-sights of Marx and Weber have now been absorbed, but they are usually qualified by an emphasis on accidental factors of geography, specific and un-repeatable convergences, and the plurality of transitions. Many ideas now associated with the West have clearly been derived from other cultures. The dominant position of the West within the increasingly global structures of capitalism has depended on processes of production, surplus-extraction, and coercion that are worldwide. History is being challenged by histories that put the European age into a broader context.

Now, it seems, we are besieged by histories. The myths of History may still beguile, but, as a particular construction of the past, it is itself becoming an historical artifact. There may be a clear sense that the rise of capitalism has brought all societies into active participation in one another's affairs. There may also be an emerging sense of both our interconnectedness and shared vulnerability to the dangers of the modern world. But this intercon-nectedness and this vulnerability are interpreted in different ways and on the basis of distinct historical experiences. If one part of the problem in try-ing to establish some perspective on contemporary events is that we might once again be seduced by the evolutionary myths of progress and develop-ment, the other is that we might be overwhelmed by the cacophony of voices now trying to make themselves heard.

The call for a just world peace rests on a shared sense that this is a crucial historical moment. It also rests on a recognition that, in trying to interpret the dangers and opportunities of the modern world, it is necessary to listen carefully to the way that people in diverse circumstances struggle with these dangers and opportunities on the basis of quite different historical experiences.

Once one is prepared to listen, the multiple voices of the oppressed can be heard most insistently. They are recorded by journalists and by novelists, by statisticians and by poets. A lot is now known about the world made by the industrial working-class and the world made by slaves. The recovery and reconstruction of working-class history has long been vital to labor movements everywhere. The recovery of precolonial history, as well as the portrayal of colonial relationships from the viewpoint of the colonized, has been central to movements of national liberation and independence. These histories have already made their mark. More recently, the recovery of women's histories, the emerging consciousness of the commonality between women's experiences at different times and places, has become one of the most potent sources of modern political transformations.

Some speak to affirm their own identity. Some speak to affirm a solidarity of class, creed, ethnicity, or gender. Some speak to affirm their consciousness of and support for the abused and marginalized across all ages and societies. Their stories may be romanticized or incomplete, embellished with footnotes or folk songs, heroic or tragic or mythic. They may depict events of long ago that explain the troubles of the present despite the subsequent departure of the oppressors. They may explain the barbarities of the present—rape, apartheid, disappearances, starvation—in terms of deeply rooted historical processes. These stories are seen on television screens around the world, insufficiently perhaps, distorted certainly. But they may now only be ignored through a myopic blocking of the ears.

The voices of the oppressed and excluded are only a beginning. Riding the wide-bodied jets may convince a privileged elite of the essential homogeneity of the modern world. But for most people, a sense of where we are going depends on where we live. Historical perspectives differ from India to Sweden, from Egypt to Chile, from Japan to Senegal. They even differ—increasingly so in many cases—between different regions in these societies. The pursuit of a just world peace cannot be nurtured through ethnocentricism. The meeting of different historical perspectives emerging from different regions has to be a critical part of any thinking about the future.

This is not to invite the replacement of an arrogant ethnocentricism with a romanticized or relativistic appeal to cultural traditions, which would be merely to reproduce the false choice between modernity and tradition in another form. Cultural tradition cannot justify the kinds of violence that are so often committed in its name. But it is to recognize that access to the modern world is no longer possible only through paths elaborated by the mainstream West.

It is not enough to recognize that judgments about where we are vary considerably according to our location within both geographical-cultural regions and structures of political, economic, and social inequity. Temporal horizons are also expanding rapidly. There is increasing awareness everywhere of the continuing vitality of cultural and civilizational traditions other than those of the West. The past is now interrogated not only in terms of the last four centuries of Western supremacy but also of the remarkable transitions that produced the wonders of India, China, or ancient Greece, the great river valley civilizations of Egypt and Mesopotamia, or life in the Americas before Columbus stumbled into the New World. No longer can it be said that a Rhodes "discovered" Rhodesia or a Columbus "discovered" America. Histories merge with archeologies as the origins of human endeavor are pushed further and further back in time. The "primitives" and "ancients" have begun to be rescued from their relegation to the dark antithesis of contemporary "enlightenment."

Even the geologists, those specialists in the longest and slowest of rhythms, have had their impact on the way we relate to the past. To all these proliferating histories, they add the perfect antidote to the feverish hubris of the present.

All this is to belabor what is becoming increasingly obvious. It makes a vital difference whether we orient ourselves with the compass of a mythological History or by listening to the dramatically different dreams and aspirations that may now be heard from so many societies around the world. The historical imagination necessary for thinking about a just world peace must be able to build on these experiences, as well as on a sense of the structures that link so many people together. It must try to understand what a meaningful future might look like to a child in Soweto or the South Bronx, in Beirut or Managua, in Khartoum or Amritsar, in shantytowns or refugee camps, confronting a short life of grinding poverty or contemplating a quick death in a nuclear firestorm.

Despite the seemingly marginal role of social movements in the modern world, it is their capacity to draw on this multiplicity of historical perspectives on the contemporary human condition that now makes them potentially so important as interpreters of the challenges and transformations of the modern world.

CRITICAL SOCIAL MOVEMENTS

Social movements have always arisen under conditions of social distress. They now grow up around all the multiple crises of modern life—problems of poverty and economic dislocation; threats of war and processes of environmental degradation; the abuse of human rights and oppression of gender, ethnicity, and race; the search for meaningful cultural identity. Social movements are in fact a very good guide to some of the major lines of fracture in the modern world.

Although there have always been social movements, they have usually been fragmented and scattered. They have responded to specific injustices in particular places, with little continuity over time, or connection from region to region. Their histories usually remain unwritten, their failures and even their achievements largely forgotten. This pattern began to change in eighteenth- and nineteenth-century Europe as a consequence of challenges to the old feudal aristocratic order. These challenges precipitated struggles for a more democratic form of politics that continue to the present day.

The initial move came from the rising bourgeoisie and was rooted in the logic of the emerging market economy. Eventually, a fairly narrow species of democracy—one deeply influenced by the needs and assumptions of that economy and expressed through institutions of representative government—became embedded in state power itself. Broader challenges to feudal privilege, as well as to this once radical but nevertheless restricted conception of democracy, remained limited to the barely organized masses until relatively late in the transition to industrial capitalism. The resort to the barricades in the great revolutionary years of 1789 and 1848 contrasts quite sharply with the more systematic practices that developed after about 1860. From that point on, the increasing integration of the world economy was accompanied by an increasing integration of movements struggling in response to rapidly changing economic, social, and political conditions.

The most important points of convergence and integration involved attempts to change the relationship between employers and workers and to assert national identities within territorial states. Much of the subsequent history of Europe—and of much of the rest of the world—is written in terms of these increasingly integrated socialist and nationalist movements. Much of that history concerns the deep tensions between the claims of class and those of nation. Contemporary debate over political values, ideologies, and the proper meaning of democracy still reflects options articulated in that era. Liberal conceptions of democracy remain tied to a market model of political life and reflect the close historical connection between the capitalist economy and state power. Socialist and nationalist traditions challenge the narrowness and elitism of the liberal view and press for more equalitarian and communitarian forms of democracy based on the effective participation of particular peoples or of people as such.

In contrast with most of the sporadic and fragmented movements that came before, these movements were remarkably successful. They have become part of the primary political structures of the modern world. This is not to say that their great visions have been adequately realized. Far from it. But it is impossible to deny their impact on what we have now become. They have been successful precisely because they have been able to build strong organizational forms around a sense of common identity.

For nationalism, this sense of identity is primarily cultural and territorial. For socialism, it is rooted both in a universalist conception of humanity and in the presumed capacity of class struggle to enhance the realization of our common human potential. In both cases, the expression of identity has been the state. Both nationalism and socialism share with liberalism an overriding concern with the state as the locus of political power. However suspicious particular nationalists and socialists may have been of the state, both nationalism and socialism became organized in relation to state institutions. Both associated the possibility of political change with gaining state power. Many states became nation-states. Many others have attempted to do so. In spite of the internationalism of socialist ideology, and even of many strong antistatist socialist traditions, socialist organizations quickly became national in structure and sought to attain power within particular states. There were in both cases important debates about how state power was to be attained—whether through persuasion and reform or through force and revolution. But the crucial connection was firmly established between these increasingly integrated movements and state power.

Whether grounded in a culturally cohesive nation, in a socioeconomic understanding of class struggle, or in the historical experience of exercising state power itself, the predominant contemporary understandings of political life in general, and democracy in particular, have emerged from movements characterized by systematic organizational structures and institutions. For most conventional categories of political analysis, in fact, the presence or absence of such organizational structures and institutions is the main criterion for judging whether a social movement is to be taken seriously.

Judged in the context of the great socialist visions of the past, new movements may appear to be in need of incorporation into the primary struggle between capital and labor. For nationalists, particularly in postcolonial contexts, movements tend to be judged in terms of the primary aim of resisting imperialism and dependence and achieving national autonomy and dignity. For liberals, movements may appear as mere expressions of group interest, as something between a pressure group and a political party. In all these cases, the presumed object is state power—which, after all, is what politics has been about for so long and for so many people.

The emergence of liberalism, nationalism, and socialism is obviously a very complex affair. But the presumption that politics involves the capture of state power seems increasingly inadequate when trying to understand contemporary social movements. Such movements have not completely abdicated any desire to capture state power. Nor do they represent a return to the scattered and fragmented pattern of an earlier era. But neither of these historical experiences provides a sufficient understanding of what is going on now. The theme of the primacy of histories in the modern world is of particular significance in this respect.

Both the form and the aspirations of the classic socialist and nationalist movements of the past century or so have been strongly indebted to a clear sense of a universalizing History. Socialism, building on a long liberal tradition, has been deeply influenced by a vision of progress in which reason, history, economic development, or political struggle makes possible a promised land of freedom and plenty. The number of variations on this theme is enormous, but the theme itself has been all-pervasive. Formulated abstractly, this vision has often encompassed humanity as such. Formulated more practically, it has tended to encompass the single state. In either case, the possibility of progress in History has acted as a kind of guarantee of the possibility of emancipation in politics.

Nationalism, by contrast, has been explicitly grounded in a sense of historical pluralism. Even so, it is a pluralism with distinct boundaries. There are many more nationalisms in the modern world than there are nation-states. The multiplicity of possible histories is contained within a relatively few national histories. Historical and cultural pluralism is captured by the state. Moreover, nationalism has become caught up in the interplay between more-powerful and less-powerful states as well as in the dynamics of the world economy. It has become as much a matter of resistance by the weak against the strong as an expression of particular histories. Universalizing History has been the prerogative of the well-off. It can even inform the nationalism of states like the United States, which can afford to believe that what is good for them is good for everyone else. For the most part, nationalism has become part of the mobilizing ideology of weaker states. It is paradoxical that nationalism may even become a way of mobilizing state resources for pursuing the path to modernity projected by universal History. In any case, the dialectic of universal and particular, History and histories, has become caught up in the historically specific dynamics of imperialism and international politics.

Contemporary political life is now marked by a renewed resurgence of social movements. There are peace movements, human rights movements, environmental movements, women's movements, urban movements, movements of indigenous peoples, and movements for alternative forms of economic life. Massive popular movements have challenged authoritarian regimes and demonstrated opposition to specific policies. Grassroots movements have sprung up everywhere. They are visible even in societies in which popular mobilizations have been most powerfully expressed in relation to postcolonial nationalisms.

Although it is possible to interpret the character and significance of these movements in different ways, it is not possible to ignore them. No analysis of modern political life can leave them out of account. But neither can analysis rely on conceptions of History or understandings of the nature of social movements rooted in an era that is now drawing to a close. Contemporary movements grow out of the particularity of historical experience. They resist the incorporation of those histories into the generalizing categories of class, nation, or state. And they are deeply skeptical both of the myth of History in the singular and of the view that the plurality of human experience is exhausted by the claims of either national culture or the isolated individual struggling in a competitive economy. They suggest that the old antithesis between universalizing History and the histories captured by nation-states has almost run its course.

Despite the tenacity of conventional interpretations, there is an emerging sense on the part of both the participants in these movements and a wide range of academic analysts that something new is going on. Such movements have a sense of vibrancy and a willingness to articulate alternative ways of knowing and acting that put the claim to politics as usual into serious question. They arise, as always, under conditions of social distress. They respond to a future that is seen as threatening. But their response does not easily conform to the conventional accounts of what political practice involves.

Of course, many movements do adhere to more conventional practices. In societies like South Africa, the Philippines, or South Korea, large-scale movements have challenged state power in ways familiar to students of past revolutions. In the case of the environmental movement in West Germany, party politics has proved to be an influential model of political participation. Many social movements try to engage with existing political energies in one way or another. Yet, many are also unlike either large-scale revolutionary movements or political parties.

Even where more familiar revolutionary movements or political parties dominate the political landscape, smaller movements are visible, acting in ways that challenge prevailing conceptions of political practice. To speak of emerging political energies in the Philippines, for example, is to engage not only with the "people power" that toppled the Marcos regime but also with all kinds of small-scale movements in particular communities. Whether these movements focus on creating more appropriate forms of development, or on agrarian reform, or on questioning presence of U.S. military bases, the ambiguous success of the 1986 rebellion cannot be separated from ongoing attempts by popular grassroots movements to reshape the process of political change itself. Similarly, the visibility of the West German Greens as a political party easily obscures the sense among many environmentalists that other forms of political practice are more appropriate. To try to interpret the practices of, for example, women's movements or antinuclear movements or community economic development projects within conventional political categories is to end up with caricatures that few can take seriously.

It certainly cannot be said that all the movements now emerging provide grounds for optimism about the future. Many movements are deeply reactionary and parochial. Many others act as a mere safety valve, as tame critics coopting or deflecting the energy available for fundamental change. Critical social movements are not always easily distinguished from either movements of reaction or cooptation. Indeed, in this book I will suggest that the exploration of what it means to be critical or emancipatory at all is central to what such movements are doing. The meaning of "critical" and "emancipatory" has to be discovered rather than stipulated in advance.

Nor do I suggest that critical social movements are the only political forces relevant to the pursuit of a just world peace—still less, that they are or are about to become the main political force in the modern world. There is an ebb and flow to their behavior that makes it difficult to judge their strength at any particular time or place. Neither the world economy nor the states system is likely to succumb to them. For those who believe that these large systems are coextensive with social and political reality, movements are likely to remain invisible or, at least, minor disturbances at the margins of vision. Although it is possible to show that they are a novel and significant presence in modern political life, critical social movements obviously face severe problems.

One of their main challenges is to generate creative connections with other, more-established political actors, whether socialist and nationalist movements or political parties. Whatever connections they do make, their overall achievement must involve a capacity to enhance the struggle for more authentically democratic forms of political life than those so far achieved under the banners of liberalism, nationalism, or socialism. In this sense, critical social movements may be understood as part of a much longer process. As part of a much longer process, the deeply ambivalent relationship between critical social movements and state power is particularly important. But it cannot be taken for granted that the capacity to influence or exercise state power is the *only* ground on which the importance of movements is to be judged.

Whatever the challenges they face, some of the most creative energies available for fundamental historical change now come from critical social movements. They present a sober assessment of specific challenges that have to be met. They offer some idea of how the grand visions and aspirations of the past need to be reworked and of how to respond more coherently to the conditions of the present. Critical social movements raise crucial questions about the nature of political life in a world of rapid change, both in terms of where political action ought to take place and in what form it ought to occur. They hint at ways in which new forms of political identity and human solidarity may be emerging despite all the evidence to the contrary.

Whether they will grow in vitality and significance cannot be predicted. As forms of political practice, their future has to be àchieved. But listening to such movements provides at least as good an indication of the trends of our time as the official statistics of government agencies. This is not least because whereas official statistics carve the world into analytical categories, social movements are forced to identify the interconnections between the structures and processes that mold people's everyday lives. In bringing so many experiences and histories from different circumstances to bear on the connections that are recreating the way people live, social movements not only tell us where the most important changes are occurring—and where they are most dangerous—but also make us more sensitive to the future trajectories these changes and dangers may bring, as well as the possibilities these trajectories disclose.

CHAPTER THREE

Structures

A WORLD OF CONNECTIONS

If contemporary thinking about human affairs is now characterized by challenges to a universalist view of History and the assertion of a plurality of histories, it is also important to pursue the argument in the opposite direction. For the inescapable fact remains that, whatever the variety of historical experiences that inform contemporary political practices, we do live in a world of global structures. These are the structures that make the scenarios of No World or Two Worlds so plausible. Although the easy evolutionist myths of universal History must be rejected in favor of a greater openness to the conversation between proliferating histories, it is also necessary to come to terms with those concrete historical structures that have made us all participants in a world of global connections.

The precise character of these connections is difficult to specify. Different theoretical and ideological perspectives have tended to privilege particular structures and processes rather than others. This tendency has been particularly strong among academic and technical analysts guided by the highly specialized concepts and languages of modern social research. A very high premium has been placed on analytical skills that enable scholars to examine narrowly defined phenomena with great care and precision.

Analytical concepts have been defined particularly sharply in the case of two of the most obviously important structures in the modern world: the system of states and the world economy. Although it may be fairly obvious in general terms that these two broad structures are in fact very closely interrelated, attempts to understand them in any detail tend to focus primarily on one or the other. Each has been said by different groups of scholars to be the primary determinant of the possibilities open before us.

The structure of the contemporary states system has depended ultimately on the legitimacy of war. This is perhaps the greatest irony of the European political tradition. The great search for legitimate authority and progressive enlightened civilization within states presumed the inevitability of bloody conflict between states. With nuclear weapons, this fundamental contradiction has become almost unmanageable and certainly ethically intolerable.

Economic processes have brought all states into varying degrees of interrelationship and even interdependence. But the claims of universal

33

progress and development that emanate from the centers of economic power and privilege turn bitterly sour in view of the huge disparities in the well-being of peoples in different societies and classes. The possibility of nuclear annihilation may be the foremost concern for some people. For others, annihilation is a present reality. Poverty is deadly. The contradiction between processes bringing all states into a universalizing world economy and those bringing uneven development, marginalization, and exclusion is not new in principle, but is now more insistent than ever.

Both sets of contradictions—and they are far from simple, far from suggesting any necessary or desirable resolution—are made more complicated and more dangerous by powerful new technologies. Hardheaded analysts tend to point to these contradictions with an air of inevitability. International competition, they say, is a permanent feature of the modern human condition, whether concerning the game of power politics between states, the logic of the world economy, or the dynamics of technological innovation. In fact, these supposedly permanent features of the human condition are the product of historical processes, and they are always subject to change.

Such analysts are also prone to treat these structures as cold, remote, and abstract, as huge determining forces beyond the reach of ordinary people. In fact, they are the historical products of very concrete human activities. They depend on people going about their normal everyday tasks. They absorb muscle and sweat, contemplation, emotion, creativity, and corruption. People may be caught up in huge structural transformations over which they have little direct control. But structures are produced and reproduced by the practices and rituals of everyday life. They may seem natural or inevitable, abstract and remote, but they depend on people doing things, or not doing things, on the way people organize themselves collectively, own things, produce things, talk, think, pursue routines, and treat each other. Challenges to these structures depend on a clear recognition of this insight.

Moreover, not only is it all too easy to treat the states system and the world economy as completely separate, but it is also tempting to treat either or both of these as the only sites of real power. The immediate crises of modern life do often occur as economic and political necessity. Other aspects of human existence—those that are usually forced into the elastic category of culture—are often treated as secondary, as determined by the needs of economy and state. Yet, it is becoming more and more obvious that the workings of neither the states system or the world economy can be easily separated from cultural processes. Some of the most pressing modern problems—such as racism, sexism, or abuse of the environment—involve enormously complex interactions between processes that are conventionally labeled as political, economic, and cultural.

In any case, it is in terms of cultural practices—of ways in which people come to understand and participate in the world—that people comprehend how the world might be changed. Far from being largely irrelevant to considerations of power, as so many analysts have supposed, cultural processes have always been central to the way power is constructed, legitimized, and transformed.

Whether one begins with the states system or the world economy, with new technologies or with cultural processes, it is becoming clearer than ever that accounts of contemporary global structures that try to treat any of these in isolation are necessarily misleading. In this chapter, I will present each of these starting points in turn in order to sketch a broad context in which to examine the way critical social movements respond in practice both to a world of proliferating histories and to emerging patterns of connection that defy conventional analytical and ideological categories.

THE STATES SYSTEM

Systems of states are relatively rare in human experience. The modern states system was slow to crystallize. Its origins go back to Renaissance Italy and the changing economic, technological, and social changes that allowed for the effective autonomy of city-states. With the Treaty of Westphalia of 1648, this principle of autonomy was formalized in an agreement that wars would only be fought over the secular interests of competing states, not over the universalist claims of religious doctrine. With the nineteenth century came a fusion—often ragged and incomplete—of nationalism and the territorial jurisdiction of states. Only since decolonization has the states system become the primary political structure everywhere.

The most important thing about the states system is its fragmentation. This is what distinguishes it from an empire, in which authority is structured in a hierarchical manner from a single center. Interpreted positively, the states system provides considerable diversity in the arrangement of human affairs. It allows for a freedom from centralized hierarchical control. It encourages the emergence of different social and cultural traditions within relatively secure territorial areas. It permits the kind of division of labor and economic competition that is often claimed to be important for material progress and has certainly been crucial for the creation of the modern world economy.

Most significant, it embodies a fundamental contrast between life inside and outside the state. As early European commentators such as Machiavelli and Hobbes argued, within the state it becomes possible to live the "good life": to become a citizen; to establish society, community, culture, and nation; to trade off obligations with freedoms. Between states, on the other hand, any overarching sense of a community of people as people is essentially abandoned. It is at this point that the interpretation turns sharply nega-tive. In fact, international politics is conventionally seen as a realm of wars, force, and violence; of deviousness, intrigue, and diplomacy; and of power politics unfettered by considerations of justice and legitimacy. It is not neces-sary to glance back very far or very often to see how this negative interpreta-tion can be very persuasive.

Even so, a conception of an underlying community somehow holding this system together has rarely disappeared entirely. Some have tried to pre-serve a sense of a shared natural law. Some have appealed to the essentially "rational" nature of all peoples. Others have predicted the eventual integrat-ing potential of commerce and economic life. For the most part, relations between states have been organized by all kinds of pragmatic and fragile accommodations. There have been customs and rules, unspoken agree-ments, and codified laws. There have been vague principles about balancing power against power in order to preserve order. The "great powers" have been expected to play a central role in organizing the system as a whole—to their own advantage of course. There has even been the emergence of regu-larized decision-making procedures, from international organizations like the United Nations to meetings of heads of the most powerful states to semiformal policy coordinating bodies concerned with financial and trade matters. Some analysts have gone so far as to call this a "society of states," implying that all is not purely anarchical and that, despite the incipient threat of a resort to force, some kind of order is possible.

Even so, whatever may be said in favor of the states system, the resort to force and war has remained one of its central features. And although it is possible to see some continuity in the underlying competitive logic of the states system since the seventeenth century, industrialization, technologies of mass destruction, and the growth of a world economy have fundamentally altered the dynamics of interstate interaction and the character of contempo-rary warfare. It is now fairly obvious to most people who examine the work-ings of the modern states system that our capacity to live with both the logic of this system and with modern nuclear, chemical, or biological weapons is exceedingly precarious.

To begin with, although the resort to war has been formally delegiti-mated, war retains a central place in contemporary political life. The accom-modations worked out under the rubric of nuclear deterrence reflect an understanding that the states system can no longer rely on war as a mechanism of system change. Deterrence theory, with its emphasis on the threat of "mutual assured destruction," has involved an attempt to keep the system going without actually engaging in overt warfare. But these accom-modations have always been rather fragile. Deterrence theory itself has not been a particularly good guide to the way weapons are actually deployed. New technologies threaten to replace the deterrence principles of war avoidance with those of war fighting. Nuclear war between superpowers may have been delegitimized, but competition between them has persistently erupted in the form of conventional wars all over the world. Add political elites susceptible to extremes of self-righteousness, as well as the usual tendency for things that can go wrong to go wrong at the most inopportune moment, and we arrive at our present chilling waltz along the precipice of self-annihilation.

Moreover, the principle of sovereign equality among states has always been something of a fiction. Inequality between states has been justified on the grounds that it allows the larger states to preserve "order" in the system as a whole. Yet, following a long tradition, the contemporary superpowers have often behaved less out of any sense of responsibility for maintaining a reasonable degree of international order than out of the unilateral pursuit of their own supremacy. The very scale of their power means that the modern states system also contains a good deal of the logic of empire, as the inhabitants of Nicaragua and Afghanistan, among others, are discovering yet again. Thus, the logic of the modern states system brings not only the promise of war between states but also the ongoing domination of strong states over weaker ones.

Whatever may be said in favor of the states system as our primary political structure, we now find a remarkable convergence of people who, from quite different backgrounds, raise their voices in horror. Some draw attention to the divergence between the codes of conduct traditionally associated with the "society of states" and the way states in fact behave. Some focus more specifically on the destabilization of nuclear deterrence through technological innovations. Others stress the fundamental incompatibility between a system that assumes both war and the domination of the strong over the weak to be legitimate and forms of militarization that take political struggle and war into a realm of mutual extermination.

Questions of war and peace remain central to those who examine the workings of the modern states system. But although the possibilities of nuclear war in particular remain the most spectacular concern, understanding the states system is no less important for understanding problems of environmental degradation or the abuse of human rights. On the one hand, the states system depends on the principle of sovereign territorial jurisdiction, whereas ecological processes tend to ignore territorial borders. On the other hand, the logic of the states system poses problems of national security, and national security is perhaps the easiest rationale available to any regime wishing to engage in internal repression or establish more effective curbs on democracy.

For all these reasons, many people have identified the states system as the primary problem that now confronts us. It is easy to see why better options are sought in attempts to replace the fragmentation that is the primary characteristic of the states system with some form of integration or global community. In this context, peace has come to be understood primarily—and simplistically—as the absence of war, and the absence of war has come to be understood primarily in terms of the centralization of authority.

The major debates on this issue have been framed as a choice between such a centralization—through the United Nations, international law, and so on—or renewed attempts to make the society of states more coherent through more effective arms control, better diplomacy, and so on. Fewer and fewer people believe that tinkering with the system is enough, and those who push for global centralization are confronted with the problem of identifying the concrete historical forces that could bring such centralization about. States themselves seem unlikely to do so. The self-identified agents of History, whether in the guise of transnational corporations or superpowers, would seem all too likely to favor a centralization reminiscent of authoritarian empires. In a world of histories, solutions posed as the simple need to move from fragmentation to integration seem quite inappropriate. And in any case, most debates on these themes have arisen out of an analysis that treats the structure of the states system in isolation. They have largely ignored the relationship between the states system and the modern world economy.

THE WORLD ECONOMY

Nineteenth-century thinkers could already see that the dynamic economic life set in motion with the transitions from feudalism to capitalism in Europe would soon expand to create a world economy. World economy has now become a reality. Even if some states, like the Soviet Union and China, have not been drawn into it completely; even if states respond to it in many different ways depending on internal social, political, and cultural arrangements; even if there are a great many forms of economy in different states; and even if protectionism remains common, everyone is now affected by patterns of production, distribution, and exchange that are global in their scope.

The workings of the world economy are complex, often mysterious, and certainly subject to sharply divergent explanations. Yet three features stand out no matter what political inclinations color the analysis: First, the development of the world economy has been very dynamic. There have been periods of rapid growth but also periods of severe crisis. The third quarter of this century, for example, was a time of unprecedented economic accumulation. The severe malaise that followed still affects us. Periods of economic crisis are sometimes the result of cyclical downturns. More significant, they are sometimes the result of fundamental contradictions between various parts of the system that can only be resolved by a restructuring of the system as a whole.

We are now living in just such a period of fundamental restructuring of the world economy. The dominance of the United States, which was so important to the way the world economy became structured after 1945, has been challenged on many fronts. The economic center of gravity seems to be shifting geographically from the North Atlantic region to the Pacific Rim. Information and communication are replacing raw materials as capital assets. Above all, there are major changes in the international division of labor, as well as both an increasing reliance on capital-intensive forms of production and new patterns in the exploitation of cheap labor. The consequences of all this are now clearly visible even in the world's most prosperous societies, particularly in high unemployment in regions that once thrived on heavy manufacturing.

Second, the overall trajectory of this dynamic development has been toward greater and greater internationalization. This is what has made the myth of History so powerful. Internationalization became particularly important in the post-1945 era. The Yalta agreements may have symbolized the continuing importance of divisions between states—or at least between groups of states—but the agreements at Bretton Woods symbolized a concerted attempt, led by the United States as the dominant power, to institute a world economy based on the principle of comparative advantage: a world of free trade with the dollar as an international medium of exchange and a management of "interdependence" by U.S.-dominated institutions such as the World Bank and the International Monetary Fund (IMF). This era saw an enormous extension of world trade and international investment, the emergence of multinational corporations and international institutions, greater integration of the economies of many states, particularly the wealthy states of the Organization for Economic Cooperation and Development (OECD), and the internationalization of the banking and financial markets.

The pattern of internationalization is undergoing substantial change once again. New information technologies link London, New York, and Tokyo more rapidly than companies in any of these cities could communicate only a few years ago. The "world car" has become a symbol of the way production is becoming organized on a worldwide basis. The development of a global capital market has become particularly significant. World trade in goods and services in the late 1980s amounts to around $3 trillion a year, foreign-exchange transactions amount to $35 trillion, and turnover in London's Eurodollar market, where major financial institutions borrow from each other, comes to about $75 trillion. Investments tend to be made more and more by nation rather than by industry. Although policy makers in the major economies can together control world money supply, they are decreasingly able to control money supply within their own countries.

Third, the growth of the world economy has been fundamentally uneven. Costs and benefits have been unequally shared. Owners of capital have had a relative advantage over the owners of labor power. Capital has been increasingly concentrated. Huge disparities have resulted from the dynamics that are set in motion between "more-developed" and "less-developed" economies. There is undoubtedly much to be said for the achievements that have accompanied the recent periods of economic growth associated with this internationalization of economic life. But unequal development puts all these achievements into serious question. Economic life in Western societies is now dominated by mass unemployment, attacks on real wages, the erosion of social services, and the abandonment of regions and peoples that do not fit into the new patterns of international production. The economies of socialist states are clearly in difficulty. The so-called Third World is stricken with huge debts, falling commodity prices, mass unemployment, and increasing levels of poverty, even in societies where overall economic wealth is increasing.

The Two Worlds scenario has become especially plausible in this context. Whereas myths of History and theories of development have assumed that everyone will be climbing up the same ladder sooner or later—given the right sort of aid, institutions, and government policies—nationalists and theorists of imperialism, dependence, or the internationalizing of capital have stressed the divergence of possibilities available to those at the center of the world economy and those on its periphery.

This divergence occurs both between and within states. Whether because of their relative position in the international division of labor, or of processes of unequal exchange between raw materials and manufactured goods, or of the tangled strings attached to foreign aid, IMF credit, and corporate investments, poor states constantly find themselves at a relative disadvantage. They find it difficult, and for some perhaps even impossible, to escape from a vicious cycle of poverty and maldevelopment.

Moreover, only certain sectors of such states become tied to this international economy. National economies become divided into a modernizing urban sector, based at least initially on exports that make capital accumulation possible, and a peripheral sector. The latter tends to be characterized partly by traditional ways of life and partly by the consequences of the impact of the modernizing sector, as when cheap manufactures and capital-intensive technologies destroy the basis for traditional economies and communities.

Contrary to the old theories of linear development, therefore, such conceptions of the world economy refuse to attribute poverty and maldevelopment to any innate backwardness of tradition and point instead to the way in which modernity itself, in the form of an inequalitarian world economy, sucks the energy and resources out of poor societies, undermining their capacity to develop on their own terms. Moreover, because the political elites of such societies are caught up in all the tensions that are bound to arise in such a dualistic economy, yet have effective support only in the modernizing sector, they tend to resort to more or less authoritarian or military forms of rule. This is, in turn, reinforced by the possibility of foreign intervention.

Of course, it is possible to come up with versions of this analysis that are just as oversimplified as those found in the classic accounts of development as a series of stages along the highway to modernity. In practice, different states show different patterns, depending on existing traditions, class structures, political institutions, and so on. Some states have managed to break out of the cycle of dependent development. Even so, the divergence of opportunities remains a central characteristic of the contemporary world economy.

The issue of international debt is particularly important in this respect. This is a problem that is often framed in terms of the threat posed to international banks by big debtors like Mexico, Brazil, and Argentina. But from the point of view of those in debt, the situation of many small states is much more worrisome. For them debt is both a symbol of their vulnerability to the vagaries of the world market and an instrument readily available to the IMF, the World Bank, and multilateral development banks in the imposition of loan conditions. In fact, for debtor countries in general, the dynamics of international finance are becoming more important than the dynamics of production and trade.

In the poorest of societies, the gulf between those people who are able to participate in the world economy and those whose capacity to survive has been undermined through processes introduced by the structural demands of the world economy seems to be widening. Declining industrial states like Britain, with such a sharp contrast between the industrial rubble of its north and the affluence of its south, exemplify the appearance of parallel patterns in what is conventionally thought of as the First World. From fears about a disappearing middle class in the United States to the savage immediacy of mass starvation and malnutrition among marginal peoples in so many societies, inequality remains a central characteristic of the way human beings live together.

It is perhaps in the context of the dynamics of the world economy that the possibilities before us remain most obscure. Just as, when considering the states system, it is easy to become obsessed with the immediate threat of war and to ignore its impact on, say, ecologies and human rights, so also it is possible to be overwhelmed by poverty, unemployment, and so on, understood only in formal economic terms. But it is just as important to be concerned about the quality of economic processes—about the nature and meaning of work, for example, or the way basic needs are turned into commercially stimulated desires through advertising and popular culture.

Further than this, analysis of the world economy is obviously subject to complex and sharply contested arguments. Tensions run especially high between those who stress the beneficial consequences of internationalization and those who point to the consequences of inequality. On the one hand, the conventional economic wisdom and policy emanating from the centers of economic power stress the need to extend and manage the latest phase of internationalization, a need wrapped in promises of trickle-down for all. On the other hand, those who look at the fate of weaker states or peoples see that the universalizing character of the world economy has brought not development and equality for all but the present reality of poverty for millions and the promise of complete exclusion for those who are being made dispensable to the functional needs of the world economy as a whole. Similar analyses motivated the socialist and nationalist movements of the past. But it seems increasingly unclear to many socialists and nationalists alike, not to mention democratically inspired liberals, just what response is appropriate now.

The problem of appropriate response is especially difficult given the changing relationships between the state and the world economy. For most of this century, and for the most influential political ideologies, the state has been treated as an instrument capable of redressing at least the worst aspects of economic inequality and alienation. Whether as the nation-state resisting the pressures of colonialism and underdevelopment, the socialist state with its stress on collective ownership and centralized planning, the welfare state simultaneously acting to meet the needs of an expanding economy and to provide at least a minimum level of social services for everyone, or, indeed, the state as the essential agent of economic development and modernization everywhere, the state has generally been regarded as an essentially progressive force.

Of course, states have always been regarded with some suspicion in this context, not least because of the way they have advanced the interests of particular classes and elites. But with the increasingly internationalized and capital-intensive nature of contemporary economic life, judgments about the essentially progressive character of states have become even more uncertain. The market, not the state, has been resurrected as the primary source of solutions to all economic problems. The welfare state has been seriously eroded. Inequality has become increasingly respectable. Demands for law and order have become louder than demands for social justice. The poor and marginalized are more and more likely to be castigated as social deviants and subjected to surveillance and control. As the more progressive elements of states are gradually whittled away, the idea of a national economy, subject to the sovereign authority and control of state actors, becomes more and more difficult to sustain. The claim that it is possible to do something about poverty and inequality by taking over state power becomes more and more illusory.

TECHNOLOGIES AND POLITICAL ECONOMY

One of the main difficulties in understanding what is going on in the modern world is the complexity of the relationships between the states system and the world economy. This remains a serious challenge for contemporary scholarly analysis, influenced as it is by traditions that have treated politics and economics as separate enterprises. It is especially important in trying to make sense of the modern state. The relationship is more difficult to disentangle given the important role played by factors that are often analysed in noneconomic or political categories.

The role of technological innovation is particularly important in this respect. The impact of new technologies on so many areas of human existence has even led to the elaboration of powerful theories of technological determinism. Such theories must be resisted. Technologies arise from and enter back into very complex social, political, and economic processes. In the context of the states system, they amplify dangers that are already present in the structures of fragmentation and in superpower dominance. In the context of the world economy, they reproduce and intensify patterns of unequal development that are central to the way the world economy is organized.

Nor is it very useful to see technology in terms of the classic choice between optimism and pessimism. Many of our modern technologies are magnificent achievements. It also remains true that many of these technologies are implicated in terrible barbarisms. What counts in the end is not the technology as such but the character of the social structures that channel their energies into developing and using particular technologies. To take examples from the field of health, the simple technologies of sewage treatment and the provision of adequate food and shelter have had a far greater impact on human well-being then all the sophistications of the artificial heart. New technologies are a worrying issue for those pursuing a just world peace, not because they determine everything, nor because advanced technologies are necessarily inherently destructive in themselves, but because in their present forms they intensify the dangers already arising from other social processes.

Technological innovation has been particularly important in contemporary military affairs. It has always been necessary to understand the consequences of specific technologies for the relationship between offense and defense. Keeping abreast of new technologies in this context has now become a full-time and almost obsessive occupation.

The advent of nuclear weapons, for example, has undermined any reasonable calculation of a balance between ends and means in warfare—although old ways of thinking linger on among many all-too-influential groups. The basic premises of nuclear deterrence are undoubtedly flawed in principle, but even if they are accepted, new technologies are rapidly putting them into ever more serious question in practice. The requirements of "second-strike" capability or "mutual assured destruction," for example, are threatened both by the increasing accuracy of new missiles and by the sheer complexity of all the refinements that have been presumed necessary to keep deterrence "credible." The proposals for a new regime of 'Star Wars,' or the Strategic Defense Initiative, (SDI), now intensify still further the concern—felt among most analysts who are familiar with contemporary strategic affairs—that the whole regime of nuclear deterrence is becoming obsolete. Even politically conservative observers have concluded that many new technologies in this area reduce rather than enhance national security. There is no doubt at all on the part of many analysts that the security of people in general is decreasing in an unprecedented manner.

While the mind-boggling military technologies being deployed by the superpowers against each other occupy center stage, conventional weapons continue to become more and more deadly. Miniaturization proceeds apace. Biological and chemical weapons are still being developed, and the taboos against their use seem to be crumbling. Everywhere, it seems, the resolution of political differences is being conducted with increasingly expensive and increasingly nasty technologies of destruction.

Technological innovation is no less critical for contemporary transformations in economic life. Its impact on the creation of new patterns of wealth are particularly significant. On the one hand, new technologies can lead to greater productivity, quality, and profitability. On the other, they can make people and their skills redundant, increase the proportion of repetitive, low-paying jobs, and increase the relative advantage of management over labor.

Such tendencies have been particularly important in the way states have responded to structural crisis in the world economy. Throughout the 1970s a new international division of labor between North and South appeared to be emerging between high-technology industries and advanced services, on the one hand, and assembly operations, low-skilled manufacturing, and extraction of natural resources, on the other. As the consequences of the technologies involved became clearer, it became even more apparent that a simple North-South distinction obscured more than it revealed. The very idea of a homogeneous Third World became particularly outmoded. States often lumped together under this label now participate in distinct and often contradictory processes. They are affected by and respond to new technologies in quite different ways.

The so-called newly industrializing countries—such as Korea, Taiwan, Hong Kong, Singapore, and possibly Malaysia—have used technologies both as a way of modernizing industry and as a product for the world market. With strong government direction, they have managed to shift from an export strategy based on low prices to new forms of industrial competitiveness based on new indigenous technologies. Such countries are often touted as the new model that other "developing" societies could follow. Yet, on the whole, they stand by themselves. The major oil producers have accumulated great wealth, but wealth alone has not been sufficient to stimulate effective industrialization. Other countries, like Thailand, or the Philippines, have been susceptible to dependent forms of industrialization organized by multinational corporations on the basis of cheap labor and deplorable working conditions. These states have been able to benefit from the way new technologies permit the dispersed organization of production around the world. But increased automation also undermines the cost advantage of such locations, eventually reinforcing the position of already more technologically advanced economies. In such cases, technological development seems to lead to economic dependency.

Larger states—such as Brazil, Mexico, Argentina, China, and, to some extent, India—are able to envisage a process of technological modernization aimed at both the domestic market and the world economy. They can aim to increase their competitive edge in the world economy through a combination of technological modernization and cheap labor, as well as to extend their industrial capability on the basis of large domestic markets. But, in such cases, technological modernization largely remains dependent on the transfer of technology from the more technologically advanced economies. This process depends in turn on the multinationals, who are usually willing to make such transfers only in return for access to these large markets.

Thus, development is again likely to involve greater dependency. Attempts to increase protectionism in order to develop indigenous industrial strength are likely to result in a restriction of technology transfers. Opening up the market to multinationals is likely to make it difficult to increase indigenous industrial strength. In any case, the kind of technological modernization currently necessary to compete in the world economy is unlikely to increase employment significantly. It is more likely to increase the gap between those sectors that are integrated into the world economy and those that are not.

The patterns of exclusion visible within the larger states are even more clearly apparent in the case of those societies that are being more or less bypassed by current technological transformations. This is true for most of Africa. Modern technology may appear in the form of consumer electronic products, links to world communication systems within the cities, or even military hardware. But, for example, new agricultural technology tends to increase labor redundancy, to turn agriculture from a domain of women to one of men, and to accelerate rural-urban migration. Most such societies are already suffering from a relative decline in commodity prices. The development of new synthetic materials even makes some of those commodities obsolescent. The chances of entering the competition in new information technologies are remote. Consequently, a world of gleaming gadgets coexists with a world of unemployment, misery, hunger, illness, and violence, all of which are on the increase in the most disadvantaged parts of the world and, particularly, in the urban centers.

Emerging technologies seem to enhance even further the contrast between those who can and those who cannot participate in the world economy. They also indicate the shift in power within the industrialized parts of the world from Europe and the eastern United States to the Pacific Basin. As new technologies help reshape both the location of economic power and new forms of inclusion and exclusion, the leading industrial states, particularly the United States, Japan, and Europe, put more and more resources into even more advanced technologies, knowing full well that control of them is vital to their attempts to maintain and improve their position as the wealthiest and most powerful states in the world.

Whether in terms of military hardware or economic production, technological innovation is a critical variable in the way the major structures of power are now being transformed. Yet beyond this are a number of other more troubling questions. Some of these concern the consequences of relying on technologies—such as nuclear power—whose social and environmental costs are already clearly enormous. The symbols of technological carnage are usually related to the atrocities of war: the fields of Flanders, Dresden, Auschwitz, Hiroshima, Nagasaki, and Kampuchea under Pol Pot. With Chernobyl and Bhopal, such symbols come closer and closer to the infrastructures of everyday life.

Technologies now becoming available—particularly those involving data processing, communications, and, above all, biogenetic engineering—seem certain to radically transform the conditions of human existence in even more unpredictable directions. The way technological innovations are so tied to the interaction between the contemporary states system and world economy gives ample grounds to see them as threatening, whatever promises they hold for a few.

Beyond the problems associated with particular technologies, or the relations between technologies and the organization of production, lies the way that technology as such has become the dominant metaphor of our times, a metaphor foreclosing philosophical, aesthetic, ethical and political options. It is a metaphor in which the primary questions—What? Why? For whom?—are ignored in favor of the most instrumentally calculating question—How?

CULTURE, DIFFERENCE, POWER

The problems of the system of states are usually understood to concern either the difficulty of managing strategic relationships—through diplomacy, negotiation, and arms control—or the likelihood of nuclear war if present trends continue. On the whole, state elites tend to believe that effective management is still possible. But millions of people, including military experts, arms control specialists, and academic analysts, are convinced this belief is naive and myopic.

These problems are serious enough, but in an important sense they are only symptoms of something deeper. The structure of the states system is implicated in all kinds of other problems, from a failure to cope with ecological collapse to the abuse of human rights. Taken together, all these problems put into question the underlying ethical, cultural, and political legitimacy of the state itself. Short-term concerns with particular missiles also raise very serious questions about how and why people live together in the way they do. After all, if one of the most basic justifications for the state has involved its ability to ensure the security needed to pursue a good life within its borders, the fragility of national security in a nuclear age puts the old distinction between citizen and foreigner, us and them, onto very flimsy foundations indeed.

Similarly, the primary problems of the world economy may be framed in terms of attempts to manage an increasingly complex set of worldwide processes, on the one hand, and the devastating effects of uneven development, on the other. But much more is at stake than this, including the particular understanding of economics—the kind of work, production, distribution, and so on—that gives rise to the present form of world economy in the first place. Concerns about particular policy problems quickly give way to more basic questions about the ethical, cultural, and political character of capitalism, industrialization, materialism, and modernity.

The same goes for problems posed in terms of technologies. Particular technologies may bring obliteration or redundancy, but the character of contemporary technologies reflects all kinds of cultural and ethical values as well as the needs of economic processes and interests. Technologies depend on processes involving science, education, and even aesthetics that are usually treated as somehow less important than the hard realities of guns and money. Even so, the adage that knowledge is power is particularly relevant to the contemporary age. It is becoming more and more unreasonable to treat what are usually classified as "cultural" forces as any less important than the more easily identifiable dynamics of economy and military strategy.

Concern with the seeming inevitability of the oppression of women by men almost everywhere is particularly important in this respect. Analysis of "patriarchy" is an even more contentious enterprise than the analysis of modern economic life. There are people who refuse to recognize the problem at all, or who accept it as a simple fact of life. There are also those who see gender relations in general, and men in particular, as the source of all problems. But the most serious difficulty is the great variety of patriarchal processes in different societies and the complex ways in which gender relations intertwine with the economic structures and cultural traditions of those societies. We are faced here less with any coherent theoretical account of patriarchy in general than with multiple descriptions of discriminations in different societies and with ongoing attempts to liberate the interpretation of these descriptions from the conventional categories of economic and political analysis.

For women, the world appears immediately as a realm of "difference." And difference becomes an opportunity for all kinds of injustices and oppressions to crystallize. These occur as systematic physical abuse and disfigurement, as reduction to the status of chattel, as objectification to the status of commodity, or even as a vaguer sense of entrapment within routines, roles, and obligations over which women have little or no control.

There is the direct physical violence of rape, sexual abuse, and domestic battering. And there is indirect violence resulting from women's position within economic, social, and cultural processes. Women may occupy particularly oppressed roles within the production process or become caught up in new demands for migrant labor or for tourist-based prostitution. They may be subjected to abuse because of social policies on abortion, contraception, and divorce. They may be the victims of cultural traditions involving dowries, veils, or *machismo,* as well as the violence of pornography and of the international ideal of desirable femininity.

Violence slides into multiple discriminations. Property rights are usually monopolized by men. Women are effectively absent from the centers of power almost everywhere. Even supposedly progressive political parties and states usually preserve the patriarchal values of the states they seek to transform. Minority women usually find themselves subject to double discrimination. And when push comes to shove, women often suffer disproportionately from additional privations.

Recent feminist scholarship is particularly concerned with forms of power that have remained largely invisible, obscured through the cultural codes and socioeconomic practices through which oppression has become accepted as normal and common sense. In Western societies, for example, gender relations have cohered primarily around the fundamental division between public and private that runs through so much political, economic, social, and cultural life. Within the supposedly private realm, women are located within the structures of the family and given the roles of mothering and housework. Such roles have conventionally been distinguished from "real" work but have been none the less important for economic activity as a whole.

Feminist scholarship shows that gender is itself an historical and social construct. Whereas "difference" may be partly determined by biology, it is abundantly clear that the actual articulation of difference—and oppression—is a consequence not of some presocial and essential human nature, but of specifiable social, economic, and cultural practices. Feminist scholarship directs attention to the historical connections between the construction of gender identity and almost every other aspect of social life, from the economic division of labor to religious symbolisms, received traditions of philosophical and political speculation, methodologies of scientific research, pictorial representation in high art, and the commercialization of sexuality in mass advertising. In this way, patriarchy appears not only as patterns of violence and discrimination but also as the embodiment of entire ways of life. The feminist critique of patriarchy thus becomes the indictment not only of political and economic structures but of civilizational values that have been assumed as given for centuries.

A questioning of the character of dominant cultural forms and values is obviously not limited to the critique of patriarchy. Cultural politics are at the center of concern in many societies. As with History, so with Culture: It has been subject to the presumption of universalization. Analysis of the rise of the West and the world economy typically merges with the analysis of a dominant form of consciousness. The story is usually concerned with the emergence of claims to objective knowledge and promises of utilitarian efficiency. Science and technology have become guarantors of truth and progress. In this sense, the rise of the West has become coextensive with the spread of modernity. And modernity has then been located at the far end of the line down which all societies are progressing. Thus the term "development" has become synonymous with the term "modernization." It has become the opposite of "tradition," the antidote for myths, superstitions, and religions, the remedy for poverty and violence, and the presumed fate of all other cultures.

Modernity is now visible in all parts of the world, although as with the spread of the world economy that has been its principle driving force, it has been a very uneven process. It has certainly not been benign in its consequences. Most obviously, the culture of modernity has been diffused globally not because it has any monopoly on access to truth, beauty, or goodness but because it has been an intrinsic part of the most powerful forces in recent history. Whether understood as an extension of specifically Western cultural traditions, as a consequence of specifically capitalist forms of economic life, or even as a consequence of a particular form of patriarchy, the culture of modernity is not so much universal in any absolute sense as it is an historically dominant expression of the claim to universality.

In part, this dominance has been reflected in relations of inequality expressed in cultural forms. Racism is the primary issue here. As with patriarchy, the violence of racial oppression is often very difficult to disentangle from class conflict understood in more economic terms. The violence of racism is usually obvious enough. South African apartheid is only the most brutal attempt to legitimize power and privilege through the discriminations of color.

But straightforward racism slides into more sophisticated readings of the "other" as morally inferior and, therefore, as legitimately subservient. Much has been made in the past decade, for example, of the way in which Western scholarship about other societies has been infused with stereotypes and assumptions arising from an imperialist presumption of superiority. Whether in terms of anthropologies of the "primitive" and the "oriental" or propaganda about the "enemy," racism may be as insidiously invisible as it may be overtly violent.

Similar themes arise from the way that cultural interaction is organized globally. Whether we think of the way cultural forms are packaged and sent around the world to be consumed through television, or the way "news" is constructed and distributed, or of the recent development of satellite communications technology, cultural life is increasingly subject to forces that are at once global and expressions of the interests of the most powerful. This is precisely why the appeals of the late 1970s for a New International Economic Order to redress the most glaring injustices of world trading patterns were accompanied by equally ignored appeals for a New World Information Order. In an era in which control over knowledge and information is becoming increasingly crucial, the tension between the claims of universality— "One World," or "global village"—and the realities of cultural imperialism and loss of control over one's own cultural identity is an ever more pressing item on the political agenda.

The primary response to processes of this sort has been nationalism. Nationalism is undoubtedly a very complex phenomenon, one that cannot be grasped in cultural categories alone. But it can be understood at least partly as a counterpoint to the cosmopolitan pretensions of the dominant powers. Cultural life—especially the appeal to lost traditions, the recovery of histories, and the construction of alternative national identities—then becomes channeled into resistance of the meanings and aspirations encouraged by the more powerful alien forces.

As a form of resistance, nationalism has always had serious problems. It has tended to be preempted by a particular class, or even by particular "nations." Nationalism has often become a means of legitimizing a class rule that is not only organized within the institutions of the modern state but is directed toward the very path of universal modernization that nationalism as a doctrine has claimed to be resisting. Moreover, nationalism has often involved an over-romanticized and dogmatic appropriation of local traditions. The claim that one's cultural identity is encapsulated in centuries-old texts is no more edifying than the claim that all nonmodern cultural traditions are obsolete. Nationalism has often taken the form of an excessive appeal to particularity as the appropriate response to an excessive appeal to the universality of dominant cultures. Most significant, nationalism has involved the identification of particular cultural traditions with the political apparatus of the modern state itself. Culture here becomes less a matter of resistance or reassertion than the cooptation of particular values within the broader dynamics of the states system and the world economy.

Yet, if there is, on the one hand, considerable skepticism about statist nationalisms as the appropriate vehicle for resistance to dominant and power-laden cultural forces, there is, on the other, no less skepticism about the staying power of those cultural traditions that have been dominant for so long. This may not be immediately obvious from the rhetoric of political leaders. As a political force, the culture of modernity remains immensely powerful everywhere. Beneath the surface, however, the internal critique of that culture is now quite far advanced.

At the heart of the culture of modernity lies an insistent dualism. An autonomous knowing subject is presumed to be gazing at an objective world to be known. Knowing is then linked to the possibility of control of the known. Whether one thinks of the great philosophical systems of Plato, Descartes, or Kant; or of the heroic artist separated from but reproducing the world around him; or the political categories in which individuals are somehow assumed to be completely autonomous from the society in which they live; or even the division between the secular world of people living in time and the sacred space of eternity, the presumption of a radical split between human being and world is always in the background. In the foreground lies a cultural life permeated by debates about the relative claims of objectivity and subjectivity and the ever-present lure of utilitarian or instrumental calculation.

This underlying dualism has been the unerring target of critique within the culture of modernity itself. At the popular level, "science" may remain a potent incantation supposedly offering protection from charlatans and subversives. But the actual conduct of much scientific research reveals a fundamental rejection of the dualistic categories constructed by Galileo and Newton—the categories that have become the prevailing "common sense" of modernity.

Nor is it possible to avoid the darker side of modernity so readily visible in this century. From wars and extermination camps to impersonal bureaucracies, from the lonely isolation of the supposedly autonomous individual to the transformation of human life into a procession of commodities to be bought and sold, there has been no shortage of opportunities for skepticism about the progressive character of modernized life. And whether in terms of philosophy or science, of social thought or of aesthetics, there has also been no shortage of attempts to revitalize the cultural traditions that have been dominant for so long and to take them in more creative and emancipatory directions.

It is important to recognize the complementarity between these two forms of cultural politics—that which results from the meeting of more-powerful and less-powerful cultures and that which is occurring within the dominant culture itself. This complementarity arises not least because they both confront essentially the same process: the increasing grip of an instrumentalist, consumerist culture all over the world. This culture may have had its origins in a particular region, the West. But like the world economy, it has ceased to be the preserve of the West alone. This culture is well entrenched among elites everywhere. Its attractions are increasingly coextensive with the attractions of the world economy. These attractions are offered universally but are attainable only on a very selective basis. And even as attractions, they have now lost much of their former energy and glitter.

Ideas about what it now means to belong to the human community have been largely preempted by the claims of modernist universalism, on the one hand, and by nationalism, on the other. Tensions between these claims are presumed to have been resolved primarily through the political apparatus of the modern nation-state. Looking at the modern world from the standpoint of History, this resolution has seemed perfectly adequate. The plurality of states is presumed to satisfy the need for cultural diversity, whereas the participation of states in worldwide political and economic systems is presumed to satisfy the equally necessary participation of all people into a common community of humankind.

Yet the standpoint of History provides a view from the top down. This standpoint offers a powerful image of the cultural dynamics of wealthy societies and of the privileged elites of poorer societies. It is deeply rooted in an underlying presumption of a necessary move from tradition to modernity, from undeveloped to developed, from parochial to universal. It is blind to both the intrinsic problems and the historically specific character of the cultural values that are presumed to be universal. It is also blind to the great diversity of people's cultural experiences and aspirations visible beyond the world of increasingly homogenized elites.

In fact, beyond the horizons of History lies an often perplexing vista of cultural politics. Nationalism retains considerable vitality, particularly in postcolonial situations where it is not always easily coopted by modernizing elites. There has been a renewed emphasis on cultural and ethnic identities below the level of the state. It is clear that the map of nations is now much more complicated than the map of states. Claims to religious identity complicate matters still further, not least in regions like the Middle East, Central America, or the Philippines, where political life is now particularly volatile. In many poorer societies, there has been an increasing awareness of the "modernity of tradition" and attempts to rethink the meaning of development in the context of indigenous values and practices. Even in the more affluent states, concern with the way that the culture of modernity has brought alienation and violence into societies that pride themselves on progress and enlightenment has become a central theme of modern political debate. In this context, the claims of the nation-state to be able to resolve the cultural contradictions of the age seem increasingly tenuous.

The vista of cultural politics is particularly perplexing because the issues raised here under the category of "culture" feed back into issues raised in terms of political and economic structures and technological innovation. Like "world economy," "states system," or "technology," the category of "culture" is just one way of cutting into the confusing trajectories of the modern world. All these terms presume that it is possible to separate out distinct realms of human life. What has been said so far should indicate that such a presumption cannot be sustained.

CHAPTER FOUR

Struggles

GLOBAL STRUCTURES AND PARTICULAR STRUGGLES

Cultures and economies, technologies and the international system, race and gender, guns and butter: No matter which way one cuts into an analysis of global structures, there are enough concrete problems to make one's head spin. The demand that something be done has never been more urgent. The sense that many of these problems are getting out of control has rarely been so widespread, so loudly echoed in technical data, policy reports, annual statistical surveys, academic analyses, and the sheer accumulation of information and images from all parts of the world. It is now easy enough to draw up a list of impending disasters or to identify the problems that arise from processes labeled as economy, society, politics, culture, technology, gender, or race. But it is much more difficult to understand how all these fit together.

One obvious way of thinking about the interconnected nature of modern life is in terms of the way poverty and human misery have become inseparable from the degradation of the physical environment in which we live. There are now about 5 billion human beings living on the earth. Some analysts and commentators question whether the planet can support many more people. Others question whether so many people can support the planet.

Seen from one direction, the primary problem is poverty. About half a billion people are estimated to suffer severe malnourishment. A further 1 billion are estimated to be undernourished to a lesser degree. Seen from another direction, the primary problem is the physical deterioration of the earth itself. Air, water, land, forests, and other ecological systems that support life are reported to be undergoing permanent damage. Particular concern is expressed about the depletion of the ozone layer, climatic change, and the mass extinction of plant and animal species. Both sets of analyses may easily seem divorced from each other. But famine in Africa cannot be separated from processes of soil erosion and the spread of deserts. Poverty in India is made even worse by the commercial deforestation that deprives people of the firewood that is their primary source of fuel.

Similar themes emerge from the seemingly endless studies of contemporary war and militarization. "There are more wars," goes one annual statistical report, "and more people killed in them. Four times as many deaths have occurred in the 40 years since World War II as in the 40 years preceding it. Increasingly the geopolitical designs of the major military powers are being worked out on the soil of other countries and with other peoples lives (Sivard, *World Military and Social Expenditures, 1985*, p. 5)." The inevitable connection is then made: "In a world spending $800 billion a year for military programs, one adult in three cannot read and write, one person in four is hungry." Military expenditures are approaching $1 trillion annually. At the same time, the United Nations Children's Fund estimates that $500 million could save the lives of about 3 million children who die each year because they cannot receive vaccinations against measles, lockjaw, and whooping cough. This connection puts into serious question any attempt to explain wars within the structural dynamics of the states system alone. Now, more than ever before, the accumulation of weapons has to be explained not only in terms of military and strategic interests but also of much broader economic, social, and even cultural processes of militarization. It is increasingly difficult to think of states entering into conditions of war and peace just on the basis of their sovereign self-interests. States are caught in complex patterns of dominance, dependence, and interdependence. Weapons have become vital components of economic policy and international trade.

Sickness and disease remain serious problems in many places. Malaria, sleeping sickness, yellow fever, cholera, and diarrhea are still endemic to many poor societies. Cancer and heart disease now plague the affluent. But in neither case can these diseases be grasped in medical terms alone. They are related to malnutrition, environmental contamination, and the commercialization of agriculture and diet.

Similarly, large-scale migrations both within and between states pose problems for many societies. Many cities—Addis Ababa, Abidjan, Kinshasa, Mombasa, Ankara, Bogota—have major slums. Such slums result from the influx of people from the countryside. This influx results from processes that have to be understood in the context of the wider world economy. Conversely, the grand geopolitics of international conflict are expressed in refugee camps and illicit border crossings. The ebb and flow of employment in industrial societies produces invitations to "guest workers" and the hardline rejection of "illegal immigrants" in countries that are themselves almost entirely populated by immigrants.

No matter what specific problem or group of problems is taken up, there is no getting away from either the interconnectedness or the global scope of the structures and processes that now shape people's lives. This is what makes the scenarios of No World and Two Worlds so plausible. Yet, neither the precise character of this interconnectedness nor the contours of what some analysts have begun calling a "world system" or "global society" are easily captured in a single theoretical account. The world of connections remains relatively elusive, both for those who try to grasp its broad outlines within grand theoretical schemes and for those who act within it. This elusiveness is partly a matter of complexity. Scholars have also become increasingly sensitive to the dangers of deterministic theories in which one structure or force becomes the key to understanding all the others. Perhaps more significant still, the character of global connections appears in a rather different light depending on where the observer stands.

Geography counts. Warsaw is not Johannesburg; Santiago is not Cairo. Marginalization in Liverpool is not the same as marginalization in Manila. The problems faced by women in Tokyo, Moscow, or Delhi or in the villages of Mali and Mexico cannot all be reduced to any simple common equation. It is difficult to characterize even the operation of the states system in a way that captures the preoccupations of those living in the Middle East as well as those in Australasia or China. Those living in Eastern Europe are preoccupied with their relationship with the Soviet Union. In Western Europe or Canada almost everything seems to hinge on relations with the United States and the political economy of the Atlantic Alliance. In the Middle East, the interplay of regional and global geopolitics with religious and secular cultural processes creates a complex politics that is difficult to interpret on the basis of experiences elsewhere. Central America, Latin America, Japan, Pakistan, Indonesia: Each region, each society interprets the world in terms of its own place within it. In fact, the very attempt to develop a general theory of global interconnectedness begs the question of the point of view from which the analysis is to be conducted.

The problem is more than geographical. For most people struggling to cope with violence, poverty, and injustice in the modern world, talk of global structures is simply alien and unreal. Scholars and politicians may speak of the world economy or the international system. They may attribute powers of determination to them. People may be told that sacrifices have to be made to the World Bank or the "national interest." But these seem to be sacrifices to remote gods, disembodied from the aching grind of everyday life.

The world economy and the international system are certainly referred to in textbooks and government documents. They are the "realities" invoked by hardheaded academics and policy makers. But for most people, it is difficult to ascribe reality to such huge abstractions. Reality appears as immediacy, as the touch, taste, and smell of particular communities in particular places dealing with particular people and institutions. Friends, relatives, and lovers are taken away just before dawn. A neighbor is thrown out of work. Particular communities are singled out for abuse and discrimination.

People live in a variety of circumstances. They are subject to all kinds of pressures from a great number of sources. To understand individuals, it is necessary to have some idea of where they stand in relation to their economic, social, cultural, and geographical environment, to know their genders, personalities, personal histories, and so on. Of course, if taken far enough, this way of thinking can lead to the dissolution of all explanations of social processes into mere accident and contingency. Yet, without going so far, it is essential to be open to the sheer diversity of human experiences as well as to try to understand the larger structural forces of our time. Structures cannot be separated from histories.

Six Questions

For many people, it is enough to be concerned with the problems at hand. These are often overwhelming. To engage in immediate struggles of life and death is to have little time for reflection about the struggles' wider relevance. Reflection may come later, or from those who recognize parallel concerns from afar. Again, such reflection can remain concerned with relatively specific concerns. The elimination of nuclear weapons or the eradication of famine, say, seems enough work for several generations. But more is at stake here than what is to be done about specific problems. To try to understand the contemporary convergence of global structures and plural histories is to raise six groups of very serious questions about how to even think about what is to be done about the pressing problems of the age.

The first group of questions concerns what it means to act in a world of global problems, of global structures and connections. More and more people may be aware that we live on a small and vulnerable planet, or that the structures that determine how we live are worldwide in scope. Yet the fact is that, despite the claims of superpowers and transnational corporations and the best intentions of international organizations, our political processes remain fragmented. To speak of democracy or authority or accountability in such a situation is to engage in a considerable amount of wishful thinking. The structures of democratic participation are increasingly remote from the dynamics of global power.

A *second group of questions* concerns the character and significance of the modern state. After all, it is to the state that one is supposed to turn for answers and policies for pressing problems. But states, as the primary claimants to the legitimate use of power in the modern world, are themselves caught up in the structures they claim to control.

States undoubtedly do have the capacity to respond to many serious problems. India, for example, has managed to achieve self-sufficiency in basic food. Greece, New Zealand, and the Philippines have attempted to limit their participation in nuclear military structures. The Soviet Union has tried to pursue far-reaching negotiations about nuclear arms reduction as well as a more open society internally. Argentina, Brazil, Uruguay, Haiti, and the Philippines have recently made transitions from dictatorship and military rule to some sort of constitutional order. China has achieved a remarkable deceleration in its population growth. And so on. All these cases may be controversial on many counts, but they do suggest that states can achieve a great deal.

Although states undoubtedly have a capacity to respond to many of these problems, the problems themselves may also be seen as mere symptoms of much deeper forces, forces that are beyond the scope of short-term state policies alone. Some of these forces are perhaps comparable to those historical transformations that brought the modern state into existence in the first place. They are certainly likely to change the character of the state and its relation to economic, cultural, and political processes.

A *third group of questions* concerns the way people organize themselves in response to both emerging global structures and existing states. The character of the familiar mass movements of socialism and nationalism as well as specific organizational forms, like political parties, is relevant here.

Nationalist and socialist movements, as well as the broader struggle for democracy over the past few centuries, have been able to articulate connections between the particularities of people's experiences in seemingly diverse circumstances. Whether in terms of class consciousness, of a sense of national identity, or of ideas about the rights of all peoples to exercise some control over the forces that shape their lives, political thinkers and activists have sought to show how diverse experience can be transcended through participation in broad struggles rooted in a shared community or potential solidarity. In one way or another, such movements have sought unity by seeking to reduce diverse experiences into one underlying common identity: the nation; the proletariat; a free agent in the market economy. This claimed unity has been reinforced through the identification of the state as the primary source and objective of political power. This identification is also central to the way political parties have become the primary organizational intermediary between states and individual citizens or the way trade unions participate in the relationships between workers, corporations, and states. The development of new patterns of global interaction and the way states are responding to these changing patterns seem likely to require serious rethinking of the appropriateness of these conventional images of political organization.

Conventional political ideologies also seem to have lost much of their vitality. A *fourth group of questions* thus concerns the extent to which these can be revitalized or whether changing circumstances call for radically different ways of envisioning the future.

A *fifth group of questions,* growing out of all of these, concerns the spirit in which it is appropriate to try to respond to the most pressing problems of the age. Is it a matter of finding the right agent, like the state or alliance of states? Is it a matter of putting the right people in charge of existing institutions? Is it more appropriate to find the right method of administration, to eradicate petty jealousies and major intrigues in order to allow some meritocracy to organize things according to criteria of common sense or utilitarian efficiency? Is it a matter of finding more appropriate policies; or is it more a matter of wholesale political transformation? Most significant perhaps, is it not too easy to be caught up in untenable choice between pragmatic tinkering with the status quo and the search for yet another prophet of salvation? If we recognizing that the status quo cannot hold, the image of the charismatic hero—whether as an individual or a special privileged group—provides an all-too-seductive Archimedian point through which all problems may be identified and resolved.

All these themes converge, finally, on *the sixth group of questions,* about the emergence of novel political forces and, particularly, about the significance of social movements. Large-scale transformations always bring forth new political actors and new forms of political action. Social movements are particularly significant in this respect. They have always arisen to express opposition to dominant power structures as well as to respond to structural dislocation. They have always provided a good indicator of the character of social change, both in the past and at the present time.

Emerging Political Practices

Social movements have been associated primarily with Western industrial societies, where they are identified in terms of specific struggles around nuclear weapons, feminism, and ecology. But there are fairly well known movements elsewhere, especially in Central Europe, India, and Latin America. In many poorer societies, movements are still largely motivated by nationalistic attempts to preserve a country's political, economic, and cultural autonomy. Yet even in these societies, there are many movements struggling around a great variety of specific issues, such as deforestation, access to water, bride burnings and communal rape, the protection of ethnic minorities, local community development, and the plight of the urban poor.

Questions about what ought to be done about particular problems and about appropriate political practices may be posed in many different contexts. They may be asked of those who see the state as the only significant political actor, or of those who see international organizations as the best forum for problems of global concern, or of those who remain satisfied with conventional political ideologies and forms of political organization. But it is in the context of emerging forms of political practice that such questions seem most dynamic, most likely to encourage a capacity to slip through or behind the familiar clichés and dead ends of contemporary debate about peace and justice.

In an age of histories, none of the traditional claims to political community or solidarity is necessarily privileged of necessity. The state is not going to disappear, though it will undoubtedly be transformed. Class consciousness or national identity may still be indispensable in some situations. The pursuit of democracy is certainly at the center of all emancipatory projects everywhere. But not only is it unhelpful to rely on a single account of the emerging relationships between states systems, world economy, and so on; it is no longer possible to take a single view privileging the perspective of any particular group of people.

On the contrary, in an age in which it is so important to try to understand the relationships between the seemingly fragmented forces that affect us, it is equally important to try to understand how different people actually experience these relationships on an everyday basis under different circumstances. This is why it is necessary to try to understand the emerging connections between the most powerful forces of our time—and the opportunities and dangers to which they give rise—from the point of view of people who are trying to respond to these forces in different situations, who are engaged in highly specific struggles.

Scholars point to structures that are worldwide. All kinds of social movements are now responding to intolerable conditions in particular places and situations. Conventional political strategies try to respond to both global structures and specific injustices through the power and authority of the state. Whether for scholars or politicians or movements, the need to interpret the interconnectedness of the modern world is crucial. Scholars may have sophisticated analytical tools for mapping the patterns of contemporary human affairs. Politicians may have the power of the state at their disposal. By comparison, social movements can compete neither in analytical sophistication nor in overt power with which to respond to pressing problems. Yet movements are particularly sensitive to connections that may be invisible both to those with refined analytical categories and those who wield the instruments of power.

The struggles of particular movements can and must be understood in their specificity. Indeed, it is just as difficult to make sense of the great variety of contemporary social movements as of the interconnected character of the modern world. Some of the best-known movements are concerned with problems in particular states. Mass movements have been particularly prominent in South Africa, the Philippines, Chile, Poland, South Korea, and Iran. Other movements have coalesced around specific problems: women's movements, environmental movements, antinuclear movements, consumers' movements, and movements struggling for human rights. Combining geographical location and struggles around specific problems is already enough to understand the diversity of even the best known social movements. Yet, in many places, modern political life is characterized by hundreds of much smaller and much more specific movements, centered in particular urban areas, for example, or concerned with education and health care, or arising from particular religions or cultural groups. Some are concerned with challenging threatening megaprojects such as dams, nuclear facilities, or military installations. Some promote alternative forms of technology or education or agricultural methods within local development initiatives. Movements that encourage local theater groups or increase awareness of the benefits of breastfeeding draw on similar energies and strategies as do movements attempting to convert military production into socially useful goods or to stop toxic waste disposal or campaign on behalf of political prisoners.

The bigger and better-known movements often resemble conventional nationalist movements or political parties. The smaller ones are difficult to distinguish from the normal groupings of everyday social life. They may look like interest groups trying to press their advantage in a competitive environment or like community groups trying to express their collective identity. Some push for particular goals; others seek more general transformations.

There are serious limits to the extent to which it is possible to categorize and analyze movements in this way. There is always a danger of imposing premature classifications onto political processes that have not yet run their course. The available empirical research does not yet encourage fine distinctions. It is possible to point to fully formed movements, such as women's and environmentalist groups, as well as to almost inarticulate stirrings or to groups as different as the Muslim Brotherhood or Moscow Trust Group that are exceptionally difficult to categorize at all. To use a label like "fundamentalist" is to obscure distinctions between movements that insist on an exclusivist interpretation of a truth claim and those engaged in a more open politics of cultural resurgence. Categories like "revolutionary," "reformist," or "counterrevolutionary" are notoriously slippery. Indeed, the difficulty of theorizing about social movements in general gives an indication why they have become so interesting to people seeking to find some way through the conventional horizons of contemporary political debate.

Even so, although social movements struggle in specific situations, many of them—those that can be called critical social movements—are able to look beyond the immediacy and specificity of their struggle to understand at least some of the wider connections in which they are caught. It is the capacity to interpret connections that gives certain kinds of movements a vitality and significance that goes beyond the claims of scholars and politicians, claims that are in any case often rooted in relatively limited interests and assumptions. It is this capacity, present in varying degrees in many different kinds of movements, that is of particular concern here.

This interpretive capacity begins with a recognition of three closely related ways of understanding the broader context of particular struggles. First, in trying to respond to specific problems and forces, movements are forced to broaden their understanding of the processes that affect particular struggles. They discover that to act in a specific arena is to respond to structures that, although seemingly remote, have a tremendous impact on immediate experiences.

Second, they discover connections between processes that are conventionally understood to be separate. The conventional analytical categories force apart what to movements appear as complex webs of continuity between, say, culture and economy, technology and gender, or children's play and missile deployment.

Third, movements learn to interpret the ways in which people's everyday lives are inserted into seemingly remote structures and how these structures are in turn registered and integrated into language and emotion, into fantasy and everyday routine. They recognize how the big questions about war, violence, poverty, and ecological malaise are related to the myriad minor injustices that crop up every day. Movements begin to understand that large-scale structures are always dynamic and that people are always in varying degrees of resistance and accommodation to them.

Specific struggles are pursued by particular groups for their own reasons. But this capacity to interpret and act on connections is central to the way that many movements in quite different situations have begun to learn from each other. This capacity makes it possible to make some initial distinctions between critical social movements and movements of a more conventional or reactionary character. On the basis of this capacity, critical social movements confront important challenges of imagination and open up the possibilities of a just world peace in new ways.

RESPONDING TO CONNECTIONS

Connections and Economy

Movements responding to conditions of economic inequality have usually been at the forefront of social and political change. Now, in placing considerable stress on the need to recognize the connections between economic processes and other aspects of our social life, contemporary labor movements and movements for alternative forms of economic development repeat one of the most powerful messages being given by critical social movements everywhere.

As we all know, wealth is concentrated within all societies according to hierarchies of class, gender, color, and so on. This is not just a matter of distribution. It is also a matter of the way that production priorities are arranged. Societies organize their economies in order to produce things for particular groups.

Wealth is also concentrated in some regions of the world, particularly within the OECD states. Resources and energies are invested in wasteful and counterproductive ways, not least on huge military systems. Many people are not working, and others are exploited where they work. Land is uncultivated while millions have little, if anything, to eat. People live in ill health and deprivation, undernourished. They suffer premature death. In a world that produces enough to keep everyone currently alive living at a fairly tolerable material standard, millions live in conditions of degradation and with the imminent possibility of starvation.

Reports on modern economic inequalities are even more striking than reports on the militarization of so many facets of human affairs. Even in the more affluent societies, the consequences of the restructuring of the world economy are apparent to all but the most privileged. There may still be many who remain convinced that everything is simply the consequence of a normal cyclical downturn. Yet more and more people know that mass unemployment is here to stay and that poor housing, declining standards of health, cuts in social services, and so on, are symptoms of a much more serious long-term trend. Large numbers of people leave school knowing that they will never find the full-time jobs they had been brought up to expect. Even amid a society of plenty, the promise of material prosperity for all remains an unfulfilled dream. Centrally planned economies are also characterized by slow "growth" rates and inefficiencies, rising prices, and declining living standards. Problems are made worse by international indebtedness. In the least affluent societies, things are obviously very serious indeed.

Nowhere is all this made more apparent than in accounts of conditions under which so many children are now living. Although children are unable to reflect in any sophisticated way on the social processes in which they participate, we have come to know a good deal about what children living in different circumstances may expect from the world they are just beginning to recognize. Cold statistics speak for children. About forty thousand of the world's young children die every day from hunger-related causes. Millions more are malnourished, blinded, brain-damaged, and disabled by preventable infections and poverty. Even in the center of affluence, in New York City, about 40 percent of the children live in families with incomes below the official poverty line.

Such suffering remains part of the human condition. From all over the world it is clear that present forms of economy, although still presented in a rhetoric of hope and progress, in fact bring despair and threat to the survival of millions of people.

Economic injustice has always brought protest and revolt, moral indict-ment and political revolution. People around the world continue to resist intolerable economic conditions. It is perhaps in the context of economic struggles that a capacity to see a clear connection between local problems and wider structural dynamics has been developed most powerfully. Nineteenth-century coal miners in Wales quickly learned to see the connec-tion between their problems and the broader pattern of ownership and con-trol at a national level. Twentieth-century tin miners in Bolivia have made similar connections between their local struggles and the need for a na-tional response to the ravages of multinational investment. Attempts to en-hance South Korea's standing as a "newly industrializing country" are clearly at the root of harsh working conditions and the abuse of human rights.

Most of the best-known struggles of the present day confront such con-nections quite starkly. Whatever the complexities of its internal support, the Aquino government is very seriously constrained by the location of the Philippines within webs of economic pressure and geopolitical force. Politi-cal revolution has not brought land reform. The fate of the Palestinians is juggled around between many layers of regional and global interests. The persistence of apartheid in South Africa cannot be separated from the per-ceived security and economic interests of external powers. Abuses of human rights in Latin America, Central Europe, and elsewhere depend on the interplay between local interests and the ever-present arm of a super-power. In such cases, the connections between local struggles and global structures are relatively obvious, at least in broad outline. For many move-ments, the need to clarify precisely what these connections are becomes compelling when it becomes apparent just how far they constrain the pos-sibilities of any purely local progress.

Economic movements have also been in the forefront in making a second kind of connection, that which involves putting into question the compartmentalized categories in which modern life is understood and con-structed. Thus, although most struggles around economic processes do in-volve attempts to reduce inequality, they also often call for a reconstruction of the nature of economic activity itself. It is becoming more and more obvi-ous to many people, particularly those who act collectively around eco-nomic problems at a grassroots level, that economic crisis is not just a matter of lower profits, mass unemployment, and starvation, but is also a crisis in the way wealth is produced.

There is nothing new in this realization. It has been a recurring theme of progressive labor movements for a long time. Even so, there is now a re-newed critique of the alienation created by existing forms of production, including the devaluation of skills and forced migration. Similarly, there is a widespread critique of the way in which, in so many places, economic development has led to the destruction of cultures, traditions, and communities, as well as the physical environment. There is also a growing awareness that particular forms of economic life interact with and intensify different forms of social conflict, particularly those around gender, race, ethnicity, and even age.

Nothing is more indicative of what is at stake here than the increasingly controversial character of the idea of economic development. The very term "development" has become one of the most bitterly contested words of our time. Once it embodied proud hopes. It promised a future written as an extrapolation of History. The grand vision of progress from barbarism and superstition was busily translated into economic categories, policies of foreign aid, and the standards of national behavior expected by international financial institutions.

For many people, at least a vague approximation of this vision has been realized. Others can hope for it to materialize in the foreseeable future. But for millions of others it has been a cruel mirage, a prize beyond reach and quickly receding from view.

Political leaders may try to improve the position of their societies within the world economy. They may search for a more appropriate niche within the system, concentrate their resources in areas of comparative advantage, call for the stabilization of commodity prices, or encourage a solution to the international debt crisis. For many people, even those strategies are quite irrelevant. For the most vulnerable and marginalized peoples, the promise of development handed down by abstract economic theory, by multinational corporations, and by superpowers is not only unattainable but also often undesirable. This form of development itself has come to threaten their chances of survival. They search instead for alternative forms of development, ones that are more in keeping with indigenous traditions and local needs.

A parallel process is occurring in the more affluent societies among established labor movements, whose concern is less with the fate of the already marginalized than with the changes occurring as a consequence of the worldwide flexibility of capital and the increasing resort to capital-intensive forms of technology and production. On the one hand, labor movements attempt to preserve the achievements of past struggles, especially for those within well-established manufacturing sectors. On the other, there are signs of an attempt both to respond to the needs of workers who are in the process of becoming marginalized and to cope with the consequences of global economic transformations in ways that go beyond conventional considerations of profit and wage-labor relations.

The search for alternative forms of economic development in marginalized societies and innovations in thinking about the nature of economic life among established labor movements seem to be part of a common pattern.

In both contexts there have been significant attempts to create alternative forms of economic organization. In relation to the scale of the primary dynamics of modern economic life, these attempts are perhaps rather minuscule. Yet, they are indicative of a significant rethinking of the nature of economic life that is occurring in quite different situations.

In more affluent societies, similar energies have been directed toward the establishment of cooperatives and community or worker-owned enterprises. The response by workers to cutbacks at Lucus Aerospace in England in the mid-1970s, for example, has encouraged attempts elsewhere to demand the right to work on socially useful and needed technologies. In societies threatened by development from the spread of the world economy, local movements try to work with local resources and traditions, using technology that is appropriate both to the prevailing environmental conditions and to the special idiosyncrasies of the local social structures. In such cases, it becomes clear that tradition is often a good deal more efficient and less destructive of people's lives than the capital-intensive methods introduced by outside experts. What happens when people lose control over the economic processes that affect their lives is brutally displayed in the development disasters that are at the core of recent African famines.

In both cases, there is an emerging sense that economic activity is not the only issue, or perhaps not even the major issue, involved in these situations. Alternative development movements quickly discover that poverty is not a purely economic problem. It is a function of the location of the poor within complex economic, social, and cultural structures that divide those who have access to global patterns of economic growth and distribution from those who are excluded. Movements of forest dwellers and tribal groups in India understand that to challenge a specific dam is to engage in a movement for better housing. Like movements organized around the Chico Dam in the Philippines or the Dona Kor environmental action group concerned with damming of the Danube in Hungary, they know that to challenge a specific dam is to challenge the economic, political, social, and cultural assumptions of a whole society. Movements demanding more adequate housing understand that squatting in vacant dwellings is to put into question the gap between the conventions of entrenched property rights and the failure to provide for the basic needs for people's survival.

Struggles with economic vulnerability have to engage not only with structures of economic class, but also with those of caste, ethnicity, gender, and age. The narrow categories of economics expand to encompass the establishment of social, cultural, and political rights of the poor. Similarly, movements attempting to create alternative economic forms outside the structures of corporate capital and market exchange become especially sensitive to the dehumanizing myth of the rational and isolated individual that stands at the heart of modern economic theory. They see instead that we are social beings, for whom work and collective enterprise can have meaning as well as material reward.

If viewed in a longer historical perspective, this challenge to contemporary conceptions of what we mean by an economy is hardly surprising. The currently dominant conception of economic life is of relatively recent origin. It has evolved along with the modern world economy and has depended on a process of separating out various spheres of human activity from each other and then subjecting them to specialized treatment. Economists have invented their own rather bizarre ideas about what constitutes rational behavior. These ideas often jar disconcertingly with the way people act in practice. What is more serious is that these ideas have enabled people to stop thinking about how to create forms of economic life that are appropriate for human development. Conversely, it has become very easy to treat human development as coextensive with a narrowly instrumental—and intrinsically inequalitarian—form of economic life.

Thus, from the point of view of those who struggle to help people respond creatively to the economic crises of our time, it is not enough—though it is urgently necessary—to put an end to the worst scandals of poverty and degradation. It is also essential that we reconstruct the way we all produce and reproduce ourselves through economic activity. Such a necessity is not so simply because contemporary economic structures are not working very well, although this is undoubtedly true; but it is more crucial because any attempt to create more effective economic forms has to begin by stressing, rather than forgetting about, the close connections between economic processes and all other aspects of everyday life.

Connections and Gender

This sensitivity to both the need to react to the intolerable and the need to understand connections is characteristic of movements around many other issues. Many women's movements, for example, are particularly insistent on this point. The very recognition of patriarchal structures is itself a recognition of connections that have usually remained hidden. Women's movements see that problems of gender inequality are merely the surfaces of power relations than run very deep within economic and cultural structures. They see that the achievement of greater power for women depends on an ability to decode the connections between the objectifications of scientific discourse and the objectifications of mass advertising, between the stereotyping of gender roles and the dynamics of race relations, between the labor process and the family as a site of repression, violence, and the reproduction of labor. They explore the intimate connections between the sexual division of labor and the economic division of labor, between gender and class. Without this ability to make such connections, and thus the capacity to see the possibility of reconstructing them in different ways, women's movements would lose most of their contemporary vibrancy.

Connections and Environment

Environmental movements have become politically significant only recently. Except perhaps for the cases of the Green party in West Germany and of Greenpeace, their public profile has remained rather low. They also tend to encompass a wide range of political persuasions and are as likely to draw on conservative or romantic forms of reaction as on more critical energies. But then again, they are also able to interpret what it means to engage in conservation or to reconstruct more traditional ways of life.

Environmental movements are particularly important as interpreters of connections. This is not just a matter of showing how ecological destruction results from states pursuing their own self-interest without regard for the global commons or the way the world economy depends on pollution and the ravaging of natural resources in return for short-term profits for a few. Nor is it only a matter of pushing for a greater sensitivity to the biospheric systems that allow us to live and warning of the fragility of these systems when confronted by the despoilation of modern societies. Disappearing forests, vanishing ozone, poisons in the food chain, mercury in the rivers, lead in the air, lifeless soils, desertification: These are all very serious problems in their own right. But they also pose questions about the economic, political, technological, cultural, and even philosophical systems that caused these problems to arise in the first place. The way we treat the planet becomes a measure of the way people treat each other.

Although environmental movements are best known in Western societies, they take particularly interesting forms in societies that have seen long-established economic and cultural traditions incorporating a strong sense of ecological harmony disrupted by processes of rapid modernization. In India, for example, many movements have resisted the destruction of soil, water, and vegetation systems as a result of irrigation projects, dam building, and the pollution of fishing grounds. The Chipko, or "Hug the Tree," movement is the most famous of these. It began in the early 1970s when village women in the Himalayan foothills responded to flooding and landslides precipitated by deforestation. They challenged lumber companies to cut them down first in order to get at the remaining timber. This illustrates both the spontaneous, grassroots character of such movements and the way that resistance to specific vulnerabilities leads people to recover philosophical and ethical traditions as a guide to future possibilities.

As a tactic, hugging the trees proved successful in several important cases and quickly spread to environmental actions in other areas of the country. But beyond the successful skirmishes with more powerful forces,

Chipko stimulated a broader critique of dominant social, economic, technological, and cultural processes. Environmental movements everywhere have been especially successful in challenging atomistic and reductionist conceptions of scientific knowledge and drawing attention to the possibilities of more appropriate forms of technology. They have also begun to articulate credible conceptions of sustainable life for people through genuinely collective management.

In modern industrial societies, a concern with environmental problems easily turns into a romanticized idealization of premodern life. In the case of movements like Chipko, environmental movements act in the context of cultural and philosophical traditions that retain considerable vitality and which allow for the conceptualization of more ecologically sensitive practices in a way that is directly meaningful to people's everyday lives. In this context, it becomes clear that steadiness and stability do not necessarily mean stagnation and that balance with nature involves considerable— though not capital-intensive—technological sophistication. The notion of a deeply rooted contrast between tradition and modernity so essential to dominant economic and political categories is again seriously undermined. The experience of remote forest dwellers in India resonates very clearly with the struggles within more affluent societies, such as that in British Columbia in the face of the ecological devastation brought by half a century of plundering of timber resources. It resonates with all those movements for whom access to wood and water is a matter of survival, a matter of basic human rights.

Connections and War

Despite the sheer size of the antinuclear movements in Western societies, their concerns can sometimes appear fairly specific and even parochial. But even here, the central message is once again a stress on connections. These movements gained considerable strength in the wake of the collapse of détente between the superpowers in the late 1970s. The deployments of increasingly provocative weapons under the pretext of the "modernization" of NATO was a particularly important stimulus. In view of explicit shifts from nuclear deterrence to war-fighting postures, of the visible contempt for processes of arms control, and the crude rhetoric of renewed cold war, even normally conservative and apolitical people have recognized that something is seriously wrong. Under these conditions, it is not necessary to be radical, subversive, or pacifist to know that contemporary forms of "defense" are becoming more dangerous than any conceivable enemy.

But although much of the energy in the contemporary antinuclear movements has been directed at changing specific policies, much more is at stake than a narrow response to the so-called arms race. In fact, it has become clear to many people that the term "arms race" is thoroughly misleading. Weapons deployments are understood to be less the result of competitive responses by states heading toward some well-defined goal than they are the result of the nature of available technology, the condition of the economy, allocations made for defense budgets, pressures from armed services and bureaucratic institutions, ideological fervor, and so on. Weapons systems themselves are known to be not only a matter of defense requirements but are thoroughly integrated into social, economic, cultural, technological, and political structures of immense complexity. It has become clear that the problems posed by nuclear weapons cannot be separated from questions about, for example, development or environment.

Although people's deepest fears may be concentrated on "the bomb," contemporary antinuclear movements have come to recognize that the structures and processes that support nuclear weapons are already deforming, maiming, and killing. These structures and processes extend into all spheres of normal everyday life. They infiltrate games, toys, languages, and fantasies. They induce a sense of powerlessness and incomprehension, undermining both the legitimacy of the state's claim to provide security and the processes of democracy through which people are supposed to exercise some control over matters of their life and death. For some, these structures and processes are overt, immediate, and physical. For others, their effect is more insidious. People recognize that they have simply become used to living in a civilization that places the preparation for mass murder at the center of its agenda.

Thus European peace groups, particularly European Nuclear Disarmament (END) have been understandably obsessed with the overt dangers of specific weapons systems like Pershing II and cruise missiles. But these missiles have also become symbols of a much wider project. They raise very broad questions about the relations between Western Europe and the United States, about the need to rethink the division between Western and Eastern Europe, about the lack of democracy in the formulation of European security policy, and about the connection between fears of future war and the present consequences of violence and hatred induced by the cold war. These questions will remain even if the most provocative weapons systems are removed.

Similar connections are raised by the Hibakuska movement of radiation survivors. Meeting forty years after Hiroshima, victims of exposure to nuclear weapons have begun to demand an acknowledgment of the connection between the dropping of nuclear bombs and the suffering of those who have been exposed to radiation from uranium mining, production, and waste dumping as well as from weapons testing in the Marshall Islands, French Polynesia, and Australia. Again, the stress is on the connection between threats of future extermination and ongoing deceptions, secrecy, suppression of human rights, and the distortion of socioeconomic life.

In many parts of the world, movements concerned with national security issues are much less concerned with nuclear weapons. They focus on more familiar forms of state aggression and push for more effective forms of security within a continental or regional setting. There is no doubt that the confrontation between superpowers impinges on security problems everywhere. Nevertheless, in some places security problems arise primarily from the more local hegemonies of particular states like South Africa, or from continuing border disputes of the kind familiar in the history of Latin America, or from the introduction of ever more deadly weaponry as a result of the growing trade and aid in armaments. Even in these situations, however, it is clear that a concern with security leads directly to a greater awareness of the complex forces that combine to create insecurity in specific settings.

Connections and Human Rights

Such forces are of equal concern with what are usually called human rights movements. Although abstract principles have been enshrined in internationally sanctioned declarations, abuses of human rights remain epidemic. And although the abstract principles have been expanded beyond narrow Western liberal conceptions of political rights to encompass social and economic considerations, many movements insist on the achievement of an even broader understanding of what the struggle for human rights involves. Organizations such as Amnesty International find plenty to do by acting within the bounds of established legal norms. Mass movements have managed to topple brutal dictatorships.

But in the long run, the most important human rights movements are those that have been forced to change from resistance to brutality to a thorough rethinking of the political conditions under which fundamental rights can become assured. Some struggles for human rights become linked to struggles against the interventionary diplomacy of superpowers or the coercive apparatus of the nuclear national security state. Others explore the way that political or economic conflict is channeled into the repression of ethnic, religious, and linguistic minorities, such as Sikhs in India, Tamils in Sri Lanka, Kurds in the Middle East, Eritreans in Ethiopia, and Chinese in Indonesia and Vietnam. Still others recognize connections between human rights violations and attempts to "modernize" a state from the top down to comply with IMF conditionality and the requirements of capital formation, as in South Korea, Taiwan, and Singapore. It is precisely the recognition of connections of this kind that has led so many human rights movements, like those in Latin America or Eastern Europe, to become so concerned with the need to enhance processes of democratization.

Connections and Culture

Many other people are concerned with problems of a primarily cultural character, particularly with threats to their individual and collective identity.

The meaningfulness of human existence has become especially problematic in the twentieth century. Modern intellectual histories are in large part accounts of a crisis in values, of a disenchantment of the world, of a loss of meaning within the iron cage of bureaucracy and instrumental reason. The global spread of functionalism and modernity has swamped cultures and civilizations. People are torn from traditions that have lost their conviction and enter global systems where conviction is only skin deep. Global communication accompanies the erasure of local conversation. Whether celebrated in angst or ambivalence, in romanticism or unabashed relief, the modern age offers a cold heart.

Movements that respond to these themes often express at the level of culture forces that are as much economic, social, or political as they are cultural. This has always been true of nationalism. It has been true more recently in the resurgence of Islam in so many societies. The case of Iran is fairly typical, for it shows how the convergence of religious and cultural traditions with political revolution may be a response to the combination of rapid political development and geopolitical penetration that has been such a common experience for so many societies.

Cultural politics are always difficult to interpret, never more so than in the late twentieth century. Cultural assertion may be primarily a form of political resistance. It can involve a recovery of self-consciousness on the part of peoples who have been told that they are obsolete. It can involve a dialogue between the still vital energies of different cultural traditions, including those that are usually understood as modern. Khoumaini offers one vision of what is possible; Gandhi offers another. Depending on the circumstances, the pursuit of cultural identity can lead to the assertion of rights of self-determination, to the revitalization of political life in local communities, and to experimentation with alternative forms of property ownership, such as those now proposed in aboriginal land claims in parts of Canada and elsewhere. In all these cases, a primary concern with cultural issues leads into a concern with the way societies as a whole are organized.

The theme of connections emerges from the struggles around cultural themes in two particularly important areas. First, it leads to questions of identity and community. If one is attached to a particular community, what is one's relationship with people in other communities, or indeed with other human beings as such? Cultural life has been primarily particularistic. This is why the proliferation of histories has so often been articulated as a diversity of cultural identities. This particularism has been institutionalized within the states system, and the states system has formalized a clear-cut division between the claims of national citizenship and the claims of humanity as such. Nationalism and the claims of national community remain very powerful. But ethnic nationalisms not formalized within states are also powerful and in many situations cut across state boundaries. Other cultural movements—from women asserting their identity as women to intellectuals as-

serting their participation in a cultural life that transcends national boundaries—intimate the emergence of quite new forms of cultural interaction
and community. The conventional forms of cultural allegiance, with their
reliance on a clear-cut division between insiders and outsiders are often becoming more fluid.

Concerns about cultural identity and community also involve questions
about relationships, not with people in general or with citizens of particular
states or members of particular cultures, but with the emerging structures
of inclusion and exclusion being created by modern political and economic
processes. If one is attached to the universalizing values being spread by the
world economy, what is one's relationship with those whose own sense of
identity is being crushed? How is it possible to engage in a cultural politics
that does not depend on a stark choice between modernity and tradition,
universal and particular, dominant and dominated?

Second, the theme of connections leads to questions about appropriate
forms of knowledge. If we recognize the frailty of those conceptions of
knowledge, normative aspirations, methods of analysis, and so on, that have
arisen both out of the culture of modernity and out of other cultural traditions, then thinking about the future requires considerable exploration of
new ways of knowing the world. With the dissolution of the contrast between tradition and modernity, as well as the internal critique of modernity
itself, it is clear that no cultural tradition has a monopoly on truth. This realization is not a matter of nihilistic relativism, but it is a recognition that our
understanding of what constitutes knowledge is always changing and is
changing under social conditions.

Struggles of Connection

The terms used here to describe all these groupings of social movements
are both general and conventional. They do not discriminate very well between the many different kinds of movements that can be forced into the
categories of "feminist," "environmentalist," and so on. They cover up in
generalizing language thousands of different movements, some large
enough to make governments tremble, others small and disorganized. For
the moment, this matters less than the way the most interesting of these
movements are involved in struggles of connection. They may not intend to
be. They may begin around very specific problems. But they find that they
have to be. To be effective in dealing with specific problems, movements
have to learn to recognize and act in a wider world.

The real problem with these conventional terms is not their overgener-
ality but the way they force movements into categories that are much too
narrow to encompass what they are doing. Movements may begin in one
context, but they often move very quickly to others. To struggle on the

ground of human rights in Latin America is to come up against the problems of national debt, economic penetration, and disputes over territorial boundaries between states. The victims of nuclear weapons tests in the Marshall Islands of the South Pacific have caught the world's imagination because what has ruined their lives threatens to do the same for everyone else. The people struggling against poverty in the fertile Philippine Island of Negros understand very well that they are engaged with structures that reach much further than the degraded personal behavior of the Marcos regime. The difference between movements of women and of environmentalists is a shifting frontier. To engage in struggles around health, refugees, homelessness, or urban ghettos is to engage not with a single problem but with a field of structures and processes, some very local, others with unmistakable global reach.

The world is not short of information about the perils of the age. The experience of social movements in this respect merely echoes the warnings of volume upon volume of data, statistical projections, computer models, and sophisticated theoretical speculation. We are overloaded with information. Similarly, in stressing the need to interpret such warnings in the context of an understanding of the increasingly interconnected nature of the modern world, movements are also corroborating the commonplace conclusions of scholarly observers everywhere. There may be squabbles over details, but the overall picture is well known despite the lack of theoretical clarity about how the interconnected character of the modern world ought to be specified. What movements add to the better-known analyses of overall trends issued by international organizations, state bureaucracies, universities, and research institutions, in academic jargon and populist prose, is a sense of what it means to live at the intersection. Governments know, but they postpone action if possible. Movements know and are forced to act. Governments know but believe old prescriptions will still work. Movements know, and they are also more likely to recognize an outdated prescription when they see one.

CHALLENGES OF IMAGINATION

The movements that have been mentioned here are clearly very diverse both in their aims and their organizational forms. Sometimes they seem quite familiar. They extend the experiences of labor movements, or turn into political parties, or combine to topple dictators. Yet they also fit uneasily into our conventional understanding of what political life is all about.

The difficulty here is not just the lack of convincing classifications of different kinds of movements but the way existing classifications draw on ideological traditions that are themselves increasingly in question. The way some movements respond to certain kinds of connections is important not least because many of these connections undermine our most powerful guides as to how political life should be conducted. Critical social movements both evade classification in terms of and challenge the very principles that give rise to our prevailing images of political power. Scholars may still find refuge in elaborate variations on well-worn themes, but movements are forced to struggle just as much with the limited horizons of dominant ideologies and visions as they are with more concrete problems. The superpowers and other influential states, too, no longer convince many people that they offer attractive models of the way ahead. Bhopal, Chernobyl, and the Strategic Defense Initiative symbolize a failure of the contemporary imagination on a colossal scale. Critical social movements everywhere are faced with a growing sense of the inadequacy of the great political doctrines—liberalism, socialism, and nationalism—that have dominated political life over the past century.

In its concern with the individual, the vitality of civil society, and democratic processes and institutions, liberalism has been a source of very creative inspiration and energy, though it has always been compromised by its intrinsic connections with forms of economic life that resulted in very illiberal inequalities. The credibility of liberalism has been put into particularly serious question as a result of the ravages brought about by recent transformations in the world economy. The postwar period of compromise and accommodation that—in Western industrial societies—brought Keynesian economics, the welfare state, and various forms of social democracy is being left behind. The bureaucratic state, which attempted to mediate the claims of individual freedom with those of social equality, has fallen under intense suspicion. A more reactionary form of liberalism, one extolling a narrowly conceived economic freedom in theory while aiding and legitimizing the unequal power of international and corporate capital in practice, now characterizes the policies of many of the world's most powerful states. It is becoming increasingly uncertain whether the more imaginative and emancipatory promises of liberalism can be maintained.

Socialism is perhaps the subject of even greater skepticism, not least because it has been tied for so long to the difficult experiences of the Soviet Union, China, and Eastern Europe. Indeed, in all these places there are encouraging signs of a willingness to admit past mistakes. Perhaps even more significant, signs indicate a recognition that some of the problems of socialist experience have been the result not of mistakes or particular personalities, or even of the way socialist societies have been challenged and undermined externally, but of deficiencies in the formulation of doctrine. The connection between socialism and the centralized state has been particularly suspect. Even so, socialism remains a terrain of considerable intellectual vibrancy in some places, particularly where attempts are being made to rethink fundamental theoretical positions or to engage with all kinds of social movements.

Nationalism, also, remains a very potent force. Even today, it is the dominant ideological thrust in those societies whose primary experience has been colonialism and dependency. Yet, although nationalism has been liberating for some, it has played an essential role in some of the most appalling events of this century.

It is not so much that liberalism, socialism, or nationalism fail to express values and aspirations that remain potent. It is more that both the ambivalence of the historical record and serious doubts about the way these ideologies remain trapped in the intellectual prejudices of an earlier age have combined to deprive them of popular conviction. There is instead a widespread sense that the aspirations they express require reformulation and revitalization.

Much the same is true of more visionary or utopian impulses. There has been an increasing recognition that utopian schemes for the future have usually involved an artificial separation of theory from practice and that the future has to be made rather than merely thought into being. There has been an increasing awareness that the best-known utopian schemes have involved the ethnocentric projection of Eurocentric concepts that do not translate very well into other cultural or socioeconomic contexts. There has even been an emerging sense that attempts to bring grand designs down to earth in this century have often involved the kind of violence that makes the creation of the envisaged world simply impossible.

Some explanation of the exhaustion yet tentative renewal of both grand ideologies and utopian traditions is to be found in difficulties inherent in some of the basic categories and concepts of modern political thinking. What, for example, is meant by "security"? In a world of multiple insecurities, the equation of security with national security is increasingly tenuous. Similar problems arise with the concept of "development." It is clear that the deep-rooted distinctions between developed and undeveloped, and all their synonyms, must be abandoned. We confront rather, a world in varying degrees of maldevelopment. And what does it now mean to speak of "politics" or "democracy"? In a world where power is dispersed in so many different directions, it is difficult to know where or how power is to be exercised or controlled.

It is disconcerting to know that cherished guidebooks are out of date or incomplete. But to recognize that this is in fact so is a precondition for creative politics in the late twentieth century. This is why the capacity of some kinds of movements to react to a world of connections is so crucial.

Not so long ago it was respectable to speak of the forthcoming "end of ideology," of a convergence toward a world where all doctrinal differences would be erased by the inevitable march to modernity. To make similar claims today is to invite ridicule, despite the increasing influence of global economic structures and the spread of cosmopolitan cultural styles. The Nicaraguan passion for baseball, for example, can hardly be taken as an indication of cultural or ideological convergence.

Rather, the modern world is characterized not only by global structures and cosmopolitan cultural forms but also by a bewildering array of political movements and stirrings. Some are familiar—the revolutionary movements, the pressure groups, the political parties—but many are not. And the stress on the way movements respond to connections makes it possible to specify two important distinctions between critical social movements and movements of a more familiar character. These two distinctions underlie the way critical social movements respond to the imaginative horizons of our age.

First, conventional forms of political life are concerned ultimately with the question of state power. For all their other differences, the claim that it is necessary to capture state power unites revolutionary mass movements with moderate parties employing electoral strategies. Yet, so many of the stirrings now visible around the world are less concerned with taking state power than with challenging more basic principles of everyday life. Women's movements are exemplary in this respect. Judged conventionally, these stirrings may not even appear to be political at all, precisely because they do not have state power as their primary goal. They may not even last very long or achieve any coherent institutional form.

The way some movements respond to connections is crucial precisely because many of these connections challenge the presumption that states must be treated as the center of political power. Rather, such movements show that in a world of connections, power is decentered, a matter of global relationships and local practices. They show that the patterns of inclusion and exclusion that are reproduced in the state in so many cultural processes must be and are being challenged, both by large structural forces and by seemingly disparate social movements. An openness to connections is, in short, openness to the way power is being reconstructed in the modern world.

Second, among the many stirrings now visible, many are clearly reactionary. Indeed, in purely quantitative terms, reactionary movements often seem to dominate the political landscape. But these movements are essentially closed. They look inward or backward. They separate believers from nonbelievers, saved from damned. Looking to the past, they annihilate histories. Whether as Klu Klux Klan, as religious fundamentalisms, or through slogans about evil empires and the magic of the market, the reactionary forces of our time maximize exclusion, render complexities in sharp strokes of black and white, and reject connections in favor of keeping their backs to the wall and their weapons point out.

There are many variations on the theme of reaction. The resurgence of Islam has rather different political expressions than does Christian fundamentalism in North America. Religious fundamentalism has to be distinguished from the return to Adam Smith or the images of former national greatness that have strangled the imaginations of so many national leaders. Yet, a common thread is the way so much energy is devoted to grasping at the simplest certainties at any cost. A common premium is placed on the literal interpretation of texts and traditions and on the exclusive and privileged insight of those who know how to read these texts clearly. This is why, whatever the populist or democratic rhetoric, movements of reaction exaggerate hierarchies and justify the need for order from above. These forces of reaction are profoundly antidemocratic.

To be alive to the threatening complexities of modern life is to be susceptible to cynicism, even fundamentalism. There are many ways of closing oneself off. There are many ways of saying that there is no alternative to what already is, many ways of arguing that optimism, even a skeptical optimism, is only for the naive or well-to-do. There is obviously no shortage of political actors, including many social movements, now engaging in a politics of closure.

Nevertheless, there are also many political actors engaging in a politics of openness—to the complex connectedness of modern life, to the uncertainties of a world of imminent dangers, to the need for renewed vision in a world of fragile categories and old dreams. To be open in a time of danger is to be especially vulnerable. But it is this very vulnerability, this willingness to refuse both the intolerable and the conventional wisdom, that makes critical social movements such an important source of thinking about a just world peace.

This capacity to respond to connections and to remain open sets critical social movements apart both from the familiar mass movements, interest groups, and political parties whose primary concern is to challenge state power and from the wide range of novel movements whose primary characteristic is closure. This is not to say that critical social movements can always be easily distinguished from these more familiar forms. Nor are critical social movements themselves immune to a politics of closure. On the contrary, they are often subject to external pressures or failures of imagination, which allow hierarchies, elitism, parochialism, and self-righteousness to undermine their critical potential. Yet, precisely because of the way they have to respond to a world of emerging connections that are largely missed by conventional political actors, critical social movements increasingly discover that an openness to connections is a condition of their success. Similarly, many movements associated with the New Right in the West also have a fairly clear understanding of the need to respond to connections. But this is an openness to connections that rests on a fundamentalist faith in the capitalist market as the source of all solutions.

The real source of hope embodied in critical social movements does not lie in their overt physical power. Nor does it lie in any clear vision they offer of light at the end of the tunnel. Movements fail and fade away. Sometimes they are crushed. They struggle against very powerful forces. But they are a source of optimism. It is important to be aware of the problems and limitations on what such movements can do in specific circumstances. But it is also important to see that, whatever their diversity, movements suggest a number of insights that must be taken up if the struggle for a just world peace is to have any lasting meaning.

First, partly by virtue of their marginality, but also partly because of a deeply rooted skepticism about the character of contemporary political life, movements discover new spaces in which to act politically. Although they experience a tightening up of the structures that threaten No World or Two Worlds, they also find that there is a loosening up of the spaces in which it is possible to act. Second, they formulate new ways of acting politically, both within existing political processes and in these new political spaces. For many movements, in fact, to find new political spaces is to discover new forms of political practice. Third, and as a consequence of these new forms of political practice, movements are able to articulate new conceptions of knowing and being. They reconstruct the horizons of the possible. Fourth, movements are able to explore not only the objectively interconnected nature of contemporary life, but also the connections that may be achieved between seemingly different movements struggling in different situations. They rework the meaning of human community. Finally, because critical social movements are only one of many kinds of actors struggling for peace and justice in the modern world, they explore the concrete connections that may be made with other more familiar forms of political action.

In the next chapter I will explore each of these themes in turn. Through a grasp of these five insights, it is possible to see how, despite their apparent lack of overt power, critical social movements are able to be both symbols and agents of a constructive politics at a time when closure is so inviting.

CHAPTER FIVE

Explorations

EXPLORATIONS OF POLITICAL SPACE

Political life is most easily grasped as a matter of government institutions and policies, of competition between interests and parties, of clashes of powers and ideologies, of intrigue, persuasion, and force. This appears to be what politicians do. The immediate day-to-day character of political life is certainly largely about these things, and it is easy enough to be overwhelmed by the complexity and detail of political events understood in this way as they unfold in all their variety in different societies.

Yet some of the more important aspects of political life often remain hidden by a preoccupation with day-to-day details. Political life is, in fact, not quite coextensive with what politicians do. When examined in a broader historical perspective, for example, political life seems to reflect the deeper structural patterns associated with transformations in the world economy; political categories begin to fuse with economic, sociological, and cultural categories. The overt activities of politicians and governments then appear only as the visible component of a much more complicated process.

More significant, in the present context, the nature of political life—the dominant understanding of what political life is all about—is itself always the subject of sharp political dispute. This is particularly the case in periods of social and economic transformation. Political change is not just a matter of replacing one group of politicians with another, nor even a reordering of government policies and institutions in response to large-scale social and economic transformations. It also involves serious challenges to prevailing conceptions of human community, of the philosophical assumptions guiding people's conceptions of what human community can possibly become, of what kinds of activities are to be considered political, and even about where political activity is supposed to occur. The claim to have effective answers to these questions is a crucial element of political life everywhere.

To try to understand what critical social movements are doing, and what it is they might be able to do in the future, is thus necessarily to go beyond asking questions about their successes and failures within the existing conceptions of political life. In part, they have to be understood as responses to broad structural problems and transformations of the kind sketched earlier. In part, they have to be understood in terms of the way they challenge the constitutive principles of the existing political order—the principles taken for granted both by politicians and in most of the analytic and ideological categories through which people try to make sense of political life. To challenge these principles is not necessarily to have any fully formed alternatives, but it is to engage in an exploration of what such alternatives might be. It is to explore, to begin with, new understandings of where political life is supposed to occur, particularly in relation to the modern state.

Rethinking the State

The state easily appears to be the great unchanging given of our collective existence. Whether in terms of security, of cultural identity, or of the organization of economic activity, the territorially bounded state has successfully claimed not only a monopoly on the legitimate use of violence, but also a monopoly on how and where political activity occurs. Critical social movements are often concerned at least as much with other social, cultural, economic, and political processes, but it is in terms of the modern state that their challenge to established conventions is perhaps most visible.

Although the state dominates our understanding of what political life is all about, our understanding of the state remains rather vague. There is not a single theory of the state but a series of competing accounts arising from different theoretical traditions. The emergence of the state as the primary political formation is a complicated historical episode. The state is not given by nature. Moreover, the character of states has changed considerably over time, and states vary enormously in character in different parts of the world. These variations are as important as the fact that states as such have become the primary political formation everywhere.

The processes that have created the modern state have not stopped but are being transformed. The state may remain the primary locus of political activity, but all states are now caught up in processes of economic, technological, social, cultural, and political transformation that are likely to provide both the need and the opportunity for new forms of political practice.

Although interpretations of the recent history of states vary enormously —tending to be more positive, for example, in postcolonial societies—increasing skepticism has been expressed concerning their capacity to do much about the larger problems of our time. The very logic of a system of autonomous states assumes the inevitability of war. States still seek their own advantage in the world economy. Those that are better off show little concern for those that are weaker. Few states can claim much success in reducing economic inequality within their territories. Most remain the preserve of strongly patriarchal forms of power. Most have been extremely reluctant to address environmental problems. They are often inhospitable to minority cultures and aspirations. Western societies have been experiencing the effects of global economic changes on the capacity of the welfare state to guarantee minimum universal standards of health, education, and employment. They have seen governments try to control the effects of international economic forces only to see them confront the stark reality that no state can now maintain autonomous control over its own economic policies. Even in societies that viewed nationalism and the state as liberator, equalizer, and modernizer in the wake of colonialism, people feel a sense of betrayal. States have become captured by classes and managers, by ethnic groups and technical elites, by propagandists and transnational enterprises.

The history of the state in this century has largely been a history of the centralization of authority and the encroachment of state power upon more and more areas of social life. This has occurred at a time when states have become caught ever more firmly between the pressure of increasing internal demands and decreasing room for maneuver with respect to the world economy and the states system. Although it is with respect to the state that we have come to understand what is meant by democracy, states are caught up in processes that make democracy more and more difficult to achieve.

Reliance on a strong internal security apparatus has become more and more apparent everywhere. Even in those societies, essentially Western, that distinguish between state and civil society, between the overtly political processes of government and the seemingly nonpolitical social processes of everyday life, it is clear that in practice it is often difficult to distinguish between the state and, say, the mass media, education, or the surveillance that accompanies the provision of social services. In many societies, political life is monopolized by the close cooperation between large corporations, large labor organizations, military forces, and government bureaucracies.

Such critiques of the modern state are now well known, even conventional. Yet, an even more significant line of thinking about the state has begun to emerge from many critical social movements, a line that distinguishes many of them from more traditional labor and nationalist movements. It involves skepticism about both the possibility and the desirability of taking over the state as the primary object of political activity. On the one hand, the centralization, bureaucratization, and militarization of states, as well as external dependencies or the probability of foreign intervention, now make the capture of state power a very daunting task. On the other, and perhaps more significant still, the capture of state power in this century has not always been an encouraging experience. The "revolution betrayed" has been a recurrent and depressing theme of modern history.

Skepticism about the state varies enormously from society to society. It is obviously greater among critical social movements in Europe, for example, than in the Middle East. But it does provide one very important context in which to understand the character of critical social movements. For it is often said that movements are quite weak and act only on the periphery of power. In some ways this is obviously true, but they do not act at the periphery of power only because they have to. They are also engaged in a potentially far-reaching struggle to rearticulate the character of political space.

Rethinking the Meaning of Local

One of the most obvious characteristics of critical social movements is their emphasis on what seems to be local action. This emphasis reflects both their marginality and their skepticism toward states. Local space is, after all, what remains most relevant for most people. It is where they belong, where they live, work, love, and die. For many movements, it is the local level at which real dialogue between people is possible, where basic needs can be met, where effective decision making can occur. Thus, much of contemporary political life has been characterized by attempts to increase decentralization and local participation, whether in terms of establishing workers' councils, workplace democracy, and local credit organizations; enhancing community development and local government; or restoring local knowledge and traditions. Yet the term "local" is somehow insufficient to convey the scope and diversity of what is going on when movements act in highly specific circumstances.

In some ways, the geographical sense of the term "local" certainly is appropriate. Most social movements are firmly rooted in a specific topography. This is so, for example, of movements organizing for alternative forms of development. This is precisely what is meant when it is said that such movements grow from the grassroots.

Alternative development movements have grown up in many different places, particularly in South and Southeast Asia, Latin America, and parts of Africa. Of course, many alternative development projects rely on external aid or state support of some kind. Yet most of them do so knowing very well that attempts to encourage development from the top down have often been disastrous. They try to use what resources are available in order to work with the rural poor, helping them to undertake collective initiatives, to become more aware of the forces that affect their lives, and thus they help people to empower themselves. Movements like Chipko in India do this by encouraging people to become aware of the close connections between the physical environment, traditional philosophical and religious thinking, conflicting economic interests, and competing conceptions of what development ought to entail. The Lokayan project, also in India, attempts to foster convergences among excluded peoples, grassroots activists, and committed intellectuals in specific communities. In the Queen Charlotte Islands of British

Columbia, the Haida Indians have struggled successfully to defend one of the world's outstanding natural habitats from a particularly rapacious combination of lumber companies and provincial politicians.

A stress on specific location is equally important for the movements that have grown up in urban areas. In fact, cities have become highly complex political arenas, especially given the way they are tied into global processes of production, distribution, and communication. They attract people from the countryside who are looking to participate in the promises of the world economy. They are the site of rapid social change as well as intense contradictions and conflicts between different social groups.

Such conflicts have generated all kinds of movements around squatters' rights, social equality, poverty, urban planning, and housing based on human needs rather than profit. Urban areas also tend to be the focus of movements concerned with more general themes such as human rights, peace, and feminism. Even in the midst of reactionary forms of political life at the national level, pressures from urban movements have been able to turn the administration of some cities in very creative directions, the now-defunct Greater London Council having been a significant case in point.

The distinction between town and country has always been complex, and it is not surprising that social movements reflect the different location of urban and rural populations in relation to emerging global processes. Movements rooted in the countryside tend to stress the potentials of more traditional ways of life, to reflect a greater sensitivity to the environment, and to be wary of the attractions of modernity. Urban movements, by contrast, are more likely to see themselves trying to fulfill the promises of modernity, to struggle for rights, freedom, and new forms of political community.

But not all movements are confined to local spaces of this kind. Many try to articulate the importance of different kinds of geographical spaces. Environmentalists urge us to think in terms of ecological regions on the grounds that existing administrative boundaries prevent effective action in ecological systems that transcend such boundaries. Cultural movements urge the creation of political jurisdictions that recognize the more fluid or mosaic-like patterns of ethnic identities or that give legal status to historically rooted territorialities like those now giving rise to native land claims in Canada. Peace movements urge the creation of nuclear-free zones in Europe or in the Pacific. They urge the need to refuse the spatial exclusions of Yalta and the cold war. They reinterpret the meaning of security in terms of regional or global rather than national space. In all these cases, it is possible to see a refusal of the conventional political map carved up into sovereign territorial jurisdictions and an insistence on a wide variety of other territorially defined spaces.

"Local" may refer to social and political space as well as to territory or geography, involving, for example, working within the spaces of civil society

as a necessary complement to the attempt to democratize state power itself.
Polish Solidarnosc has become a paradigm case in this respect. Confronted
by a strong regime, a superpower looming in close proximity, and an international structure paralyzed by cold war, Poland has been regarded as one
of the least likely places in which to resist state power. But, the impossibility
of changing this overwhelming structure directly has led to a concerted attempt to redefine the space available for political action. In a manner
echoed in other Eastern European as well as Latin American countries, Solidarity has been less concerned with challenging the state directly than with
speaking to people, suggesting that real victory comes not from gaining state
power but from remaining truthful to oneself. Thus, civil society rather than
the state apparatus becomes the site for revitalization of political life.

The experience of Solidarnosc has been particularly interesting to social movements in societies in which the state apparatus is very strong. In
such societies, finding the right space is an important key to effective action.
It may involve increasing democracy in the workplace, revitalizing existing
institutions and procedures, developing networks, or just working with a
circle of friends. It may mean learning to recognize the immediacy of power
in societies in which the penetrations of the state are less obvious—in
schools, workplaces, prisons, mass media. To stress the political character of
civil society is not to forget about the state entirely. State institutions also can
and must be the site of democratic renewal. But contrary to the main trends
of twentieth-century political experience, critical social movements have become wary of concepts of political life that treat the state as the only space in
which serious political activity can occur.

Finding new spaces in which to act, movements seek to create new social norms and identities, to reshape existing institutions, to enhance resistance to minor dominations. They act to politicize places of work and family
relations, to sensitize people about their relations with nature or their standards of rationality and progress. They try to revitalize and maintain democratic processes already achieved and extend democratic participation into
hospitals, schools, welfare services, and housing programs. They make visible what has become invisible and remember what has become forgotten.
In those situations in which religious institutions play a prominent role in
the activities of movements, the provision of enclaves of sanctified space has
become important. The Sanctuary Movement, for example, which involves
several hundred churches in the southwestern region of the United States,
offers sanctuary to Central American refugees, especially from El Salvador,
despite efforts by the United States to deport such "aliens" under authority
of immigration laws.

Apart from the way social movements tend to act within a great variety
of spaces, both geographically and socially, there is a third sense in which

they focus on the local. They emphasize the responsibility of individual action. This is not the atomistic individual portrayed by some versions of liberal ideology, but exactly the reverse—individuals who recognize that they are always acting, on an everyday basis, to reproduce or change the world in which they participate.

Women's movements have been particularly important in this regard, especially in trying to understand the relations of power that are embedded in distinctions between public and private, social and individual. In Western societies in particular, where the public/private distinction has been especially sharp, women's movements have shown how many of the most important political problems in the modern world now deal directly with "private" life, with fecundity and birth, reproduction and sexuality, health and death. This is not simply a matter of treating private life as an appropriate realm for political action. It is more a recognition of the extent to which private life is necessarily part of the public sphere, not a refuge from it.

The important point is that in all these cases, local action has the potential to extend people's horizons. Peace, environmentalist, and women's movements perhaps insist on this point most forcefully. For them, the real challenge is to create more effective forms of political life, not just for one part of humanity, but for everyone on earth. Working with highly specific themes or locations leads to a greater sense of the broader connections in which local actions are constrained.

To struggle for local development alternatives is to become increasingly aware of the penetrations of the world economy. To try to move beyond the narrow categories of economic analysis when reflecting about appropriate development is to question the philosophical and ethical assumptions that are necessary for thinking about economic alternatives. Experiences with inappropriate technology can stimulate a critique of objectivistic and instrumental conceptions of science. Attention to local circumstances brings an awareness of the wisdom embodied in local cultural traditions; it creates an openness to more dialectical or ecological conceptions of the relationship between people and the world they live in. The replacement of abstract development plans with local grassroots initiatives encourages a different kind of learning activity. Education then becomes a participatory process rather than the consumption of predigested expertise. Consumer movements, like those in Penang or the international campaign against canned substitutes for mother's milk, foster awareness of the usually unspoken costs of production, such as waste, poisoning, and the manipulation of demand through advertising.

Above all, to discover that to act locally is to become aware of connections with a much broader universe is also to become aware of the need to find new ways in which to act politically.

EXPLORATIONS OF POLITICAL PRACTICE

With explorations of new spaces for political action come reconceptualizations of the nature of political practice. The practices of critical social movements redefine the meaning of social action itself. They present both concrete and symbolic challenges to dominant structures. In many respects, the way critical social movements act is as important as the goals they pursue. Much of modern life is characterized by a separation of ends and means, allowing means to turn disconcertingly into ends. Aware of this, critical social movements have become highly conscious of the way means and ends are dialectically related. These movements understand that the processes through which changes occur set limits to the kind of transformations that are possible.

Redefining Power

Again, the starting point often amounts to a celebration of small-scale local action. There is a pluralist and indeterminate character to the way many of the most interesting movements act that seems at odds with the seriousness and global scope of the problems to which they are responding. They resort to short-term tactics rather than long-term strategy. They may celebrate diversity and show considerable tolerance for tentativeness and uncertainty. They may show deep ambivalence about existing institutions. They pursue small victories.

Instead of looking for the necessary and sufficient conditions for change to be found in a reading of History or structural contradiction, critical social movements look for unusual historical developments, rare convergences of favorable conditions, the possible, or partial advance. The state is seen as necessary and progressive in some circumstances, or in some aspects, but not in others. Instead of searching for the most powerful social force to which others should be subordinate in organizing political change, critical social movements are reluctant to assign priority. They resist the incorporation of a new "subject of history." Instead of grand utopian plans, there is a tentativeness about the future, a suspicion of premature foreclosure. There is an emphasis on the diversity of confrontations, on the impossibility of privileged saviors—philosophers or priests, party leaders or chosen people—immune to the contaminations of existing power. Unlike either the great revolutionary movements of the past or the fundamentalists of the present, many contemporary social movements seem to consciously refuse the false comfort of knowing exactly where they are going.

Small-scale local action, ambivalence, uncertainty: These are hardly signs of an emerging potential for significant transformation, at least judged by conventional images of political life. Like the spaces in which movements act, the way they act can seem marginal and even frivolous. Yet, there is in many of these practices a sophisticated appreciation that real political power is not a simple commodity that can be measured by the accumulation of weapons or wealth. It is a much more complex affair in which less tangible things like credibility and legitimacy are immensely important. Indeed, a capacity to redefine the nature of political power is itself an important element of political power.

The more one is able to define what is legitimate, or necessary, or sensible, for example, the less one has to rely on direct physical force. Critical social movements are able to understand very clearly that to challenge the prevailing standards of "common sense," or to use official claims and principles in order to judge the extent to which particular policies fall short of them, is not marginal at all. It is to recognize that dominant powers are never omnipotent; if they have to rely on force alone, then their strength is brittle, subject to fatigue and unexpected fracture.

It is always possible to struggle for the normative initiative, to show that dominant forces may in fact claim nothing more than that might is right, to show that *machismo* is laughable as well as violent. Above all, it is always possible to recognize that every person can work to define and redefine the character of social reality. It is always possible to realize that political life is not something that occurs "out there" among professional politicians or elites but is implicated in everyone's daily life, whether they recognize it or not.

This sense of the need to redefine political power makes critical social movements suspicious of the procedures of conventional politics, especially in those societies that have managed to institutionalize a democratic framework of political rights, parties, and elections. This suspicion makes these movements especially sensitive to the way bureaucratization presents a major challenge to all forms of emancipatory politics. Thus, critical social movements are usually organized as networks of small groups submerged in everyday life, requiring personal involvement and experience. They tend to be informal and ad hoc, discontinuous and sensitive to specific contexts, equalitarian and participatory. There is a fusion of public and private roles, instrumental and expressive behavior, organization and community, membership and leadership.

The effectiveness of organization by networks rather than through command from above is particularly striking in the case of European and North American antinuclear movements. The resort to mass demonstrations and civil disobedience may not be new, but such tactics now grow out of loosely organized networks and coalitions. These movements are notably without leaders. Initiatives tend to come from below, from locally organized groups in churches, schools, city councils, and so on. Similar patterns of networking are important to women's and environmental movements.

Some of the most interesting attempts to develop new conceptions of political practice in this way have occurred in Eastern Europe. Here movements are often said to be engaged in "antipolitics" or to have a 'self-limiting' character. They seem to be less concerned with taking over state power, at least in the short term, than with the democratization of local and functional systems, developing new forms of participation, creating processes that can inhibit the excessive use of state power. Polish Solidarnosc and Charter 77, for example, have been particularly difficult to understand in terms of categories that simply assume revolutionary action must be concerned with taking over state power. Judged in terms of our conventional images of what political change or revolution must involve, many of the political practices that have been developing in Eastern Europe seem highly constrained. But it is not possible to dismiss them as insignificant. Indeed, some of the most interesting experiments with workers' control and community participation have emerged in these countries despite the legacy of centralized planning from above.

Such movements pursue a vision of cooperation among individuals who have been battered by the excessive power of the state. They encourage openness, truthfulness, autonomy of action, and trust as principles of everyday conduct. A refusal to submit to a politics of deceit is to defy the ethical basis of states that depend on systematic distortion. Critical social movements act so as to recognize and resist the presence of repressive state power within each individual's everyday life. They recognize, not the impotence of individuals before an all encompassing state, but the power of each individual to act in the immediate circumstances over which he or she exercises some control. It may not be possible to confront the militarized state or the monopolistic corporation directly. But it is possible to recognize the extent to which one has absorbed and internalized the expectations of the militarized state—or, under different circumstances, the monopolistic corporations—and to do something about the way these expectations determine how one acts toward other people.

Movements can try to react to the intolerable, even where people cannot agree on grander visions of the desirable. They can locate specific situations in which an alteration of power is possible even where the grand structures of power seem almost unmovable. They can try to make convention and common sense seem dangerous and odd. They can turn politics into the art of daily democratic resistances. They can refuse to become trapped in an uncompromising attitude of all or nothing as well as refuse to compromise basic principles. They can fuse an attitude of moderation with an attitude of intransigence.

Practices of this kind are often almost invisible. In fact, many movements are explicitly concerned with avoiding premature or visible institutionalization in order to avoid early identification and elimination.

More significant, practices of this kind can challenge power where it is most invisible and thus most powerful. A large part of the difficulty of analyzing contemporary political life arises from the way power is neither where nor what it seems to be. To explore the invisible—the unseen connections, the forgotten histories, the taken-for-granted routines of everyday life—is to challenge power not only where it is most effective but also where it can be most fragile.

A Politics of Nonviolence

One of the most interesting aspects of the practices of critical social movements is the explicit rejection of violence. This is particularly important given that it is very difficult to dissociate the idea of revolution from the belief that violence is inevitable. Yet, for many movements it is becoming increasingly clear that the essence of revolution is not bloodshed and cruelty but the practices through which it is possible to bring into being a society in which violence and cruelty becomes unnecessary.

Conventionally, violence is an unfortunate prerequisite for revolution. For critical social movements, it is an inhuman mode of being and must be eliminated. Movements find it difficult to see how violence can be eradicated through violence. To some extent this reflects the influence of long-standing pacifist principles as well as the historical experiences associated with Gandhi and Martin Luther King. But it is also clear that especially under modern conditions, violence tends to undermine the very changes that movements seek. Nonviolence is no longer discussed in moral terms alone. In many situations, movements have discovered that it is a basic practical precondition for any successful political action. Ends and means cannot be separated.

It is in this context that the early stages of the revolution in Iran remain so impressive. Similarly, in the Philippines, in a situation that was ripe for change, the ability of millions of people to occupy the streets of Manila in a nonviolent manner at the critical moment has inspired movements everywhere. In neither situation has the outcome been perfect. In the Iranian case, the victory of fundamentalism over the spirit of democratic renewal is sobering, to say the least. In the Philippines, problems of mass poverty, rural unemployment, inequalitarian agrarian structures, and the restoration of cultural identity and national dignity still remain.

Even so, even among the more traditional mass movements struggling for control of states in South Africa, South Korea, and elsewhere, the struggle to create a more democratic society involves some recognition that to use violence is to risk the escalation of processes that make real democracy impossible. Similarly, despite the bloody record of murder, exile, torture, arrest, and systematic violation of human rights under General Pinochet, most

Chileans stubbornly hoped and many worked for a return to civilized political life without recourse to violence. With an attempted assassination came
a state of siege, renewed violence, and intimations of even more. Still, the
belief that violence cannot be overcome with violence remains very
powerful.

Again, it is possible to see in this belief an attempt to reinterpret the
nature of political power. Power may be understood as mere brute force, or
the ability to command and repress. In this sense, power is essentially negative. It is compatible with violence. And there remain a number of situations
in which the sheer brutality of violence and repression makes the resort to
violence as a mode of resistance almost inevitable. But power may also be
understood as the capacity to create new possibilities. This sense of power
is of greater concern to critical social movements. Whether as physical force
or as more subtle forms of pressure, intimidation, and delusion, such movements understand that violence and power are not identical. Nonviolence is
increasingly seen as precisely a form of power that makes creative political
practice possible.

A Politics of Resistance and Delegitimation

Although the use of violence has been put into question, critical movements
engage in other well-established forms of political action, giving them new
meaning and importance in changing circumstances. Thus, movements
everywhere are involved in a politics of resistance. This is clearly seen in the
emphasis on the protection and enlargement of human rights among the
movements of Central Europe and Latin America. Resistance plays an important part in the activities of groups like Ground Zero in the northwestern
United States, which is engaged in drawing attention to trains carrying components for Trident missiles. Perhaps the most noteworthy characteristic of
resistances of many movements is the appeal made to those who are being
resisted, whether these are soldiers on the march or workers in armaments
factories. The methods of resistance entail maximizing the awareness of
identity between resistor and resisted. They suggest the importance of
avoiding Manichaean dualisms of "us" and "them" in an age in which Us and
Them threatens to become No World or Two Worlds.

Techniques of resistance are closely associated with those of delegitimation. Movements engage in activities that call into question the legitimacy of
existing governmental procedures and institutions. This has sometimes involved the formation of "tribunals," such as the one set up by Bertrand Rus-
sell to inquire into the legality of policies pursued by the United States in
Vietnam. At the time, this tribunal was controversial primarily because of its
substantive allegations against U.S. war policies. Of perhaps greater long-
term significance was its implicit rejection of statist claims to a monopoly

over political life. The same is true of similar tribunals established since then. The League for the Rights of Peoples set up the Permanent Peoples' Tribunal in 1976. It has conducted some thirteen sessions on such matters as repression under Marcos in the Philippines, intervention in Central America and Afghanistan, Turkish genocide against Armenians, and Indonesian policies in East Timor. Judgments and supporting materials have been published as a way of challenging the legitimacy of specific policies and elites.

Other more ad hoc tribunals have been formed. In 1982, a tribunal on the nuclear arms race was organized in Nuremberg by elements of the West German Green party. In 1985, a group of lawyers in England organized a tribunal on the international legal status of nuclear weapons and strategies. In response to the 1982 Israeli invasion of Lebanon, a group of prominent citizens in England established the MacBride Commission to report on the international legal aspects of this event. Again, the substantive findings are less important than the way they disclose a frustration with the inabilities of governments to uphold expectations about compliance with international law and morality.

A Politics of Accountability

Processes of delegitimation are closely related to attempts to establish a greater accountability in political life. Legal aid movements have played significant roles in these attempts. One of the largest movements in Indonesia, for example, has been concerned with showing that ordinary people have legal rights in relation to the government. Some of the most effective labor organizing in Indonesia is done by the Legal Aid Institute, which has also pursued a number of class-action suits even on behalf of whole villages; it has criticized what the government has been doing to Papuans in Irian Java; and it has provided the most formidable of the defense lawyers in a series of trials arising primarily out of the Tarjong Priok riots of 1984.

Many attempts to establish greater accountability rely heavily on existing legal processes. Even in South Africa, for example, the courts have struck down a number of minor apartheid provisions and curbs on freedom of the press. Elsewhere, movements try to establish accountability in the behavior of large economic corporations with respect to their impact on the environment or the quality of their products. The international campaign against the indiscriminate use of canned milk for children not only led to the establishment of an international code setting out minimum standards of marketing behavior but also drew attention to serious problems with children's nutrition, prenatal care, and postnatal community support.

Some of the most significant activities of movements in this area involve responses to the activities of foreign governments. The French "intelligence operation" against the Greenpeace vessel *Rainbow Warrior* in Auckland Harbor is significant. The boat had been involved in the monitoring and protesting of French nuclear testing in the Pacific islands. The statist refusal to stop tests harmful to health, environment, and resources reflects the impotence of the established procedures of international society to challenge official French behavior. Only a private transnational group has been able to pose such a challenge. Operated within a framework of militant nonviolence, the *Rainbow Warrior* and its activities generated a violent reaction.

A brief commitment to a broader ethos of accountability occurred with the war crimes trials of defeated leaders of Germany and Japan held in Nuremberg and Tokyo at the close of World War II. These trials produced a body of law generalized in the form of the Nuremberg Principles affirming the importance of holding governmental leaders internationally responsible for crimes of states. The impulse here remains suspect, as it was always associated with a grand display of "victors' justice" and was never institutionalized by the establishment of ongoing procedures. Even so, the symbolism of these principles has been of significance for some movements. A Nuremberg Pledge has been circulated among professional lawyers' groups throughout the world, committing individuals as both citizens and professionals to uphold the Nuremberg Principles and to extend their application to new areas. More significant, the principles have been used to question the legality of foreign policy initiatives, such as those involving reliance on illegal weaponry or overall patterns of military action. In Europe and the United States, many peace activists have engaged in civil disobedience under a claim of right—namely, that international law binds governments and that individual citizens have a duty to secure compliance.

Many critical social movements have incorporated accountability directly into a politics of symbolism. Thus, the Great Peace Journey, initiated in 1985 by a small group of Swedish women, involved visits to the heads of governments of small and medium-sized European states in order to ask a series of questions. These questions—about their willingness to shift to more defensive forms of defense, to eliminate production and trade in weapons of mass destruction, to share the earth's resources more equally, and so on—highlight the gap between the rhetoric and the practices of existing governments, a gap for which people can and must keep demanding an accountable explanation.

Attempts to establish accountability have also been important in the responses to the disasters at Bhopal and Chernobyl. As these disasters show quite graphically, individuals are increasingly vulnerable to harm, whereas distant perpetrators may withdraw behind the safety of national boundaries. Governments are both implicated in the events and fail to respond adequately. As a consequence, civil society is challenged to fashion effective humanitarian and political responses. Young people in India, for example, have arranged to help victims in Bhopal do physical therapy over prolonged periods to recover proper use of their lungs. More general questions are raised about whether governments and corporations can be entrusted with the ultrahazardous technologies that are increasingly being relied upon in modern-sector productive enterprise. There seems to be a new awareness by all governments, even those that reject liberal democratic forms of accountability, that their legitimacy is being drawn into question by their inability to protect society from the dangers of technological breakdown.

A Politics of Knowledge

In an age in which so much importance is attached to information, it is hardly surprising that many of the practices of contemporary social movements involve challenges to existing sources of information and attempts to create more relevant and accurate knowledge. Nor is it surprising that especially in this realm movements have been able to establish important connections with more formal organizations. They have been able to act with a variety of international nongovernmental organizations (INGOs) to create reputable sources of information capable of challenging the abuse of state power.

The International Committee of the Red Cross, for example, has been able to make effective claims on behalf of the victims of war. Amnesty International makes similar claims on behalf of those tortured and prisoners of conscience. Movements have been able to engage with scholars, working in groups like the International Peace Research Association, or even with governmental organizations, such as the Stockholm International Peace Research Institute, to establish alternative narratives about weapons deployments in the face of the capacity of states to convert highly technical data into the crudest of propaganda.

Western antinuclear movements have been particularly active in raising levels of public awareness about current trends. Physicians for Social Responsibility draws attention to the medical consequences of nuclear war and the psychocultural consequences of preparations for war. Scientists Against Nuclear Arms (SANA) points to the abuse of scientific knowledge when it becomes caught up in military research. Lawyers for Nuclear Disarmament show how preparations for nuclear war contravene the Hague and Geneva Conventions. Other groups participate in vigils to make particular weapons deployments more visible, or, as in the case of the military base at Greenham Common in England, to symbolize connections between militarization and the struggles of women everywhere.

The provision of accurate information has become important to most critical social movements. The extent to which even governments have been made aware of impending environmental disasters is a major achievement. Graphic television images of the work of so many groups responding to famine conditions in Ethiopia revealed humanitarian energies that put major governments to shame. Conversely, the extent to which information about the major processes that affect people's lives is held by state agencies and large corporations remains a huge challenge. The monopolization of information in an age in which information technologies are becoming so crucial is very ominous.

Struggles over information may involve the tedious accumulation of data as well as highly charged public battles over what is to be considered credible and trustworthy. They also make education and consciousness-raising an important part of the ongoing activities of movements.

Consciousness-raising has always been a crucial element in emancipatory politics. All too often this has involved the handing down of wisdom from above, from the all-knowing leader, party, or technical elite. For many movements, this process itself undermines the emancipatory potential of knowledge. Again, ends and means are understood to be dialectical. Education becomes less a matter of teaching than of learning and discovery, a matter of knowledge as empowerment rather than as a disembodied instrument of technocratic control. Theory and practice also become understood in a dialectical manner, and the prevailing conceptions of what is meant by legitimate or objective knowledge, by science or reason or truth, become subject to thoroughgoing critique. The exploration of new spaces in which to act and new ways of acting thus leads directly to the exploration of new ways of knowing about the world and new ways of understanding what it means to be part of the world.

EXPLORATIONS OF KNOWING AND BEING

Critical social movements tend to be highly conscious of the symbolic character of modern political life. This is partly a matter of recognizing the importance of rhetoric and image in gaining and maintaining power. More significant, movements understand that political change involves transformations of consciousness as well as alterations in more tangible economic and institutional arrangements. More significant still, many of them are beginning to understand that old distinctions between concrete causes and ideological effects, between matter and consciousness, are themselves rooted in conceptions of what it means to know and to be in the world that are no longer credible.

In this context, critical social movements are often said to serve a kind of prophetic function, announcing to society that a fundamental problem exists in a given area. They fight for symbolic and cultural stakes, for the achievement of new meanings in social action. They try to change the way people understand and live their lives. They challenge the logic that governs the production and appropriation of social resources and expose the power and violence hidden in dominant symbolic codes. They contest established rules of normalcy, pose questions that are usually unasked, and search for answers among the silences of established discourse.

The emphasis antinuclear movements place on the symbolism and imagery of contemporary debate about war and peace is illustrative. The notion of nuclear deterrence is itself a complex symbolic affair. It draws on utilitarian images of human beings as rational actors, as well as on logical arguments that defy the rational imagination. It incorporates dubious metaphors, behavioristic psychologies, and contentious theologies of good and evil. Although calculated with mathematical precision, it is most appropriately decoded by students of literature and mythology. Moreover, nuclear war is by definition an imaginary war. It occurs as rhetoric and scenario, as threat and posture, as the diplomatic duplicity of meanings. Those who struggle for peace have to do so on symbolic terrain, whether for control over information, for demystification of the rhetoric of "national security," or for the achievement of meaningful conceptions of what peace might look like.

Movements thus become highly sensitive to the nature and power of language. Women's movements protest the stereotypes captured and reproduced by gendered language. Movements working with the poor and excluded protest the assumptions loaded into the term "development." Movements are always engaged in a struggle for meanings, trying to show how generalizations protect the interests of a minority or how "common sense" is neither common nor makes much sense.

Rethinking Knowledge and Power

Sensitivity to the symbolic character of politics extends to a concern with the relationship between forms of knowledge and political life. Few political thinkers of any consequence anywhere have avoided some discussion of philosophical questions about the nature of knowledge in general, if only to lend their more pragmatic speculations some additional respectability. Most radical calls for political change have stressed the need for new forms of consciousness as well as new social and economic arrangements. In this respect, critical social movements continue a tradition as old as politics itself.

As might be expected, many movements pay careful attention to the claims about science, objectivity, and instrumental rationality that inform so much of modern life. They observe the great paradox in which claims to modernity and progress through science and reason are advanced in an age in which science and reason have helped enhance our insecurity. They point to the unhappy divorce of knower and known, subject and object, person and nature, and to the reduction of organic systems to their atomistic fragments. They lament the cult of expertise, the calculus of profit, the cold wedge between fact and value, means and ends.

Alternative conceptions of knowledge have been central to many movements. Some look to abandoned cultural traditions. Others make the achievement of new forms of knowledge part of their ongoing practice. Thus, alternative development movements find "expertise" embedded in local experience and traditional modes of thought. They encourage participation by the people concerned in research conducted in their community. Consumers' movements encourage greater awareness about the commodities that enter into people's daily lives. Reflections on ecological systems, or women's experiences with nurturing, encourage more dialectical and holistic ways of knowing the world. Artificial disciplinary divisions dissolve as soon as one tries to understand what lies behind the demand for peace, economic equality, environmental harmony, human rights, and human identity.

Critical movements are more likely to be open to the unexpected, to see what remains hidden by the categories and codes of conventional ways of thinking. They are less likely to be trapped in the seeming inevitabilities of common sense. The consciousness of "modernity," for example, has been deeply indebted to the scientific philosophies of Galileo and Newton. Critical movements seem to be comfortable with the probabilities and relativities of contemporary microphysics. They feel the sharp divergence between political claims based on archaic conceptions of scientific method and the opportunities signaled by new intellectual horizons.

Politics and Spirituality

One of the most striking—and puzzling—things about many social movements in this respect is the importance so many of them attach to the spiritual dimensions of human existence. There are, of course, many accounts of social change that stress the importance of religion, most obviously those that stress the significance of Protestantism in the breakthrough to capitalism in Europe. But there is also a strong tendency among modern political analysts to interpret religion or spirituality as a substitute for real social change, as an "opium of the people" or even as necessarily a force for political reaction.

In some cases, the practices of movements are informed by an explicitly religious orientation. It is only necessary to think of Poland, the Philippines, Nicaragua, or the Basic Christian Communities that have become so important all over Latin America. These cases are often very confusing to people who have learned to equate radicalism with a convinced secularism. But it is becoming quite clear that sharp distinctions between secular and sacred, or assumptions that religion and emancipatory politics cannot coexist, are becoming problematic.

In other cases, movements reflect a more general sense of mystery and awe. This may come from a greater sensitivity to the physical environment, from the cosmic uncertainties of contemporary science, or from a greater openness to various mystical or philosophical traditions. Many movements are certainly informed by a willingness to explore realms of experience excluded by dominant forms of knowledge. In the face of a world that has been increasingly able to reduce everything to utilitarian calculation, movements struggle to acknowledge the centrality of spirit, love, and passion in human endeavor.

The place of religion or spiritual sensitivity is certainly ambiguous. There is sufficient evidence of the way those who feel threatened by the uncertainties of the age invoke fundamental validations of traditional values, including notions of separatism ("the chosen people") or moral absolutism (the holy war against the infidels). But also clear is that it is within the religious or spiritual realms that many movements seek unifying myths and images of civilizational possibilities. The reworking of Catholic doctrines under the influence of liberation theology has led to immense creative energy. In a more diffuse way, some movements seem to be engaged in reinventing what it now means to be spiritual, treating religion as a realm that opens up cultural horizons and possibilities.

Knowledge and Empowerment

Whether concerned with symbols, language, and cultural meanings, or with competing conceptions of knowledge, or with questions about more cosmic mysteries, movements are forced to challenge prevailing conceptions both of what is and what is not possible. This is not a matter of abstract philosophy. It involves a recognition of the close connection between knowledge and power. Moreover, the explorations of symbols and alternative conceptions of knowledge by contemporary movements do not imply so much a search for power over something—over nature, over others—as an empowerment through participation in relationships and processes that are powerful in themselves.

This is why, for example, the root objection to development theory, and to the conception of knowledge that it embodies, is that it gives power to those who encourage development from the outside. The resulting sense of powerlessness is no less visible in affluent societies; the celebration of wealth and freedom is shadowed by diagnoses of alienation, anomie, disenchantment, and the resort to hedonism. This sense of powerlessness is challenged directly by movements all over the world, both by the way in which they understand the world and the way they act in it.

Alternative conceptions of development have emerged from environmentalist movements and their challenge to the equation of development with unlimited economic growth. They have come from the application of spiritual traditions, as with the interpretations of Buddhism that influence the grassroots Sarvodaya movement in Sri Lanka or the Gandhian-inspired Association of Sarva Seva Farms network in India.

To rethink development is necessarily to become aware of the close connection between technologies and the way people are able to express themselves through their labor. Technology may then be seen as neither an inherently progressive or regressive force nor as a neutral instrument that can be used by anyone for their own ends but as thoroughly political in its design and use, reflecting deep structures of ownership and control of production processes. Neither Bhopal and Chernobyl nor the economic models of the World Bank can be understood without coming to terms with the conceptions of legitimate knowledge that they symbolize so menacingly.

Women's movements are especially significant in terms of their capacity to explore the connections between knowledge and power, knowing and being. In this context, the pursuit of equality within existing structures appears as only one possible starting point for more far-reaching changes. Thus, many movements have been drawn to recover and articulate ways of knowing and acting that have been traditionally downgraded as "merely" feminine. Beyond this, women's movements have been able to develop a clearer awareness of the way that our understanding of what it means to be male or female is not only historically and culturally circumscribed but is also dependent on all kinds of unspoken and dubious assumptions about how we should live. In Western societies at least, the meaning of "femininity" has been constructed in relation to and as differentiation from a male norm. To the extent that women's movements try to affirm a more authentically feminist way of life, they have to do so while recognizing that what we understand by "feminine" is itself a reaction to patriarchal norms.

A retreat to a separatist sphere of feminine values easily becomes an important refuge when the possibility of fundamental change seems remote. But essentialism of this kind easily turns into a conservative politics. It can become the mere affirmation of a conception of femininity constructed through oppression and which, therefore, is likely to reinforce certain roles in a society constructed through oppression. An understanding of the relationship between knowledge and power is thus particularly important for women's movements because they are drawn to affirm difference without subscribing to any presupposed male norm. Women's movements are necessarily involved in explorations of knowing and being precisely because they act so as both to recover and reaffirm historical conceptions of the feminine and, what is more crucial, to explore what feminine—or masculine, or childhood, or desire, or intimacy—could possibly be under new historical circumstances.

Politics, Space and Time

Critical social movements explore new political spaces in which to act. They also challenge prevailing assumptions about space itself. After all, conceptions of space have a history. These conceptions enter into grand structures and everyday practice. The rise of the West, whether understood through categories of culture or political economy, was shaped significantly by the infinite conception of space on which Galilean and Newtonian physics depended. Whether we think of the creation of the state as a form of territorial exclusion or the skyscraper as the architectural icon of modernity, spatial assumptions condition the way we act, whether we know it or not. Indeed, such assumptions are usually so deeply ingrained they are difficult to recognize.

To challenge such conceptions—on the basis of, say, other cultural traditions, aesthetic or ecological insights, or reflection on post-Newtonian accounts of space-time—is to begin to grasp the deep-rooted and far-reaching intellectual reconstructions that accompany periods of fundamental transformation. The articulation of the concept of absolute space in early modern Europe was a massive achievement. Despite their seemingly abstract character, challenges to prevailing conceptions of space engage in a comparable rearticulation of the categories through which human beings can conceive of acting together.

Similarly, critical movements act on the basis of many different histories. In challenging History, they also engage in challenges to privileged conceptions of time. Again, although seemingly abstract, conceptions of time are inherently political. The state itself has often been treated as a place in which it is possible to escape from the ravages of time. States have obviously attempted to strengthen or weaken particular temporal memories, to invent new beginnings and forget others.

It matters whether a history refers to a Western chronology, whether it begins with Plato, or Christ, Descartes, or the atom bomb. It matters whether the succession of events is coded as the inevitability of Progress. It matters that states are developing the inventories, dossiers, and records that enable them to become the official keepers of history, memory, and identity. It matters also that modern economic life effectively reduces time to efficiency and profit, to a calibrated duration bereft of memory or meaning.

To challenge dossiers or lost memories, or to recover chronologies and identities, is to engage in practices that are at the heart of political life. Alternative development movements undermine the notion of a temporal transition from tradition to modernity. Environmentalists argue that we no longer inherit the earth from our parents; we borrow it from our children. Critical social movements of all kinds refuse the categories of space and time that make emancipatory politics unthinkable.

EXPLORATIONS OF COMMUNITY

Movements organize on collective and cooperative principles. They create new ways of being together. Connections are in fact made among groups struggling with seemingly different problems. They converge and drift apart, seeing familiar struggles from unfamiliar angles. Despite their celebration of diversity and the local, movements often exhibit a clear awareness that without closer connections and greater solidarity, they can only remain weak.

It is clear that this is not an ambition to imitate the solidarity of the nation, nor that of a universal class, nor that arising from some abstract claim about the human species as such. Nor is it a matter of conventional relations between states. It is, rather, a recognition that behind the insistence on acting locally is a challenge to rework the meaning of human community in an age in which our vulnerabilities are indeed global in scale while our capacity to act is circumscribed by who and where we are.

Three major themes are at work here. First is a recognition of the global connections that have developed at this moment of history and which are increasingly powerful determinants of people's lives everywhere. Second is a recognition that global structures and connections do not imply any easy universalism, especially a universalism that generates a reading of History as a move from fragmentation to integration, from states system to global community. On the contrary, movements recognize that global structures represent quite specific forces of dominance and that the claims of such structures to universality involve explicit principles of exclusion. Third is a recognition that in spite of global structures and awareness, people actually live, work, and play in specific places in a great variety of concrete circumstances. These three themes converge on a recognition that in the modern world, communities and solidarities have to be grasped as a dialectical moment, as a sense of participation both in large scale global processes and in particular circumstances.

This sense of connection may be vague and uncertain, but it is crucial. And it is to be expected. All great moments of historical transformation have been accompanied by changes in the pattern and form of human communities.

Within the most influential conceptions of modern political life, human community has come to be understood in the context of one historically specific resolution of the opposition between universality and particularity. At one extreme, the idea of human solidarity has been absorbed into a universalist reading of the community of humankind (Enlightenment rationalism, the universal class). At the other extreme, solidarity has been denied on the ground of the radical particularity of all individuals. In between, solidarity has been largely preempted by the state. The same goes for political identity. One is either a human being in general or an individual, or both by virtue of being a citizen of a particular state. The state has managed to successfully claim not only monopoly over the legitimate use of violence but also a monopoly over the meaning of human community and human identity. But this conception of human community is not given in nature. In some parts of the world it still remains alien.

This political resolution of the opposition between universality and particularity through the state has been paralleled by an economic resolution through the concept of property. Faced with the claim that people inherit the earth in common, early European political thinkers took up the problem of justifying claims to particular parts of it by particular individuals. Rights to private property came to be justified in terms of the way that the "rational" and "industrious" mixed their labor with that which was given in common. In fact, pursuit of private interest and property came to be seen as a guarantee of an increase in general well-being.

These particular resolutions of the claims of a universalist species identity and individualist particularity at the levels of the state and private property are the achievements of Western capitalist thought and practice. Their effect on contemporary thinking about human community, and about what it means to be human at this point in time, is overwhelming. Politically, we are told that community is a matter of either nationalism, expressed through the state, or cosmopolitanism, expressed through some kind of nascent institutional framework at the global level, usually pictured in the image of a state writ large. Given that there is little sign of the creation of a global state, and that the state itself shows no sign of withering away, conventional wisdom continues to believe that states must remain the primary focus of human community and political identity.

It is common enough, for example, to hear that we live in an "interdependent" world. It is a term that suggests the growth of objective connections, the gradual move from fragmentation to unity. Again, it is liable to absorb all the arrogances of History. It is a term that has been subject to criticism both on the ground of histories and on the ground that private property has turned into structures of capital accumulation on a global scale.

From one direction, claims to interdependence are countered by claims that independence and fragmentation are still very much with us. This is a claim that focuses on the formal autonomy of states and the persistent tendency for states to try to maximize their own interests at everyone else's expense. This leads directly to the scenario of No World. From another direction, claims to interdependence are counteracted by claims that the overriding condition for most societies is one of dependence. This leads in the direction of the scenario of Two Worlds.

Terms such as "interdependence"—like "world order," "global village," "world society," and so on—have thus been subject to criticism for their explicit ideological role. In depicting what are taken to be processes of universalization, they mask the underlying reality of fragmentation and inequality. More specifically, they are said to arise from locations of privilege. They reflect the interests of those who dominate the major global structures and processes and who seek to legitimize their dominance. Thus it is always wise to keep in mind the way that an emphasis on global problems, and particularly those that seem to loom as future catastrophe, tends to arise primarily from those societies that have harbored imperial dreams.

It is not that the globalism of movements that stress such problems necessarily harbors a secret imperial agenda. Rather, the less burdensome context of the immediate reality, together with the globalist activities of corporations, governments, and media, infuse the imagination of reformers in more affluent societies with a global-scale conception of problems and solutions and a correspondingly reduced feeling for the overwhelming intensities of local and regional preoccupations. In effect, ideological unevenness exists on matters of perception that restricts communication and effectiveness. Such restrictions cannot be eliminated, although better mutual understanding can help establish the foundation for more useful types of dialogue and social action. In fact, the degree to which, for example, the women's movement has become conscious of the diversity of situations and aspirations in different parts of the world, or to which peace movements have begun to link peace with struggles for economic equality or human rights, must be counted as major achievements worthy of encouragement.

These difficulties point to a more serious problem. Although substantial empirical evidence exists of the growth of processes and structures that cut across the formal political jurisdictions of the states system, there is little agreement about how this evidence is to be interpreted. The projections of History continue to be very powerful in this respect. The prevailing images of connection embody an emphasis on universalization and centralization rather than on diversity and difference.

In fact, these conventional categories are thoroughly misleading. It is quite clear that people's lives occur at the intersection of a great many structures and processes. They are subject to pressures from, say, economic forces, from particular patterns of patriarchy, from specific ethnic cleavages, as well as from more local and personal obligations. These pressures lead to the creation of different but overlapping solidarities. Some of them may take priority in different times and places. The state has become the principal claimant of these solidarities, but it is a claim that conflicts with the multiple pressures of everyday life. Similarly, doctrines about political transformations have often claimed the overriding priority of solidarities created by particularly powerful forces. In the era of industrial capitalism, the claim to universalizing class solidarities has been preeminent. Yet, although class remains crucial, theories of political change that assert that, for example, patriarchal or ethnic domination may be reduced to matters of class alone are rightly treated with increasing suspicion.

Part of the potential of contemporary social movements is that they expose the contrast between people's experiences in a multiplicity of situations and the monopoly claimed by state and class on solidarity and identity. They show that the state is only one of a number of political spaces in which to act and in which questions about freedom, obligation, community, and so on, must be posed. They show that emerging patterns of vulnerability require more than class solidarity as conventionally understood. They require the articulation of connections between groups acting in a variety of distinct circumstances, yet which understand the interconnected nature of the forces to which they respond.

Thus, critical social movements participate in ongoing attempts to understand the increasingly global character of the forces that affect them. They may draw on more formal scholarly analyses that try to comprehend patterns of integration, trade agreements, or dependencies within sophisticated models of international "regimes," of world systems, or of the transnationalizing of capital. They may point to the obvious existence of structures and institutions, like international organizations and multinational corporations, that are both very recent and in some measure transnational. They may themselves participate within international nongovernmental organizations. Or they may point to the uneven, but nevertheless spectacular, spread of communications technologies that link people in different parts of the world in a way that was barely conceivable at the turn of this century. They see that even the most conventional of state actors now accept the need for regional, international, and global management systems to cope with worldwide processes that threaten to overwhelm the functional capacity of existing governments.

Critical social movements also respond to an emerging subjective awareness of the connections brought about by objective structural processes. In fact, although their understanding of these objective processes may often be hazy, their understanding of what an increasing subjective awareness of these connections might mean is often very acute. Their reading of the long-term implications of Hiroshima or Chernobyl, for example, is clearly more realistic than that which informs the policies of most states.

Although conventional political actors are prone to dismiss activists in peace movements as naive or ill informed, it is quite clear that antinuclear movements often have a more sophisticated—empirically, intellectually, and ethically—reading of the meaning of security than do many statist politicians. Quite apart from the understandable obsession with throw-weights and acronyms, with the contradictions of deterrence theory and the relative irresponsibility of each superpower, some antinuclear movements raise crucial questions about the changing context of human behavior. For the first time in history, war is seen as a global problem. Even though preparation for war and its technology are increasingly specialized and arcane, movements have been able to generalize the meaning of war. It is interpreted as a symbol of the planetary dimension of human existence, putting into serious question the capacity of the state to provide a convincing sense of security. Contrary to the conventional wisdom enshrined in the categories of modern political thought—wisdom undoubtedly confirmed by considerable historical experience, but now justified by increasingly dubious claims about the inherent evil of either human nature in general or a specific enemy in particular—the interests of human beings begin to take priority over the interests of human beings as citizens of states.

In this context, the meaning of "peace" itself has to change. For some, the simple absence of war would be enough. For an increasing number of others, peace implies the removal of many forms of insecurity and "structural violence." For others, it implies the emergence of a conscious and collective recognition of the capacity of human beings to produce—and destroy—themselves and the quality of their existence. The most visible demands of peace movements may well be directed at an intervention into the policies of states. But the underlying force of these movements reflects an increasing awareness of the connections between global structures and the minute routines of everyday life, as well as the historical emergence of a vulnerability that is not only shared but shared consciously.

Ethical concerns are particularly significant. A subjective awareness of emerging connections is often informed by a normative sense that, in the end, we are indeed all part of the same species. Some see solidarity itself as a fundamental human need. Others suggest that, even though one may not feel compelled to help the starving, to be human involves knowing that the very existence of processes that are already creating Two Worlds, and may be bringing No World, undermines our capacity to be human. These normative assertations may be able to draw upon long-standing religious, spiritual, and philosophical traditions. Even those religions that have been most susceptible to the tendency of dividing the believers from the unbelievers often have a more open and more cosmopolitan side that can be drawn on here. Similarly, the universalizing thrust that has informed Western unilinear views of History—whether these draw on ideas about natural law, Kantian rationalism, liberal rights, or socialist community—can be recovered from their historically specific links with the political claims of dominant forces.

Nevertheless, despite all these explorations, it is quite clear that common identity and global community do not exist. They remain to be created. Moreover, from the point of view of movements, the demand for diversity is at least as great and usually greater than the demand for unity. Whatever community may come to mean, it will necessarily involve a recognition of the claims of both identity and of difference. One of the most significant contributions of critical social movements may eventually prove to be a clearer elaboration of how these claims may be reconciled in a more creative way than they are now.

EXPLORATIONS OF CONNECTION

The most obvious problems of movements arise from their character as responses to large structural forces and transformations. They are motivated in the first instance by the will to resist; and resistance is always liable to be simply crushed.

Those trying to resist the state and to develop some autonomy from it are always in danger of physical force or of inducing a corporatist alliance between the most powerfully organized groups in society. Those trying to create space in civil society discover that civil society itself contains many structures of oppression, not least ethnic domination, patriarchy, and the market. Those responding to conditions of economic inequality are often the marginalized, those rendered functionally irrelevant by a new mode of production or division of labor.

In these contexts, social movements may become less concerned with challenging the structures of exclusion than with resisting their worst effects in particular areas, with preserving a space in which people can survive in a meaningful way. The preservation of such spaces—a special wilderness here, a few seed species there, a few groups of marginalized peoples, whole states more or less excluded from the latest reconstruction of the international division of labor—is undeniably important. But it often seems that it is all that is possible. Challenges to the big structures can seem futile.

Moreover, the experiences and potentials of movements vary enormously in different contexts, according to cultural setting, political system, historical circumstances, and location within the world economy. So many societies are preoccupied with problem solving at the level of a given state or region, or even at the level of immediate local community, that wider preoccupations can seem virtually irrelevant. The pressures of context can constrain the imagination rather rigidly.

In the Middle East, for instance, the political struggles between Arabs and Israelis and between modernizers and fundamentalists take up virtually the entire political space. There is little disposition to question more widespread patterns of reliance on violence or to give up the traditional political goal of control over state power. Africa, too, seems beset by immediacy: famines, masses of displaced persons, race war, and an array of secular problems arising out of corruption and incompetence. In such settings, concerns about nuclear war or ecological collapse can seem remote and abstract.

Where political systems and cultural settings do not regard social movements as natural modes of popular participation, their existence tends to be nominal. This is the case, for example, in the two state socialist giants, the Soviet Union and China. In China, problems of relations with foreign countries seem of paramount concern, as does the national struggle to balance population, resources, and techniques in a successful developmental approach.

To speak only of the role of critical social movements in relation to the large world-order issues of our time is to write off states in which such movements are insignificant. Many of these states, especially China and the Soviet Union, are obviously major centers of power and influence. Thus, it is necessary to keep in mind the various roles of different kinds of actors in promoting positive change under varying circumstances. The contributions made by people and governments in societies in which critical social movements are marginalized or excluded obviously cannot be ignored.

Moreover, although it may be true that movements respond to threats that arise from the increasingly global character of contemporary life—whether these threats involve immediate problems of survival and oppression or the probable effects of nuclear war or ecocatastrophe—most social movements operate within very specific settings and are necessarily preoccupied with the most immediate challenge. Perhaps notable are occasions when Bishop Tutu journeys to Hiroshima for the forty-first anniversary observances or when Petra Kelly or E. P. Thompson speak up on behalf of East European and Soviet dissidents. But these are symbolic gestures that do not go to the essence of what animates their respective movement members back home on a day-to-day basis. In some instances, leaders with a more cosmopolitan outlook lose influence, being regarded as more interested in their own image than the concrete struggle back home.

Movements are exploratory. They include a wide range of outlooks among their adherents and easily fracture under the pressures of either success or failure. These fractures are "news" and often give an exaggerated impression of disunity, an impression that itself may be influential in promoting still further disunity and demoralization. Fracturing through loss of contact or demoralization brings the need for communication, which depends upon adequate resources. Many social movements operate on tiny budgets and cannot possibly afford to create transnational networks of like-minded groups and individuals. These organizational obstacles are made even more formidable by hostile institutional responses, including efforts to manipulate such movements by insinuating informers, or even provocateurs, or to obstruct their mobility by questioning travel credentials and the like.

All these obvious problems of critical social movements notwithstanding, it is quite clear that the visions of the future that are now offered by postindustrial statists, neoconservatives, unreconstructed social democrats, technocratic modernizers, self-righteous fundamentalists, and disruptive violence-prone groups can only produce two responses, both unsatisfactory: The first is breakdown and chaos; the second is managed order that excludes the poor and marginal from participation and, over time, widens and hardens gaps separating those who are saved and those who are damned. To overcome this dark destiny requires more than politics as usual.

It is easy enough to see how the diversity and fragmentation of critical social movements may be interpreted as a sign of weakness. Indeed, conventional images of power so depend on a celebration of unity—of the state, of class solidarity, of a broad alliance or a united front—that it is difficult not to see the very character of such movements as proof of their necessary impotence.

Freed from such images, it is possible to see that this diversity and fragmentation also make movements potentially so significant. Their diversity does not always consist of mere disaggregation, randomness, and contingency. Nor is it just a consequence of the way that modern economic life has tended to produce a proliferation of atomistic and mutually isolated social groups. Still less is it understandable as just a form of liberal interest group pluralism. The diversity of movements depends on an exploration of what it means to act on the basis of acknowledged differences. Critical social movements are often deeply suspicious of all claims to unity. They explore diverse political spaces and are open to many different ways of acting politically. In exploring new ways of knowing and being, they are particularly suspicious of the way in which unity claimed in the name of Reason, History, God, the State, or Human Nature has been used to humiliate or exterminate the different, the marginal, the other.

This suspicion of universalism is not the same as a rejection of commonality. On the contrary, it arises from movements that are able to understand fairly well the interconnected nature of contemporary life and the potentiality it offers. An openness to difference and to the great variety of experiences and histories that lead people to respond to global processes in highly localized circumstances occurs simultaneously with a sensitivity to the reality of connections. This double openness forces movements to pose what is in the end the most fundamental political question of our time: Given a world of both connections and proliferating histories, what does it now mean to feel and act as a human being; what does it mean to speak of human identity and human solidarity in an age that can plausibly imagine No World or Two Worlds?

Understood as interpreters of the broad trajectories of the modern world, critical social movements identify the major challenges of the age in terms of emerging patterns of connectedness. They understand that scholarly categories of analysis that divide the world up are unable to capture the complexity of processes that fuse political, economic, cultural, social, and technological forces and that do so within structures that encompass all parts of the world. Similarly, movements understand that although they are forced to act in particular circumstances, they have to do so in a world in which those circumstances cannot be artificially disconnected from what is going on elsewhere. They recognize that in articulating new forms of political action and new possibilities for the future, they have to respond to a world of emerging connections. The recognition of connections is central not only to the interpretation of pressing problems but also to thinking about more effective forms of political practice.

For the most part, this involves the way movements are drawn toward but also tend to resist connections with existing forms of political community and practice. Movements have been able to connect fairly successfully with many other political forces, but these connections are often quite ambivalent.

In some cases, this has involved interaction with relatively progressive political parties. In Western Europe, the case of the West German Greens illustrates not only the way that some movements can even transform themselves into political parties, but can also force social democratic parties to absorb environmentist, feminist, and peace issues into their programs.

In other cases, movements engage with established labor movements and class organizations. Movements struggling for economic alternatives challenge the more established socialist and labor movements to respond in novel ways to global economic transformations and to the consequent pressure on labor costs and demands for greater productivity. The terrain of economic activity is extended beyond conventional considerations of profit and the wage-labor relation. Alternative forms of economic organization are encouraged, from cooperatives and community and worker-owned enterprises to barter systems and the sophisticated improvisations of the underground economy. The meeting between labor movements and women's movements seems likely to become a particularly important ground on which to question the form of prevailing economic structures rather than just the division of spoils within it.

In still other cases, movements may work directly with governmental institutions and agencies. The Canadian International Development Agency, for example, is fairly typical of the kind of state-sponsored agency that facilitates the participation of movements in affluent societies by encouraging more appropriate forms of development assistance.

Some grassroots movements have been able to participate in the conferences sanctioned by states to examine a number of global problems. These began with a focus on environmental issues in Stockholm in 1972. Other conferences have been held on problems of population growth, food, and human settlements. These conferences drew attention to the severity of specific problems, but also to the paralysis of existing capabilities at the international level.

Much of the vitality that did emerge from these conferences was associated with the so-called counter-conferences of people drawn to the formal event but with nonstatist conceptions of appropriate responses. Similar energies were created at the United Nations World Conference on Women held in Nairobi in July 1985, which brought together women from all over the world. Again, the women who participated, about half of whom worked within INGOs, reported on their sense of empowerment arising from the way women from diverse cultural and class backgrounds discovered powerful affinities.

In general, these global occasions create networks of individuals, groups, and more formal organizations across existing boundaries that facilitate the claims of new forms of politics. In addition, the impotence of governments in the face of evidence about problems and suffering contributes to the work of delegitimation. Indeed, these negative reactions have become so prevalent that governments have grown reluctant to sponsor such occasions, as they realize that the good effects of displaying concern about the shortcomings of the world are more than offset by the bad effects of exhibiting impotence. As a result, the creation of similar networks and global arenas will have to be staged by critical social movements themselves, not an easy task in view of the funding problems involved.

Other connections occur between North-South solidarity movements (especially in relation to South Africa, Nicaragua, Chile, and the Philippines), between peace movements such as END in Western Europe and groups like Charter 77 in Eastern Europe, within international church groups, between socialist groups, environmentalist groups, within the Council of Indigenous Peoples, and so on. Thus, for example, the specific land claims currently being pursued by the Gitksan and Wet'suwet'en nations in British Columbia are consciously regarded as a leading case in the global struggle between aboriginal peoples and governments and resource companies that want the land aboriginal peoples have historically occupied. These linkages are all but invisible unless one is participating in them. They defy any easy mapping of their scope or weighing of their significance.

Connections of this kind have been possible, yet they give rise to a range of important concerns. One of the most obvious temptations open to critical social movements, of course, involves a romanticization of the will of the people. In fact, to grant power to the people has no assured beneficial normative consequences. The consequences depend on conditions, on the experience and outlook of those who have endured exploitation and suffering, and on the quality of leadership. What counts is not a romanticized view of the inherently democratic or rational capacities of people in general, but rather the establishment of social and political practices that enhance the capacity of peoples everywhere to create effective democratic communities.

Another classic temptation involves the false extrapolation from the interests and perspectives of a particular group or class as if those interests and perspectives were universal. This is a particularly significant problem for movements that draw on a middle-class population. But it leads more generally to the very difficult issue of the way that many movements are both energized and compromised by their reliance on conflicting class interests.

A third general temptation is to ignore the very real conflicts of interest that can arise between movements. The success of movements in affluent societies in curbing environmental abuse or stopping the sale of dangerous drugs, for example, can result in the export of such problems to less affluent societies. Environmental movements and labor movements are often at serious odds. Movements struggling in the shadow of one superpower can be fairly insensitive to the plight of movements struggling in the shadow of the other one. Even so, all kinds of unlikely coalitions do occur.

These general temptations give rise to practical questions about what kinds of relationships should be established with existing forms of political expression. Again, the most persistent concerns involve the state. In many situations, particularly where the inherited legacies of underdevelopment are so burdensome, the state can be a progressive force. In many other situations, movements are able to establish links with reformist forces within statist structures. Few organizations and institutions are entirely monolithic, and there is always the possibility of movements and "moles" giving strength to each other. Indeed, the resemblances between movement proposals for a nuclear freeze and the negotiating positions of the superpowers may indicate a significant change in the interaction between movements and state actors. Movements are frequently torn between their inherent suspicion of the state and their recognition that the state is necessary in order to get certain things done. It seems likely that a large part of future political debate will revolve around the opposition between those who seek to express themselves through various movements and those who accept the need for the incorporation of all political life at the level of the state. It is essential that such debate not fall into yet another false dichotomization of the alternatives.

Similar dilemmas arise with respect to relationships with political parties. Rifts within the West German Greens have become representative in this respect. Electoral success does not automatically translate into political effectiveness. In fact the very success of the Greens has raised questions about the trade-offs between power and integrity, about where real opportunities for effecting change are, and about what political power is. In general, party activists are often resentful of the way movements siphon off the energies necessary for electoral success. Conversely, movements have often been very important in creating the political climate in which progressive parties have been able to work.

Many movements experience the dilemma of not knowing what kinds of alliances to make with social forces that are partly sympathetic to the movement yet generally act in a conservative manner. Movements pursue issues that are of concern to people of quite different political persuasions. This allows for successful mobilization on specific issues but also for ultimate cooptation. Peace movements in the West may make alliances with retired generals when mobilizing against particularly lunatic arms deployments, but such alliances are more difficult to make when movements push for a more fundamental critique of militarization. Environmentalists may make common cause with conservative groups on grounds of conservation but are then in danger of abandoning their more fundamental ecological vision, which implies a thoroughgoing transformation of social and economic structures. Feminists may make common cause with liberal professionals with respect to human rights and even with conservatives on issues of pornography and the defense of family life, but the real force of feminist aspirations may then evaporate through cooptation into the status quo. The critique of philosophical assumptions and world views articulated by many movements often resonates with critiques of modernity that are essentially reactionary in inspiration.

Similar problems are emerging in relation to the proliferation of international nongovernmental organizations. On the face of it, critical social movements have been instrumental in fostering all kinds of connections through what used to be called "voluntary" organizations, often around attempts to move toward more appropriate forms of aid and development in relations between affluent and less affluent societies. Yet many NGOs and INGOs have flourished only through state patronage. It has been all too easy to capitulate to the demands of states or international financial organizations in order to get larger grants and less harassment. Formal nongovernmental status does not free an organization from the capacity of government to organize things in their own interests. As with relations with states and parties, cooptation is always on offer.

Movements may be tempted by easy abstract universalisms—the will of the people, the projected values of a particular class, an unwillingness to face up to real conflicts of interest. They may also be tempted to link up with established forms of political articulation, a temptation that offers access to established centers of power at the cost of easy cooptation. All these things can enter into the day-to-day tactical concerns of different movements. They raise choices about alliances, organizations, leadership, and priorities.

Some of the most interesting explorations of connection of this kind involve relations with those more established movements that have tried to combine conceptions of emancipation with universalist aspirations. If it remains true that the major ideologies of liberalism, socialism and nationalism are held in deep suspicion by movements, these ideologies have sometimes embodied aspirations that have not disappeared, no matter how compromised they may have become in practice. Nationalism may have been captured by the state. But the urge to live within a culturally meaningful community remains very powerful. Liberalism has become inseparable from the unequal development intrinsic to capitalism. But this has not lessened the urgency of the aspiration toward democracy that has sometimes rescued liberalism from mere utilitarianism. Socialism retains a capacity to express the possibility of real emancipation for everyone.

All these terms may have become the dirty words of our time, but movements are able both to recognize the exhaustion of these ideologies while engaging with what remains vital in them. The sense of community that emerges from movements may be far removed from statist nationalism, but it continues the celebration of diversity and pluralism that has informed nationalist aspirations. The sense of democratic participation articulated by movements may be labeled as naive or as dangerous by those who equate democracy with representative institutions, but movements can be understood as just a new phase in a struggle for meaningful democracy that is now centuries long. Movements may seem far removed from images of socialism that involve a centralized state. They may seem to be weak precisely because they refuse to adhere to a clearly defined class based politics. But the centralized state is inconsistent with socialism. And class politics in a world of global capital has become a very complicated matter indeed. But it is unlikely that critical social movements will get very far without engaging constructively with the practices and aspirations that have made socialism a practical reality for one-third of humanity.

In all three cases, the relationship between these dominant doctrines and critical social movements is one of potentially very creative encounter. It is less a matter of whether movements can be incorporated into traditional nationalist, liberal, or socialist projects than of whether movements are able to take up the challenges of community, democracy, and solidarity and to push them in new directions.

All these explorations of connection involve relationships that movements are able to make—or resist—with existing forms of political community and practice. But such explorations are obviously only part of the story. They only begin to grasp what is at stake in a conscious recognition that as inhabitants of a small and fragile planet, our destiny is inevitably indivisible.

CHAPTER SIX

Interpretations

PRACTICES AND ASPIRATIONS

As with social movements of the past, contemporary movements warn of approaching dangers. These warnings now arise from an increasingly clear recognition of the interconnected character of modern human affairs, an interconnectedness that often eludes more formal analyses rooted in the conceptual categories in an earlier age. In this sense, critical social movements extend the prophetic role of older movements, acting as herald of coming changes and as conscience for those who are either too exhausted or complacent to understand the violence of the present.

I have suggested that critical social movements go further than this. Their special significance lies in the way they sometimes respond to the challenges they identify. They find new spaces in which to act, thereby challenging the prevailing topography of political life. They discover new ways of acting, thereby challenging the prevailing conceptions of how people ought to behave toward each other. They extend the horizons of what it is possible to know and to be as human beings, thereby challenging the boundaries of received ethical, aesthetic, and philosophical traditions. Critical social movements struggle in particular circumstances, and yet they also recognize that specific struggles require new forms of interaction between peoples, new forms of human community and solidarity that cut across social and territorial categories established under other historical conditions.

The significance of these explorations will elude those who continue to think in terms of old revolutions. In a world of connections, it is no longer possible to pretend that real power is an object located in a particular place—a state apparatus, a social elite, a conspiracy of corporations. These may participate in relations of power. Struggles with them may be necessary for fundamental social and political change in many situations. But control of them is by no means sufficient. In a world of connections, power has no center, no Archimedean point that can be captured and deployed to change the world. In the end, the significance of social movements will depend on how they respond to global connections by establishing connections and solidarities of their own.

Many critical social movements have been able to transcend their particularity. They have developed patterns of common affinity and even identity on the basis of shared commitments. Coalitions and networks have been created in local, regional, national, and transnational arenas. Movements have acted in all these arenas to promote democracy and human rights, to provide political space for exploration and reconstruction, and to create alternative forms of production, management, and human relationships.

All these explorations are diffuse, even if they arise from movements with very specific and concrete objectives. They do not add up to a common program of action. They do not point to any general prescription for what particular movements should be doing to attain these concrete objectives. Such prescriptions cannot come from on high. The presumption that they can is part of the conception of political life being challenged. Yet, it is possible to speculate on the broad implications of the explorations of critical social movements for a reinterpretation of a just world peace and the form that struggles for a just world peace might take. Such speculation is especially urgent in rethinking the relation between aspiration and practice in three related contexts that have become highly problematic everywhere: those involving the meaning that can now be given to struggles for security, for development, and for deepening democracy.

It has become fashionable, even among critical social movements, to be skeptical about posing visions of the future. It is not difficult to understand why. Crusading visions have often promised deliverance from earthly travail. Some have masked exploitation and pacification, a tendency that led Marx to refer to religion as the "opium of the people." Some have sketched grand utopias without paying much, if any, attention to the possible connections between the vision and the concrete human practices that could bring it into being. This tendency has been particularly visible both in schemes for world government and in claims that a purer inner life by a sufficient number of people can automatically bring about social and political transformation. These are both ways in which the necessity for social transformation may be avoided. They involve demands for change that leave the world as it is.

Other grand visions of the future have been linked to promises made by particular groups to effect change after gaining power, promises that have been broken either by the nature of the struggle for power itself or by the nature of the power that is attained. Too many revolutions have been swallowed by all-powerful states. Other revolutions have succeeded in taking state power only to discover that the state is relatively weak in relation to other external forces.

If crusading visions for a bright world ahead have become unfashionable, so has it become important to be wary of dark forebodings. The scenarios of No World and Two Worlds find renewed plausibility with each new report of incipient famine, of resurgent dictatorships, of nuclear winter. They are reinforced by each new act of bloody-mindedness by political leaders with massive resources and little wisdom. Yet, to listen too long to these scenarios of despair is to induce submission and passivity and to abandon the possibilities and responsibilities implied in human freedom and creativity.

To work toward better times ahead may well be to grope in the dark, to be susceptible either to the false certainty of fundamentalist retreat and future salvation or to the false pessimism of inevitable doom. There may even be uncertainty about how clear the way ahead ought to be for effective action. Clarity of vision may enhance motivation; but because it is never possible to specify the possibilities with enough plausibility, consensus, or vibrancy, the very attempt to illuminate direction can be dispiriting. But none of this means that it is necessary to wander aimlessly. The problem is not so much the lack of illumination as the expectation that the light should emanate from a single powerful source.

Critical social movements are concerned less with grand utopian schemes than with aspirations that grow out of ongoing political practices. Familiar goals are cast in a new perspective. The most basic categories guiding everyday activity are constantly subject to reinterpretation. Critical social movements may thus be understood not so much in terms of the traditions of political life that try to bring transcendent or ideological visions down to earth—traditions that have had a tremendous impact on the way the modern state has been constituted—as they may be understood in terms of traditions that recognize the dynamic interaction between visionary aspirations and the creation of new forms of political practice. The appropriate image is not that of a future utopia opposed to a dismal present. It is rather that of the always ongoing struggle to create a new language in which to understand, to participate in, and to change what is going on in the world.

Despite the influential claims of so many rationalist philosophers, language is not some abstract system of symbols imposed on a point of reference. Language cannot be grasped adequately based on any account founded on the presumption of a sharp division between consciousness and matter, between idea and reality. It is a product of concrete historical processes. To reinterpret the world is necessarily to act on the world.

Critical social movements are less concerned with abstract dreams than with the possibilities of imagining the future on the basis of ongoing practices, which is to understand that what has so far become real and concrete is surrounded by a zone of many unfulfilled possibilities. It is to know that what is might not be.

RETHINKING SECURITY

A world that can plausibly envisage scenarios of No World and Two Worlds is clearly a place of serious insecurities. The concept of security, therefore, offers a particularly important starting point for thinking about a just world peace. Unfortunately, it is often treated as the only starting point, particularly where the meaning of security has grown out of concerns about war and peace—understood as opposites—within the states system. To rethink the meaning of security in ways suggested by the practices of critical social movements is necessarily to move beyond these horizons.

Beyond Rational Security

For all its aura of tough-minded clarity, the dominant understanding of security is exceptionally flimsy and vague. As a central term of contemporary political discourse, "security" seems to have been abandoned to the propagandists and ideologues. It has become less a concept with any analytical precision than an instrument of mystifying rhetoric. Appeals to the need for security justify the most blatant abuses and encourage the resort to escalating levels of violence. Such appeals legitimize vast arsenals and the curtailment of democratic rights and procedures. The concept of security is now more a symptom of the problem than a guide to the possibilities of peace and justice.

The reasons for this should be clear from the preceding analysis. The most important use of the concept of security is linked explicitly to state power. The idea of "national security" arises from the supposed demands of the "security dilemma" in the states system, a dilemma that is claimed to legitimize the resort to war when national security is threatened.

The classic European account of the problem occurs in Thomas Hobbes's seventeenth-century depiction of the insecurities arising from competition between more or less equal individuals seeking to preserve themselves in a proto-capitalist society and making each other insecure in the process. Similar ideas are expressed in influential theories of economic behavior that assume individual self-interest always prevails over the public good. The legitimacy of state power is then claimed to derive in large measure from the state's capacity to bring order to the conflict that results inevitably from the insecurities of competitive self-interested behavior.

Contemporary thinking about national security depends on a transposition of these ideas about individuals to relations between states, a transposition often dressed up in sophisticated languages of game theory, utilitarian calculation, and a subtle hint of moral pessimism. A few refinements have been added, particularly in theories of nuclear deterrence. On the whole, thinking about security in political terms still begins with the equation of security in general with the security of states in a competitive states system.

This interpretation of security depends on a number of crucial assumptions. First, it assumes that relations between states are necessarily driven by a logic of anarchical competition, something that Hobbes himself denied explicitly. This assumption then justifies a second—namely, that security can be provided only within states. Security is then often casually identified with the interests of elites and governments (the "national interest") rather than with society as a whole. More significant, security is identified with the citizens of states and not with people in general. Indeed, this concept of security reinforces the distinction between friend and foe, self and other, on which the modern concept of the state depends. A third assumption, consistent with the first two, is that it is possible to distinguish clearly between peace and war. Within states, it is assumed that communities can develop in peace. Between states, war is inevitable. National security—the presumption that security is a matter of the defense of the citizens of a sovereign territory—becomes the crucial point of demarcation, the boundary between chaos and order, conflict and community, violence and justice.

Concerned observers, even conservative scholars and dominant elites, agree that this conception of security is both analytically incoherent and increasingly dangerous. They do so primarily as a consequence of processes that have been set in motion by the two superpowers. The most obvious theme has involved a growing recognition that weapons of mass destruction undermine the claim that there can be a rational calculation of the relationship between ends and means in war. The advent of nuclear weapons has convinced even some of the most cynical believers in the inevitability of international conflict that something has to change. They have come to recognize that the weapons supposedly deployed for defense have become more dangerous than any conceivable enemy. They worry about the outrageous accumulation of fifty thousand warheads and contemplate the depravity of a world that can unleash the destructive power of a million Hiroshima bombs.

In this context, the tough-minded aura of claims about the priority of national security starts to fracture. Even conservative elites call more urgently for serious arms control processes. They demand that security be understood as a matter of détente and coexistence rather than of supremacy and victory. They begin to embrace notions like "common security," popularized by the Palme Commission.

In terms of the perspectives emerging from critical social movements, it is necessary to go much further than this. First-strike missiles and the reduction of response times, while dangerous enough, are also just symptoms of a seemingly all-pervasive militarization of contemporary human affairs. The production of armaments has to be understood not only in the context of claimed military requirements but also in terms of complex economic forces. Indeed, the term "military-industrial complex" does not begin to grasp the complex interplay between economies and military deployments and the role of the state in fostering this interplay. Nor is it possible to stop at a political economy of arms production. Processes of militarization enter into cultural forms and symbolic codes, into what is considered appropriate as children's play or as metaphor of human interaction.

The most worrying voices here are raised by those who stress the importance of understanding the global scale of these processes of militarization. They delineate the complex patterns of integration between processes of arms production; arms deployments both between superpowers and in different regional settings; international trade; foreign aid in the forms of weapons, military assistance, or arms-related technologies; and the use of increasingly sophisticated weapons as an instrument of repression within states.

In this perspective, the drift toward a future cataclysm is certainly serious but should not detract attention from the immediate violence of processes that are already destroying people's lives and distorting whole societies. It is relatively easy to see how it might be possible to stop a process understood as a race—by persuading the contestants to stop competing. It is much more difficult to know how to respond to processes that seem to converge in the inexorable dynamics of global structure beyond the control of existing authorities.

Accounts of these broader processes of militarization are often sketchy, but they provide one essential ground from which to begin to rethink what security ought to mean in the modern world. In a world of connections between the geopolitical logic of the states system and the economic processes of military production and distribution, the groping for some conception of "common security" must go beyond the usual appeals to arms control and détente. Both arms control and détente are certainly required. Urgently. Desperately. But they do not enable us to move much beyond the treatment of symptoms.

However, even this broader perspective has serious limits. It is concerned primarily with the scenario of No World. But militarization also participates in the creation of new principles of inclusion and exclusion. The scenario of Two Worlds is just as important in this regard as the threat of global extermination.

Security and Structural Transformation

Although prevailing concepts of national security remain locked into an anachronistic account of the logic of the states system, any serious rethinking of security has to take account of at least three fundamental transformations. First, there has been a broadening of the sources of insecurity. Questions of war and peace cannot be separated from questions of development, ecological degradation, abuse of human rights, loss of cultural identity. The enemy, as has been said so often, is not someone else, but ourselves and the structures that we, as human beings, have created together.

Second, there has been a broadening of the subject of security to include people in general, indeed life on earth, rather than just the citizens of states. The concept of national security incorporates a specific resolution of the competing claims of people as people and people as citizens. It gives absolute priority to the latter. Under modern conditions, the pursuit of the security of citizens of states renders everyone more and more insecure as people. Furthermore, the emergence of new structures of inclusion and exclusion—not the spatial or territorial divisions between states but the complex social, cultural, economic, and political divisions between peoples who can and cannot participate effectively in contemporary global processes—renders one-third of humanity radically unable to secure the minimum conditions for survival.

Third, the state itself, far from being the provider of security as in the conventional view, has in many ways become a primary source of insecurity. This is true not only in terms of the processes generated by the external pursuit of national security, which involves active participation in structures that threaten everyone, but also internally where states have, so often, become a primary threat to their own citizens. "Disappearances" and state abuses of human rights must enter into any rethinking of what security can be.

The sources of insecurity in the modern world cannot be reduced to the necessities of life in a system of states. Such a reduction was always an oversimplified fiction. It is now a willful obscurantism. The distinctions between friend and foe, citizen and enemy, inside and outside belong to an earlier era. These distinctions are now simply incompatible with the search for security. And the distinction between war and peace must surely dissolve in a world in which militarization is becoming a part of everyday life and in which death through starvation is the immediate reality for millions.

It is important to stress the continuing significance of these dichotomies in conventional thinking about national security. Indeed, the concept of national security is literally unthinkable without them. They reflect an historically specific account of political space. The world is divided into discrete territorialities, each with a sharp distinction between inside and outside. Powerful states may enlarge their informal account of what is considered to be inside; some seem to regard what goes on everywhere as vital to their own internal security. Nevertheless, the conventional conception of security depends on an assumption of spatial exclusion. It tends toward a zero sum—I win, you lose—interpretation of that exclusion. Traditional ideas about a society of states, or balance of power, or nuclear deterrence try to minimize the danger of overt conflict. Recent ideas about "common security" reflect a recognition that the very notion of territorial exclusion is simply incompatible with security in the modern world. The practices of critical social movements explode this familiar spatial imagery altogether.

The Multiple Sources of Insecurity

Movements stress the multiple sources of insecurity, not the location of threat in some territorially distant "other." They treat insecurity as a product of the systematic recourse to violence that characterizes modern social structures as a whole. They link insecurity with the existence of poverty and the immediate threat to the survival of millions of people everywhere. They link it to the degradation of the environment on which human life depends, to the degradation of people subject to the violent abuse of human rights, to threats to eradicate cultural traditions that allow people to give meaning and purpose to their lives.

The traditional spatial imagery embodies a strict delimitation of the options available; security is possible only within the territorial state or in the state writ large—world government. In fact, ideas about world government incorporate the same underlying spatial assumptions as the idea of national security. This shared imagery is completely obscured in all those debates about national security that have assumed a sharp opposition between so-called realists and so-called idealists. Critical social movements insist that this is a false choice. Security cannot be located within a single site, whether state or international institution. It has to be created in many locations, at many levels.

Critical social movements stress the different forms taken by insecurity in different situations. They emphasize the need to understand the connections between different conceptions of security appropriate for different situations rather than to search for a single concept or source of security. They understand that a rethinking of security has to take account of the re-articulation of political space that has made the concept of national security so anachronistic.

Regional Security

One interesting innovation in this respect is an increasing willingness to think about "common security" in regional terms. Of course, regional security may just mean a geographical extension of the concept of national security to larger structures of exclusion and confrontation, as occurred with the formation of alliance blocs in the cold war. But it can also lead to a more creative recognition of a common interest in avoiding those very structures of inclusion and exclusion, of we and they, that by their very nature undermine the possibility of common security.

Perhaps the best-known moves in this direction occur at the traditional center of superpower confrontation in Europe. Quite apart from attempts to encourage détente in this context, more and more voices are raised calling for a European security initiative that seeks both to delink regional interests from the global designs of the two superpowers and to encourage a clearer recognition of the common interests of Europe as a whole. Such a recognition could open the way for security policies that dispense with destabilizing weapons, reduce reliance on military solutions to political conflicts, enhance the possibilities of relying on more defensive, and therefore less provocative, forms of defense, and challenge the legitimacy of superpower hegemony in Europe or East and West.

Similar emphases on regional security are visible elsewhere. Some progress was once being made, for example, in limiting naval deployments in the Indian Ocean. This came to very little, primarily because of heightened tensions over Afghanistan, Ethiopia, and oil supplies in the Gulf. Yet, there is now no overriding need for a naval presence in this region, and an agreement to turn it into a zone of peace is both compelling and plausible.

The Pacific Ocean provides another example of the pressing need to think of security in regional terms. In fact, this is a region now experiencing distinctly contradictory tendencies. On the one hand, tensions between China and the USSR have decreased; increasing dialogue takes place between Tokyo and Moscow; and despite intense competition over economic and trade matters, the Pacific is currently the site of an increasing sense of common regional interests. The continuing strength of the commitment by the people of Japan to the principle of not possessing, manufacturing, or introducing nuclear weapons is particularly hopeful. Against this, there remain continuing reminders of the aggressive capacities of superpowers, most noticeably in tensions in the Korean peninsula, in confrontational naval strategies, as well as in the powerful pressures on Japan—internal as well as external—to participate in SDI and to engage in a policy of remilitarization. Again, it does not take much imagination to see that a politics of negotiation, accommodation, and entente on a regional basis offers a more coherent way of thinking about security than a militaristic encouragement of aggression and confrontation.

Thinking about security in regional terms is beginning to be particularly significant to both movements and governments in South America. This is most apparent among those who are struggling against military regimes and the abuse of human rights. The key issue here involves questions about how to reduce the legitimacy of military regimes. One obvious response to this question, of course, is for political parties and movements to act in a manner that does not provide an opportunity for military intervention— hence, the importance of nonviolent actions and of attempts to revitalize the processes of civil society rather than to attack state power directly. Moreover, the legitimacy of military regimes is directly tied to the continuing presence of border disputes. The settling of such disputes is, therefore, seen increasingly as an important aspect of the struggle for human rights. Beyond this lies the need to dissociate the identification of regional security interests with the perceived global interests of the United States, an identification that enhances the legitimacy of dictatorial politics. Hence, a concern to enhance greater regional cooperation also puts a check on the global ambitions of the superpowers.

Such linkages between the need for a greater sense of regional security interests and the struggle for human rights extend to a recognition that in the Latin American context economic security is a more pressing problem than strategic or military security. Effective security must involve a just and autonomous participation in the world economy and, thus, the removal of the burden of international debt. It must involve a significant reduction in extreme poverty.

Ideas about such zones of peace are paralleled by demands for nuclear-free zones. Such ideas have become an important thrust of antinuclear movements in Europe, New Zealand, the South Pacific, and elsewhere.

Security, Community, and Democracy

A stress on regional conceptions of security is perhaps the most obvious expression of the way in which a sensitivity to the changing spatial context of security can help shape alternative conceptions of what security in general might entail. A similar sensitivity might also lead to a rethinking of the possibility and character of security arrangements in other contexts, from the global down to quite highly specific and local situations. Indeed, it leads on to a serious rethinking of the location and character of political processes in general.

Whatever its incoherences, the concept of national interest is at least grounded in an identifiable political community: the state. In an era in which political space is being rearticulated in confusing and contradictory ways, the incoherence of the concept of national security necessarily leads on from questions about peace, war, and militarization to questions about the direction of social and political transformation. To rethink the spatial categories in which security ought to be understood is necessarily to rethink the practices through which more appropriate forms of security might be achieved. It is to understand that the concept of national security is an insufficient ground on which to think about the possibilities of a just world peace.

Despite the conventional wisdom that security is primarily a political matter, it remains almost completely tied to considerations of military policy. All too often, it is even reduced to mere technological possibility. Yet, even when treated in political terms, security is associated with a particular form of politics. Defined as national security, it has become the preserve of state elites. It has remained resistant to the claims of democracy almost everywhere.

The call to treat security matters in a more political way is now common among those who push for more effective forms of arms control, for less provocative defense doctrines, capabilities, and postures, or for more détente and accommodation. It is a call that must be encouraged. But beyond this, the lesson to be drawn from the experiences of contemporary movements is the necessity of encouraging more democratic political processes in security affairs. The experiences of critical social movements show that to rethink the concept of security is necessarily to rethink the relationship between security and political practice.

The Latin American experience again provides a useful illustration of this. On the one hand, it is quite clear that the chances of allowing more democratic political processes to emerge depend on finding solutions to persistent threats to national and regional security. Conversely, it is also clear that greater democracy is a precondition for attaining greater security. As long as military regimes and authoritarian elites prevail, internal repressions and external aggressions will continue to reinforce and legitimize each other.

Similarly, Western antinuclear movements must be understood not only in terms of their primary stress on the dangers of nuclear weapons but also as a major challenge to the undemocratic way in which national security policies are formulated. They challenge the presumption that the primacy of national security as defined by state elites can guarantee the security of people. They know very well that under modern conditions the primacy of national security can significantly decrease the security of people and that the security policies of the most powerful states are in fact now doing so. Moreover, they raise questions about the meaning of democracy under conditions in which people are prevented from participating effectively in decisions about the most fundamental questions of life and death. They raise questions about how it is possible to exercise effective democratic control over economic, social, and cultural processes of militarization that, set in motion and legitimized by claims of national security, lead to the destruction of ways of life that on the surface seem to have little to do with security issues at all.

The challenges made by such movements involve a recognition that greater security depends on a greater democratic participation in security issues. This recognition must increasingly inform the activities of antinuclear movements if they are to do more than protest from the sidelines. Security issues cannot be left to elites capable of insisting on the necessary convergence of their interests with those of the nation. They must not be used to legitimize covert operations against foreign governments and internal repression at home. There is a need for greater discussion and public debate about security matters that are now either shrouded in secrecy or overwhelmed by systematic propaganda, the manipulation of national chauvinism, and the glorification of technological superiority. Democratic politics cannot survive without a passion to know what is going on and an informed capacity to make reasoned judgments about what is known.

Security has traditionally been an issue in which people have been willing to abandon responsibility to others who claim to know best. This is one traditional habit that can prove fatal. Security is not something that can be left to someone else. In the modern world, effective security must mean democratic security.

Security, Vulnerability, and Violence

To push thinking about security toward emerging conceptions of political space (even if only toward a greater emphasis on regional security arrangements) or to assert that security must become subject to more democratic political processes (even if democratic security remains preoccupied with national defense) is to see how an engagement with security matters necessarily leads to a reconceptualization of the basic categories in which we understand how people do and should live together. Again, the practices of critical social movements offer a number of clues about how this reconceptualization might be taken further. They suggest the need to go beyond just the insistence on a more political understanding of security or even a more democratic understanding of politics, crucial though both those things are. They lead to a more basic emphasis on the need to understand the dialectical interplay between security and insecurity in human affairs and on the need to think more clearly about who security is for.

The contrast between conceptions of security implicit in the practices of critical social movements and those implicit in the U. S. Strategic Defense Initiative is especially interesting in this respect. There are no doubt many explanations for the genesis of this gigantic exercise, but part of its underlying appeal is surely its promise of absolute invulnerability within one territorially defined part of the world. Peace, security, and national interest are taken to be assured only when security from attack from outside is guaranteed absolutely. Leviathan's most neurotic dreams meet Buck Rogers's most juvenile fantasies.

Quite apart from all the technical problems involved, this project steadfastly ignores even the most basic lesson of conventional strategic and military history: that one state's search for invulnerability is likely to make other states feel vulnerable. The more invulnerability is sought, the more vulnerability is guaranteed. The promises of vulnerability with which SDI is advertised mask still further leaps down the roads to No World or Two Worlds.

The primary problem with SDI is less its substitution of technological gimmickry for political negotiation than its symbolization of a particularly crude understanding of what it means to be secure. Whereas SDI represents a necessarily vain attempt to attain absolute security, critical social movements understand that there is no such thing as absolute invulnerability in this life. Security and insecurity are complementary.

Vulnerability is part of the human condition. People are inherently vulnerable, both physically and psychically. This is not subject to only a negative interpretation. It is part of what makes us human. To be vulnerable is to be open. To be open is to create the opportunity for communication and exchange, for learning and commitment. It is to encourage the dialogue and creativity necessarily excluded by fundamentalist or totalitarian attempts to provide absolute invulnerability. SDI is inhuman, not just because of the sheer violence inherent in its technologies, but because its basic premises involve a denial of the very capacities that allow people to engage with each other as people. Its technologies have the capacity to destroy people physically. Its premises simply deny people their humanity.

The insistence by movements that security and insecurity must not be treated as mutually exclusive opposites is closely linked to their insistence on the importance of nonviolence in thinking about security and, indeed, about all forms of human interaction. The overall thrust of the practices of movements is clearly toward nonviolence. In fact, there seems to be an emerging and encouraging normative understanding that violence must only be a last resort; and then only when it is as a response to violence, where there is an authoritative consensus on the part of the victims of violence that there is no other recourse available, where there is a conscious attempt to direct violence only at the perpetrators of violence, and even then only in the most restrained and economical manner possible. More crucial than this, critical social movements show that violence and power are just not identical. To alter the relationship between power and violence is to open up the possibility of creative and empowering practices even in circumstances in which violence seems inevitable.

Toward Security for All People

The most important message coming from movements concerning security is quite stark in its simplicity. It draws on the claim that in a world of connections, in a world of emerging solidarities, either security will be understood as referring to all people or it will not be at all. The idea of "common security" has now become familiar in public debate. Unfortunately, it is a term that remains tied to the necessary but still limited push for more cooperation between states still preoccupied with defending their own national security. The idea of "collective security" was once popular among those expressing hopes for a more effective role for international institutions in security affairs. Unfortunately, it became either a synonym for alliance blocs or a way of translating the will of the most powerful grouping of states into claims of internationalism. The underlying message coming from movements is that such terms must in the end be translatable into an effective people's security. The primary subject of security is people—not states, nor elites, nor the affluent, nor the stronger.

To raise the possibility of people's security is clearly to push the concept of security as we now know it to its limits. Whether insisting that security must be rethought in terms of the rearticulation of political space, the discovery of new forms of political practice, the exploration of new horizons of knowing and being, or the struggle to establish new forms of human solidarity, the analysis of security constantly pushes into other realms. Rethinking security is particularly difficult to separate from rethinking the possibilities of development. In fact, the concept of development provides an alternative starting point for thinking about many of the same problems, especially in societies in which the prospect of Two Worlds is immediate.

RETHINKING DEVELOPMENT

The concept of development has become problematic in an even more complex and far-reaching way than that of security. It has long been subject to bitter theoretical and ideological dispute. As a synonym for "progress," it has been criticized for all the arrogances of a universalist reading of History. As a synonym for economic growth, it has been embroiled in a century of debate about the character and consequences of capitalism, industrialism, imperialism, and socialism. In some places it is still treated as shorthand for the inevitable way forward. Elsewhere, quotation marks around it symbolize increasing embarrassment and anger. In either case, as with the concept of national security, the rhetorical power of the concept of development is at odds with its conceptual, political, and ethical incoherence.

Long-standing controversies have been heightened by recent transformations in the world economy. Countries that participated in building the postwar international economic order at Bretton Woods have found themselves in serious economic difficulties. The myth of inevitable growth has been punctured even among the wealthy. Less-affluent states that tried to create a more equitable New International Economic Order have seen their hopes dashed. The suspicion that poorer societies would continue to remain poor has been reinforced yet again. Furthermore, the restructuring of the world economy has brought new patterns of inequality, new forms of inclusion and exclusion. These patterns cannot but call into serious question the received wisdom concerning what development is about or who it is for.

Development and Maldevelopment

We live in a world in which total production is at present sufficient to sustain a basic standard of life and health for everyone on earth. The reason why so many people live in poverty, ill health, and cultural deprivation, engage in hard labor, and suffer premature death is not because of the shortage of productive resources, nor a shortage of knowledge or skills. It is because of the way production takes place and the unequal manner in which products are distributed. In this context it is not utopian to envisage the abolition of deprivation. The central question is why, when such vision is possible, people continue to live with the world as it is now.

The insights of critical social movements may be used to show that other interpretations of development, other possibilities for human well-being, remain open. These insights begin with a recognition that the spatial structuring of the world economy is being transformed. This insight necessarily leads not only to explorations of new ways of acting on economic problems but also to a rethinking of the basic categories in which the possibilities of human well-being are now envisaged.

Most people recognize that the spatial organization of economic life has been transformed radically over the past four decades. The very idea of a national economy is rapidly becoming a contradiction in terms. Modern economic activity is organized through huge transnational enterprises and is characterized by massive flows of capital around the world, a rapidly changing international division of labor, and a global market.

For state elites, this implies the need to adapt to new demands, to find an appropriate niche, to encourage investment in certain economic sectors or to increase their competitive edge by cutting social services or constraining labor still further. It also implies the attempt to create new international structures—whether by investing greater power in the IMF or World Bank, giving still greater freedom to transnational corporations, or recreating a more integrated system to replace Bretton Woods—in order to bring greater order and control to processes that are increasingly beyond the capacity of state institutions. This understanding of how to respond to the spatial restructuring of the world economy obviously implies even more control by and for the already wealthy.

For critical social movements, an understanding of this spatial restructuring as a move from a national to a global arena cannot be enough. For, as usual, the restructuring is uneven in its consequences. The world economy is not only global, it is dualistic. Some people are in and some are out. Even in Western Europe and the United States, about one-quarter of the children are undernourished. Elsewhere, even where people are not starving, millions have no access to clean drinking water, let alone to land, technology, credit, or education. In all the major cities of the world, affluence and squalor coexist in spatial mosaics that defy formal political boundaries or clear social categories.

The numbers vary from region to region. In India, for example, which now does have significant national economic growth, about 40 percent of the population are benefiting from such growth, whereas about 40 percent are becoming worse off. In Africa, about 80 percent of the people have no access to the resources assumed to be necessary for development. Increasing inequalities within countries are being created by a world economy that now brings the cities and elites of all countries into global patterns of production, consumption, and investment. Economic growth for some involves exclusion for others. In this context, neither the antitheses between developed and undeveloped nor even that between developed and underdeveloped makes any real sense. It is only possible to speak of maldevelopment for all.

This maldevelopment is not just a matter of inequality. Both economic dualism and the contemporary restructuring of global economic space is the result of identifiable historical processes. To rethink development is necessarily to go beyond identifying the patterns of inequality that give substance to the scenario of Two Worlds. It is to call into question conceptions of what it means to be human that were established with the development of capitalism in Europe. These assumptions monopolize elitist politics almost everywhere. Even if explicitly capitalist processes are resisted, the identification of modern life with the production and consumption of more and more commodities, with economic growth and the accumulation of wealth, is overwhelming and is becoming even more so.

Nor is this something to be understood within the narrow categories of the economists. Indeed, it is very difficult for economists to think about—as opposed to think within—the narrowness and historical specificity of their own categories. It is a matter of the way that these categories have influenced so profoundly the dominant accounts everywhere of what it means to be human.

From one direction, these categories—of capital and labor, of production and distribution, of property and profit, of efficiency and rationality, of self-interest and the public good, of state planning and the free market— may be understood as translations of a universalist philosophy of History into economic terms. From another direction, these categories may be understood as an integral part—both influence and consequence—of the specific economic structures we live with now. To rethink the possibilities of development is thus necessarily to engage the deepest processes of social, cultural, and ethical life. Like a serious rethinking of the concept of security, it challenges the presumptions of a civilization.

Development and Empowerment

Critical social movements recognize that the world economy is being transformed. But their understanding of what this means is quite different from the understanding of those who seek to manage it from above. Movements act in particular locations. They explore what is appropriate for local ecosystems and local needs. For them, development is not something to be grasped through the myth of History and "modernization" or the accumulation of commodities. It must be tied to the capacity of all people to fulfill their basic needs.

Thus, movements stress the need for economic processes that are rooted in the needs of specific communities. Emphasis is placed on the variety of possible developmental strategies. So-called traditional ways of life become at least as important for understanding the potentialities of different kinds of human community as the lure of modernization. And as a consequence of this, development ceases to be seen as a process imposed from the top down, something that is done to rather than by people. It becomes instead a process in which people participate in the making of their own communities, one in which economic life is intrinsically connected to the social, environmental, and cultural processes that are essential to a sustained and meaningful way of life.

The capacity of movements to understand the connections between economic processes and other aspects of modern life is especially important here. Recognizing the connections between economy and environment, for example, many movements interpret economic life in terms of the need to control, protect, and even enhance local resources rather than to plunder them. They are concerned with preserving the material conditions for life on the planet. They discover that to encourage respect for the environment leads to a greater respect for other resources, notably labor, as a valued end, not just as a means to more abundant production. Plundering the planet comes to be interpreted as one manifestation of an acute alienation; alternative conceptions of development often involve the struggle for new ways of understanding people's place in the universe.

Recognizing the connections between economy and patriarchy, movements stress the alternative conceptions of development that pay special attention to the economic role of women, in the family, as both paid and unpaid labor, as allocators of resources, and so on. To work toward nonpatriarchal forms of economy is then to become increasingly aware of the extent to which patriarchy is embedded in the deepest cultural fabric of different societies. Again, to challenge patriarchy is to seek to rethink some of the most basic assumptions that guide people's understanding of who they are.

Recognizing the connections between economy and militarization is to see particularly clearly how production and destruction are so closely entwined in modern economic processes. It is to encourage a view of development based more clearly on the creation of more socially useful forms of production.

In all these cases, recognition of connections must lead to a rethinking of the most basic economic categories in noneconomistic terms. A house may appear to be a mere thing, an object of stones and boards, of walls and roof. On closer inspection, it appears in economic guise, a piece of property to be owned, rented, sold, or demolished: as capital to be accumulated. Both appearances obscure even more complex processes. A house, both as physical thing and as economic commodity, is just one of a number of factors that allow people to house themselves. It is part of complex cultural, economic, social, and political forces that allow proper shelter for some but not for others. To struggle for housing—or food, or clothing, or warmth—is to engage with all these processes. It is to see that alternative conceptions of development must involve the creation of new understandings of work, production, and ownership that are more meaningful socially than just processes of individual or aggregate capital accumulation.

It also leads to a clearer recognition that it is neither necessary nor desirable to confuse economic development with development as such. Indeed, from the perspective of critical social movements, it is more appropriate to make the connection between development and empowerment. From this perspective, the crucial problem with dominant forms of development is that they are literally disempowering for the majority of humankind. The whole point of local development initiatives, after all, is not to keep up in the race for commodities on the world market. It is to create strong communities of people grounded in the satisfaction of human needs without destroying ecological rhythms and to empower the marginalized and oppressed to take some control over their own lives under adverse conditions.

Toward Development for All People

But if the challenge to maldevelopment must be an empowering development, it must also embody new principles of solidarity. For the primary message coming from critical social movements in this respect is again quite stark in its simplicity. It is the claim that in a world of connections and global structures, and yet a world also of increasing social and economic exclusion, ideas of development must be based on the principle of inclusivity and solidarity. An empowering development must be a development for all.

The accumulation of capacities for violence cannot be equated with power, except for the power to destroy. Thus, critical social movements must be concerned with the articulation of conceptions of security that are grounded in a rethinking of power itself. Similarly, the reduction of all human endeavor, including human life itself, to the status of things, objects, and commodities cannot be equated with an empowering development.

In both cases, critical social movements are led in a similar direction. Beginning with immediate concrete problems, they find they have to engage with the most pervasive and deeply entrenched assumptions that constitute the prevailing "common sense," "rationality," and "reality" of the modern world. Movements are forced to move away from understandings of national security and development from above that have grown out of the present logics of the states system and world economy. They are compelled to articulate new understandings of people's security and empowering development that recognize the need to engage in practices of deepening democracy everywhere.

RETHINKING DEMOCRACY

There is a strong sense in many different situations that established forms of politics do not work. For elites, this generally implies greater difficulty in managing the dominant structures of our time. For critical social movements, concerns about management amount to still more rearranging of deck chairs on a sinking ship. From their perspectives, the issue is less the failure of particular policies and institutions than the need to rethink the meaning of politics itself.

The aspiration for democracy is crucial in this respect. Democracy has undoubtedly been one of the greatest projects of the modern world. But it is by no means a finished achievement anywhere. The struggle for democracy has occurred in a world in which the dynamics of capitalism bring unequal development. Formal political democracy can thus coexist with social and economic structures in which many, or even most, people are excluded from making decisions about things that control their lives. The struggle for democracy has also occurred in a world in which the presumed realities of power have been centered in the institutions of state. Claims to democracy may thus coexist with bureaucratic hierarchies and blatantly authoritarian governments. With the transformations in global political, economic, and cultural processes that are now under way, the possibility of democracy is especially problematic.

Suspicion about contemporary political life falls particularly heavily on the state but certainly not on the state alone. Trade unions, churches, parties, mass media, international financial institutions, ideologies: All are susceptible, not only to overt criticism, but worse, to indictments of boredom and irrelevance on the one hand and cynicism on the other. A sense of powerlessness is apparent in many societies.

The explanation of this powerlessness obviously varies from society to society. In some, attention has to focus primarily on the sheer centralization and brutality of authority and physical force. These are societies in which mass revolutionary movements struggle under conditions of overt oppression, whether of racist exclusions, military rule, or other forms of state terror. Some societies have been thrown into turmoil through the traumas of rapid modernization and the global strategies of superpower confrontation. Militarist regimes and fundamentalist fanaticism bloc off any available political space. Powerlessness is tied directly to the presence of immediate physical force.

In other situations, powerlessness is less a matter of presence than of absence—of the distant and dispersed nature of power and authority. State elites may look fierce and take themselves very seriously, but they are often merely the local agents of foreign powers and, increasingly, of peripatetic capital wandering around the globe looking for an interest-rate differential here or long-term security there. Power is elsewhere, untouchable.

And then there are the scenarios of No World and Two Worlds. There are the excluded, the forgotten, the superfluous. There are all those processes that threaten everyone. And there are all those transformations that surround us, the genetic engineering and the restructuring of global production processes, whose effects we have hardly begun to understand.

It is in this context—or rather in these varied contexts—that it is necessary to understand the significance of the insights being explored by critical social movements: about where and how to act, about new ways of knowing and being, about possible forms of connection and solidarity. Taken together, these insights do not provide a coherent theory of politics in general. They are explorations, not finished achievements. Moreover, they are all grounded in an affirmation of specificity and circumstance. A general prescription for the perfect polity is contested in principle. In societies in which statist repression or fundamentalist fanaticism infuse almost all the available political space, the insights of critical social movements may seem quite irrelevant. But even in the most closed societies there are openings, interstices, connections. Fractures can occur in the most unexpected places. And the explorations of critical social movements in societies where they have emerged do suggest some directions for thinking about three sets of questions that bear on contemporary life everywhere.

Democracy, Solidarity, and Universality

One set concerns the possibility of forging a language in which to speak of those things that human beings share in common: a language in which to explore universals while recognizing the arrogances of existing claims to universality. It is, of course, a truism that we are all human. Yet, as a truism, it is likely to obscure fundamental differences among human beings; consider, for example, the violence committed in the name of a supposedly universal "human nature." A sense of common species identity is certainly not obvious on the surface of contemporary political life. It may be easy enough to speak of global processes, or planetary ecologies, or human interest, but it is also easy to forget that we do so in inherited categories, in languages arising from particular cultures, from particular interests. But there does seem to be overwhelming evidence that we all share common vulnerabilities, a common maldevelopment, and a fragile planet. A universalism framed in the arrogance of empires has to be resisted, but the possibilities inherent in connections, in shared vulnerabilities and solidarities, remain to be explored.

The evidence that does exist about common human interests cannot be simply translated into ideas about how to organize political life more effectively. This has always been the approach of utopian rationalists, and it has always involved maximizing an imposed conception of common identity over pluralistic differences. It is necessary to be particularly skeptical about claims of common identity framed in the language and categories of dominant cultures. The experience of imperialism is too close, and the universals of the dominant culture are precisely what is at stake in attempts to rethink the meaning of development and security. Yet, despite the necessity of skepticism on both these counts, it is still necessary to grope toward some sense of shared identity.

This, in the end, is the implication of the emerging patterns of solidarity in the practices of contemporary social movements. Existing claims to universalism and common identity may embody the myths of the most powerful. Such claims have to be resisted. But one of the major challenges of contemporary political life is surely to struggle toward an understanding of common human identity that does not bring with it the overt threat of No World or Two Worlds. Universalism has to be resisted and sought at the same time.

In view of the current popularity of the phrase, it is necessary to insist that critical social movements do not "think globally and act locally." This phrase merely reproduces the false opposition between general and particular that movements must and do challenge. Movements act in specific circumstances, but in order to *be* critical, to be open, to refuse the lures of fundamentalism and self-righteousness, they have to be movements of both specificity *and* connection. The problem is not the claims of universalism as such. It is, rather, the way in which universalism has come to be framed as both the opposite of and the superior to pluralism and difference. In resisting dominant universals, it is possible to retreat to particularism. Such a retreat is itself a way of accepting the dominant universals by affirming their opposite. A critique of "reason" that opts for "passion" affirms the way of life in which reason and passion are presumed to be opposites. A critique of "masculinity" that opts for "femininity" affirms the opposition between supposedly natural categories that is at the heart of the way women are identified as passive, as irrational, as victims.

Critical social movements are necessarily involved in the attempt to undermine dominant universals. They are also, and more significant, necessarily involved in trying to reconstruct our understanding of the relationship between universal and particular, between the recognition of our planetary vulnerability and identity, on the one hand, and the proliferation of histories, experiences, and identities, on the other. This is not a matter of complex or abstract philosophy. It is something that has to be explored and achieved through ongoing human practices everywhere.

The understanding of connections, solidarities, and common identities arising from the practices of critical social movements is explicitly rooted in the local, fragmented, and particularistic character of contemporary movements. It requires tentative exploration rather than imperialist assertion. Moreover, it opens up the possibility for, indeed, even the celebration of, a multiplicity of possible solidarities, possible identities. It refuses the assumption that to act locally is necessarily to be parochial. It also refuses the assumption that political life must be organized around the devastating choices between being human or being a national citizen and between being an autonomous individual or a participant in a social community. Whether in terms of the rearticulation of political space, the development of new forms of political practice, or the exploration of new modes of knowing, of being, and of connections between peoples, critical social movements refuse the categories that make these choices possible. They refuse categories through which these choices often seem inevitable.

Perhaps the real test of our capacity to move beyond the conventional categories in this respect is the extent to which it is possible to create a sense of common identity with future generations. To envisage One World, albeit a world of difference and not homogeneity—both One World and Many Worlds—is ultimately to understand the imperative to act on behalf of generations as yet unborn. Children not only give the most graphic evidence of the violence of the present. They symbolize a future already here.

The rethinking of political life must begin by struggling to reconstruct the most basic categories through which political practice is constituted. To challenge the seemingly abstract but also seeming natural dichotomies between universal and plural, between subject and object, between male and female, between self and other, is to challenge the powerful historical structures in which these dichotomies have been cast as necessities and inevitabilities, as truths and visions, as violence and authority. To act in ways that recognize both the oneness and plurality of the world in which we live is to open up options that are systematically refused by the structures that dominate contemporary life.

This involves much more than the limited diversity of nations inhabiting the same formal space of states or the crude and artificial pluralism of individuals conceived as consumers in the market place. These are both forms of diversity that capitulate to the claim that all difference must be resolved in unity—the state, the free and autonomous individual, the party. To recognize that diversity is a precondition for any meaningful sense of human community is to undercut all those dominant doctrines and institutions that presume that diversity can only be tolerated after a unified community has been constructed. That the practices of critical social movements stress localism and diversity is not a sign of weakness. It is evidence of a crucial challenge to the silent power of History and the state. It is evidence of the possibility that security and development, peace and justice, can be articulated through a recognition that we must live in One World/Many Worlds.

Democracy and Democratization

If one set of questions concerns the possibility of reconstructing seemingly abstract but nevertheless very powerful categories in which people understand their place in the world, another set concerns the hard structures of institutional power. These structures exercise control over what people can do. They can coopt even the most committed movements and activists. They cannot be ignored.

One of the main characteristics of critical social movements is their suspicion of premature institutionalization. They are not immune to bureaucratic tendencies nor even to a capitulation to charismatic and elitist leadership, but the underlying suspicion is very important, and it is necessary to be clear about why it has arisen. At least four related themes may be identified here. First, there is suspicion of the urge to build institutions before underlying principles and ideas have been sufficiently worked through. Second, there is a very powerful sense that existing political institutions embody the wrong principles and ideas. Third, there is a sense that it is necessary to think more carefully about what exactly is meant by a political institution. And finally, there is suspicion that the very idea of a political institution embodies the underlying image of yet another structure that is somehow "out there," another false dichotomy between structure and practice.

All four of these suspicions are inherent in the critiques developed by movements about the modern state as well as most other social and political organizations. They also arise whenever debate about the global character of the human predicament turns to the need for international institutions. The most significant criticisms of contemporary international organizations are well known. Such organizations remain instruments of state power. To the extent that they embody nonstatist principles, they are usually conceptualized in terms of ideas about world government, the image of the superstate. They invite skepticism, either because they are found to be impotent to deal with the world's most pressing problems or because they are found to act on behalf of the most powerful states. When particular organizations fail to enhance the interests of the most powerful, funds are cut in the shoddiest manner.

In the perspective of movements, these matters are perhaps less significant than the conception of politics that remains entrenched in the very structure of such organizations. They are conceptions of politics as government, as bureaucracy, as administration, as policy making bodies. These organizations may be novel actors on the international scene, but they reproduce very traditional conceptions of what governance is about. However, there is another side to this question. When attention is directed away from those organizations that do look like attempted superstates, particularly the General Assembly and the Security Council of the United Nations, a rather different image occurs. After all, most of the work of the United Nations is done in commissions, committees, and specialized agencies. These present an image not of failure and cooptation but of tremendous achievements. This is the image that comes from looking at, for example, the UN Children's Fund, or the UN Disaster and Relief Organization, or the UN Development Program, or the way that UNESCO has managed to protect so much of the cultural and aesthetic heritage of so many different societies, or the unmapped webs that link nongovernmental organizations, movements, and groups across national boundaries.

This is not just a matter of functional success. It is a matter of the way that such organizations work. They may still be bedeviled by bureaucratic inertia, but more often they manage to operate in ways that recall the more fluid networking characteristic of so many movements. They, too, try to find new spaces in which to act, new ways of responding to specific exigencies, new ways of connecting to other institutions and processes. Even if these innovations are difficult for the larger organizations, they are less so for the hundreds of almost invisible INGOs that interact with movements everywhere.

It is even possible to develop a similar reading of the modern state. Although it is true that in so many ways the modern state is becoming ever more centralized, ever more rigid, it is also important to remember that many movements are struggling to create alternative conceptions of the state and that in some places interesting trends are already in motion.

Movements interact with sympathetic officials within bureaucracies. Attempts are made to create less bureaucratic forms of public service and to develop new forms of ownership and control of public resources based neither on the centralized state nor on the whims of large corporations. There have been significant experiments in revitalizing local government, and there remains considerable potential for using new technologies to encourage greater decentralization. In all these there is a potential to break the seemingly inevitable connections between the state and highly centralized forms of government.

Again, the trends are unclear, but the stakes are not. They concern the possibility of generating new and humane forms of governance appropriate for a world of increasing connections. The rapid drift toward Two Worlds demands an immediate restructuring of world trade and finance as well as some capacity to effect redistribution to the most immediately vulnerable. What kind of mechanisms might this imply? In practice, such issues are left largely to the self-interests of wealthy states, to international institutions organized by such states, and to the fond hope that "trickle-down" will come from those states and corporations that effectively manage the world economy to their own advantage. Against this dismal prospect, the most benign image is perhaps that of a global welfare state. But what exactly does a global welfare state look like, how might it be generated, and how might it be managed or guaranteed? And isn't even this benign image tied to a politics of management, a management of the structures that have made us what we are?

These are not easy questions, and critical social movements, like most people, have no easy answers to them. But movements can insist that prevailing images of institutionalized politics are unlikely to be all that is needed to think about possible answers. They can insist that a humane governance has to grow out of political practices that strive for One World/Many Worlds, not the management of a false globalism of Two Worlds. Such growth will involve practices as yet untried, in which people discover new ways in which to turn new solidarities into new structures of authority and legitimacy. What these will be will depend on what people do and how they participate in political life.

Democratization and Empowerment

This discussion leads directly to a third set of questions concerning the character of political participation. Almost all societies now claim to be democratic. Even assuming that it is possible to be clear about what the term means in the first place, it is doubtful that many societies can defend these claims very vigorously. In a world in which states have a monopoly on neither violence nor legitimacy, in which the most powerful forces are global in scale, the promise of democracy to enhance the capacity of people to exercise control over their own lives is put into greater and greater doubt.

This is precisely why attempts to rethink both security and development stress processes of democratization. The problem in both cases is not only the threats of No World and Two Worlds, but the feeling of powerlessness on the part of so many people to do much about these threats. The emphasis on democratization on the part of movements everywhere is generated by a struggle to achieve some control over the forces that determine the way they live.

In this context, democracy does not have a single defining characteristic. It is not to be equated with particular forms of government—with parliaments, representative institutions, party hierarchies, or national wills. Again, the practices of movements are informed by a readiness to pursue different strategies of deepening democracy depending on circumstances.

One of the most striking tendencies is the renewed credibility of political processes once dismissed as mere "bourgeois democracy." Many movements even attempt to revitalize processes of representative government. There is a willingness to work with the processes and institutions that are available, imperfect as they may be, and to reclaim them for people rather than for elites. Hence, the importance, for example, of using existing legal mechanisms to introduce greater accountability into public life. Hence, also, attempts by movements to change not only the policies but the very form of existing political parties, to attempt to break the stranglehold of the "iron law of oligarchy."

In another direction, movements seek not only to enhance democratic processes in the formal political arena but, perhaps even more so, to democratize within social processes that are usually treated as nonpolitical. Attempts are made to rethink development by stressing the importance of enhancing democratic processes within economic systems. Where conventional debate usually turns on the relative merits of command and market economics, movements are more likely to insist that whichever of these directions is taken, it must involve greater democratization. Greater participation is particularly crucial in resolving tensions between the demand for efficiency—a demand resolved historically by the market, by bureaucracy, and by instrumental technique—and the demand for equality, community, and the fulfillment of basic human needs.

Viewed in relation to existing structures, the call for democratization involves a concerted attempt to give greater voice and influence in the decisions that affect people's own lives. The call leads to a recognition that, left to themselves, these structures will capitulate to special economic and bureaucratic interests. It also leads to a recognition that democratization is not the equivalent of voting in periodic elections. It requires an ongoing insinuation of people's participation into all aspects of public life. It requires constant vigilance about the preservation of substantive rights, about how the basic investment decisions of a society are made, about how production is organized and goods distributed, about how cultures, values, and identities are constructed.

Viewed more generally, democratization at all levels involves a refusal of any form of political life that assumes that there is a sharp distinction between politics and ordinary everyday life. Politicians of all kinds are particularly keen to identify politics as the preserve of politicians, and only of politicians. They foster the illusion that politics occurs at a particular time—when elections are held—or at a particular place—a legislature, parliament, assembly, or palace. Politics is reduced to what goes on in narrowly defined institutions, "out there," beyond the grasp of ordinary citizens. People are treated as mere objects to be manipulated from above. The increasingly sophisticated technologies of mass persuasion visible in modern Western societies is particularly troubling. Politics becomes ever more a matter of image, of the gleaming smile and the benevolent gesture.

Critical social movements challenge this ominous tendency at its roots. They understand very clearly that politics is not only about what politicians do. Women's movements know that assumptions about physiology and human nature, or the structures of family life, or the visual codes of filmmakers and advertisers all have profound political implications. Structures of patriarchy become apparent everywhere once one is sensitized to them.

Racial minorities and the poor have always found it difficult to think about politics on any other terms. For them, real political power has less to do with elections, parties, or politicians than with the multiple and often invisible constraints imposed by prejudices, regulations, and the sheer energy needed for everyday survival. They know that although the structures that dominate their lives may be large and remote, these structures are ever-present in the mundane routines of everyday life.

The sense of democratization implied by the practices of contemporary social movements draws on the clear understanding that people are always engaged in politics whether they know it or not. That we are what we eat is not just a popular slogan about nutrition. It points to connections between immediate everyday decisions about what to eat or where to obtain it and the capacity of particular economic structures to take control of people's nutrition. Multinational corporations are as close as the next meal.

The same goes for everything else in people's daily lives. This is why movements' sensitivity to connections is so important. It is not only that movements are sensitive to the large-scale connections between global economic, political, cultural structures, and so on. They are also sensitive to the wider implications of everyday conduct. This sensitivity may lead to attempts to live in greater harmony with local environmental rhythms. It may lead to a stress on the truthfulness and integrity of personal relations in societies dependent on deception and forgetting. It may lead to a critical refusal to accept the mass media as objective sources of political truth in societies where claims to objectivity mask power and inequality and turn political life into a mere spectator sport.

Circumstances differ. In some cases, the primary aim is to enhance the democratic responsibility of state institutions. In some, the stress is on the democratic revitalization of civil society. In others, what counts is the awareness that everyone has some capacity, however small, to refuse to support or legitimize processes of violence and injustice. Movements in different settings explore these insights in different ways. Together they suggest a sense of a possible deepening of democracy, of democratization as empowerment that runs directly counter to those claims to democracy that emanate from state elites everywhere.

RETHINKING PEACE AND JUSTICE

To rethink the meaning of security, or development, or democracy is to enter upon very difficult conceptual terrain. It is to move from what is to what might be. It is to strain at the limits of prevailing categories and to wrench enormously influential concepts out of their present contexts.

The most familiar concepts of security refer to the presumed "interests" of states. If we listen to critical social movements, it becomes clear that whatever security could possibly mean in the future, it must refer to the security of people. A people's security must necessarily move beyond familiar concerns about warfare and military policy. It must be grounded in a reconstruction of the way violence and vulnerability enter into social practices of all kinds. It must be able to address concerns usually framed under the concept of development.

Prevailing concepts of development are rooted in deeply entrenched concepts of economic growth that begin in the linear progressions of universal History and the rise of the capitalist world economy. Listening to critical social movements, we may understand the intrisic connection between development as economic growth and the reality of gross inequalities, exclusions, repressions, and violence in the modern world. To read the concept of development from the standpoint of the concept of security is to understand that hunger is a form of genocide. This form of development may not be discussed in the UN Security Council, but it is no less a threat to human beings than the missiles standing silently in their silos. Again, to rethink concepts of development is to grope less with issues of economic policy than with the civilizational and cultural values through which the prevailing categories of economics have been constituted. It is to insist that economics, like security, is not the prerogative of technical experts, privileged elites, and esoteric languages but is a social process, a matter of political practice.

Almost all existing political systems come with claims to democracy attached. Yet, there is deep skepticism in many different situations, not only about whether particular regimes or states live up to such claims, but also whether prevailing understandings of what democracy is, or can be, go far enough. The practices of critical social movements constitute both a critique of and an attempt to enhance forms of democracy associated with the institutions of the centralized state. They push toward a process of democratization in all spheres of social interaction. They act in ways that seem to reconstitute the underlying principles on which dominant conceptions of political space have been constructed historically.

Whether rethinking security, development, or democracy, there is a similar pattern. Problems are posed as questions of policy. Mainstream political forces attempt to answer these questions of policy, and they do so on the presumption that existing institutions and authorities are sufficient both to formulate answers and to put them into effect. Critical social movements, however are driven to move from specific problems to the demand for structural transformation. And they move from received images of the way structural transformation is to be attained—the images of political revolution as the taking of state power, the positing of grand utopian schemes to be brought down to earth—to a rethinking of the possible character of social and political transformation itself. To protest about bombs and poverty, violence and brutality, militarization and maldevelopment, is to confront the need to rethink the way people live together and act toward each other. The practices of critical social movements are necessarily directed not only to attempts to bring about better policies, of the kind usually prescribed by politicians and leaders of state, but toward a rethinking of political life in general.

Thinking about peace and justice in terms of policy prescriptions is both much easier and more difficult than thinking about emerging conceptions of what it means to act politically. It is easier because at least it is possible to point to existing actors that have a real and immediate capacity to effect change.

The most outrageous thing about the current drift toward One World or Two Worlds is not that it is occurring but that the capacity to stop this drift already exists. In the modern world neither starvation nor militarization are inevitable. If certain states acted more responsibly, we might say, the dangers of nuclear extermination would not be so alarming. If the world economy were to be organized less in order to maximize profits than to provide even a more equitable distribution of resources and the satisfaction of basic human needs for everyone, then the blood-curdling poverty of so many people would not be so extreme. The removal of the international debt burden is not beyond the capacity of existing institutions. Conservative arms controllers and radical peace activists are not always very far apart in making plausible suggestions about how to defuse the most destabilizing weapons systems. Technologies are available, at a price, that would reduce the most harmful environmental hazards. It is not difficult to think of sensible procedures that would manage some of the most pressing problems on the global agenda.

There are undoubtedly many people, including many who are active in social movements, who would be happy enough to see some particularly noxious symptoms brought under control. This is certainly understandable. But the real force of the message coming from so many movements is that the control of symptoms cannot be enough. Indeed, movements recognize that attempts to treat symptoms alone have often turned into one more legitimation of the underlying processes that create problems in the first place. The unhappy experience of so many foreign-aid programs is perhaps indicative in this respect.

The perspectives on a just world peace emerging from critical social movements do not lead to a primary concern with policy prescriptions of this kind, although they do offer criteria on which such prescriptions ought to be judged. They lead instead to a concern with more fundamental change. The pursuit of a just world peace is inseparable from struggles to find new ways of acting politically in an era of profound transformations.

The significance of critical social movements is not to be assessed only by their overt power to bring about change by themselves or by the credibility of their specific policy recommendations. It lies in their capacity to recognize, interpret, and symbolize patterns of contemporary transformations and to find new ways of being and acting that enhance the capacity of people to exercise control over the processes that affect their lives. It lies in their ability to articulate ways of being together that enhance the possibilities of justice and undermine the need for violence. It lies in their ability to act in specific circumstances while becoming more and more aware that to act in specific circumstances is to engage with processes that affect people everywhere.

Acting in particular situations, critical social movements are able to generate new ways of thinking about what it means to express solidarity with others, to share a common destiny as human beings. Their practices express new ways of knowing how to be both singular and many. From this perspective, it is clear that a just world peace cannot be a singular condition, something that can be specified in a way that is applicable to all societies at all times. A just world peace may be a universal aspiration. But no one can claim a monopoly on what it may come to be. Nor is it a static condition, an architectural procedure. It is an ongoing process, a continuous struggle. It is possible to act in a world of peace and justice—not in some distant future—but here, and now.

CHAPTER SEVEN

Possibilities

TAKING CRITICAL SOCIAL MOVEMENTS SERIOUSLY

To take critical social movements seriously is to celebrate an apparent contradiction. We live in an age that has all the makings of epochal transformation. The primary dynamics that affect people's lives arise from very complex global structures. The most threatening problems before us elude even the most powerful social forces and political institutions. Yet, as I have suggested in this book, in the face of tremendous historical accelerations, of global structures and intractable problems, small and fragile critical social movements open up particularly hopeful possibilities for the future. In a time of acute dangers and a widespread sense of powerlessness, critical social movements articulate new aspirations and create new energies. They challenge the cynicism and conventions that now make scenarios of No World and Two Worlds so plausible.

This apparent contradiction obviously invites a cynical interpretation. It is easy enough to affirm that critical social movements are marginal and powerless; perhaps it is pointless, even utopian, to expect them to be more than the site of fragmented protests. From this viewpoint, power is power. Critical social movements can then be taken seriously only if they achieve power, if they take control of states or political parties or turn into mass movements capable of challenging entrenched elites and institutions. For the cynic, for the self-proclaimed realist, or for the traditional revolutionary, power comes from the barrel of a gun, from the accumulation of weapons and wealth. Big fish swallow small fish. No one can credibly claim that critical social movements qualify as big fish.

This interpretation has obvious plausibility, and not only because critical social movements are relatively fragile. Although I have stressed— perhaps even exaggerated—the potential visible in the practices of many movements in widely divergent situations, it would be too much to claim that this potential is always fulfilled. There are no unproblematic critical social movements. There are no untarnished models, no saints or heroes that can be singled out for reverent emulation. Movements struggle in difficult and dangerous places, and their potential is often crushed by force, inertia, or lack of imagination.

Nevertheless, there is also no doubt that some movements, in some places, at some times, in some struggles, have been able to demonstrate a striking capacity for a creative politics. Such movements have been able to realize a potential for openness, for connection, and for imaginative practices in ways that have made a difference. They have been able to explore and to reinterpret. They have generated energies that empower people to get things done despite the oppressive weight of structures and dislocations, despite the barrel of the gun and the international flows of capital, despite all the fundamentalist passions and technocratic imperatives that surround them.

In fact, the cynical interpretation, although plausible, misses the point. It presumes that power is always and everywhere the same, something to be accumulated and measured in the same currency. In the ledgerbooks of firepower and wealth, critical social movements scarcely warrant a passing entry. But the power to create is not measurable in the same currency as the power to destroy. There is no universal coinage through which missiles may be exchanged for the capacity to create decent human communities. Critical social movements have to be evaluated not in terms of some timeless notion of what power is but in terms of their capacity to alter our understanding of what power can be. It is in this context that it is possible to read the significance of critical social movements not only by their ability to offer new interpretations of the possibilities before us but also in terms of the ways in which these possibilities may now be realized. For whether we refer to the state and the states system, to the world economy, or to contemporary cultural processes, neither the location nor the nature of power are as obvious as they often seem.

Viewed from one direction, the challenges of the modern age appear to arise from the logic of the states system, whereby power is identified with the capacity to seize and maintain the state, whether through revolution, election, force, or persuasion. Power is also identified with the capacity to maneuver in a world of other, often threatening, states. Whether internally or externally, success depends on a capacity to accumulate power within specific territorial centers. Many of the world's problems may then be understood as consequences of competition between these centers—a competition that now issues in the looming threat of nuclear spasm and the present drift toward militarization, authoritarianism, and the abuse of human rights in the name of national security.

Challenges to the present occupants of these centers of power may doubtless make many of these problems less pressing. Much of the most important political energy for the foreseeable future must necessarily be devoted to the removal of the more ruthless exponents of No World/ Two Worlds policies. In many situations, the capture of state power remains a precondition for any significant advance. Critical social movements everywhere will continue to participate in struggles to make the exercise of state power less pernicious.

Although the necessity for this kind of politics remains obvious, it is also clear that this necessity does not exhaust the available options. In a world of transnational capital flows, the claim that states hold a monopoly on power is naive at best. In a world of superpowers and global reach, the possibility of a successful revolution within any single state is increasingly remote. The conditions of world war and decolonization, which provided the immediate opportunity for so much of the revolutionary activity of recent memory, are no longer with us. The theme of the revolution betrayed is now etched very deeply on our historical imagination. Thus, although the image of politics as the accumulation of power within territorial centers may still dominate our understanding of what politics is about in most parts of the world, it is an image often rendered in an antique, even nostalgic patina.

To be a realist in political life is less a matter of weighing contending forces than of understanding that things are never what they seem to be and are always likely to change. To claim any sort of realism about politics in the modern world cannot be to assert the eternal and absolute sovereignty of state power, but is to understand very clearly that both the state and the states system are historical creations. They are constantly being transformed. The classic revolutions in France, the Soviet Union, China, and Cuba certainly provide an influential image of political change as the capture of state power. But another understanding of political change is offered by the large-scale social and economic processes that brought the state and the states system into being in the first place.

These two images—of statist revolution and of socioeconomic transformation—lead to rather different conceptions of political practice. Especially in places still recovering from the ravages of colonialism, the need to capture state power remains crucial. In many societies a change of regime, a shift to a more moderate government, could bring a welcome and immediate sigh of relief. Yet there are signs everywhere that changes of regime cannot be enough. They certainly cannot be the only concern for critical social movements. There are signs almost everywhere that it is necessary to encourage much more complex and much more fundamental forms of social, economic, cultural, and political transformation. In this context, critical social movements look less fragile. As seeds of a world still coming into being, critical social movements look less weary, less brittle, less clumsy than the armored might and rigid bureaucracies of many established political actors.

I have suggested that one of the most persistent insights of critical social movements is that it is necessary to explore novel political spaces. These explorations occur in the context of far-reaching rearticulations of political space associated with global flows of capital, with new information and weapons technologies, with worldwide environmental problems, and so on. The disjunction between the global structures and processes that now have such a tremendous impact on people everywhere and these centers of political authority organized within separate territorial boundaries provides the setting for a major crisis in the way we understand political life. It is now especially important to come to terms with obsolescence of the principles of absolute inclusion and exclusion on which both the principle of state sovereignty and the operation of the states system have depended.

Explorations of new political spaces accompany explorations of new ways of acting, new ways of knowing and being in the world, and new ways of acting together through emerging solidarities. Similar explorations have been central to large-scale sociopolitical transformations of the past. The European transition from the hierarchical order of feudalism to the homogeneous spaces of the sovereign state, for example, involved not only fundamental changes in economic life but radical, even traumatic, changes in social structures and cultural traditions. This transition was not brought about by the capture of state power, although it was accompanied by armed conflict and civil war. The experiences of colonial rule also brought direct physical force and coercion. But the fine texture of colonial domination also involved a complex social and cultural politics in which imperial pretensions met sophisticated resistances and refusals of imposed ideologies and rituals. Subsequent capture of state power has not meant that postcolonial societies have been freed from economic, social, or cultural forms of domination.

It is now clear that the capture of state power does not exhaust the range of options that might challenge the current drift toward No World/Two Worlds. The changing nature of the state, and its changing relationship to global economic, technological, and cultural processes, has put into question all conceptions of political practice that are concerned with the capture of state power alone. The explorations of critical social movements necessarily respond to and try to work with these emerging transformations.

This is why, for example, critical social movements have to struggle for more than the removal of particular weapons systems. To refuse the principles of inclusion and exclusion embodied in the modern states system is necessarily to refuse the understanding of security defined in terms of the interests of states. It is to force the simple, naive, but devastating question—"Whose security?"—out into the open. To push for a people's security, for an understanding of security that can contribute to empowering development and deepening democracy, is to act so as to reveal both the necessity and the possibility of new forms of human community.

From another direction, the challenges of the modern age appear to arise less from the logic of the states system than from the dynamics of the world economy. Power is identified with wealth, with resources and productive capacity. But, by comparison with the power of the state, it is even more difficult to discover where this power resides, what it is, or how it can be transformed.

The consequences of unequal wealth are easy enough to see. For many people, extremes of wealth and poverty seem as natural as rain or drought. Yet even drought is often a consequence of human interventions. It is also easy enough to identify a culprit: the national elite, the multinational firm, the conspiracy of corporations—easy, but not very convincing. It is not very convincing to identify the dynamics of the world economy with a particular elite or corporation simply because the world economy is not a thing. It has no center. It arises from very complex processes. These processes have patterns and rhythms, but no one is at the controls, not even a hidden hand. There is little point in storming the World Bank.

Until fairly recently, it has been assumed that only the state had the capacity to exercise some control over this process. Whether as state socialism, as statist nationalism, or as the Keynesian countercyclical policies of the Western welfare state, political life in the twentieth century has been characterized by increasing state intervention into economic processes that have themselves become increasingly internationalized. As capital has become more mobile, so the capacity of states to control their own national economies has become increasingly tenuous, especially for those not in the Group of Seven big industrial states nor in states partially closed off from the world economy.

Again, this is not to say that statist policies seeking to intervene in economic processes are unimportant. Protectionism has not been consigned to the scrapbook of history. It makes a vital difference whether governments seek to enhance the capacity of a few to participate in the world economy or whether they work toward generating a fair and equitable standard of living for everyone. But state policies can hardly be enough. If the world economy is not something that can be captured, the processes that give rise to it have to be transformed. And they cannot be transformed without responding to the way the world economy is not a thing out there but a process that permeates the minutest rituals and practices of everyday life. Although economic life may be regulated, managed, and even partially controlled by government policies and state institutions, it is grounded in concrete processes of work and production.

Contemporary economic life is certainly organized through seemingly remote structures, by a worldwide division of labor, by massive flows of capital and expensive technical innovations, as well as by the state. But it arises from and necessarily affects people where they work and live. People produce things to be bought and sold on a world market. People engage in processes through which their labor is turned into objects that are valued less for their intrinsic contribution to human communities than for the price they will fetch. Inequality and poverty do not result from lack of resources or from any lack of capacity to satisfy everyone's needs. They cannot be blamed simply on particular corporations or elites, although these are by no means innocent. The seemingly remote structures of the world economy grow out of the way resources are used, things are produced, and capital is accumulated.

This is why critical social movements, like many labor movements of the past, are concerned with challenging economic power—less by challenging the power of the state than by struggling to articulate new forms of economy. Just as in the context of the states system critical social movements are forced to rethink the meaning of security, in the context of the world economy they are forced to rethink the meaning of development. Movements recognize that current processes of maldevelopment do indeed generate power—for some and not for others. Maldevelopment is necessarily uneven. It brings the dual economy even in societies that have become accustomed to thinking of themselves as First World, or "developed."

Critical social movements recognize that to intervene in problems arising from the world economy means they must engage with new forms of production; with new understandings of the relationship between economy and environment, economy and social processes; with new conceptions of what it means to work. Whether in local grassroots community development initiatives, in struggles for workplace democracy, in the search for more appropriate forms of technology, in women's struggles to challenge patterns of patriarchy within the division of labor, in attempts to establish more cooperative and community-centered forms of ownership and production, or in attempts to convert the manufacture of armaments into socially useful products, critical social movements intervene in the world economy not through the state, nor by sitting on the boards of banks and corporations, but by attempting to reconstruct the social processes that make the world economy possible.

Although the challenges of the modern age are usually attributed to the workings of the states system and the world economy, these are not sufficient to explain problems that occur under the heading of culture: racism, sexism, ethnic conflict, cultural imperialism, forms of knowledge that turn means into ends. With cultural processes it is especially difficult to understand where or what power is or how it can be transformed. It is easier to assume that culture is determined by something more substantial, like an economy, or that it can be controlled and protected by something more powerful, like a state. Thus, labor movements have often claimed that it is necessary to challenge economic power before a nonpatriarchal or racially tolerant society can emerge. Nationalists have insisted that only through the state can particular cultures be nurtured in the face of cultural imperialism and the "coca-colonization" of the world.

Cultural life cannot be easily distinguished from economic and political power. For critical social movements, however, the main concern is often less the primacy of economic interests in cultural affairs than the cultural assumptions—about gender, community, knowledge, a presumed human nature—that are built into dominant conceptions of what economic life is about. For them, what is important is less a matter of the capacity of the state to nurture national cultures than of the way human communities have been built on principles of inclusion and exclusion; the way the possibility of many different communities has been preempted by the state, on the one hand, and the instrumental cosmopolitanism of the world economy, on the other.

Critical social movements challenge the reduction of economic life to processes of material accumulation. They push beyond existing horizons of what it means to know and to be in the world. They explore and invent, interpret and act. What is at stake is not the possibility of storming the palaces of culture but of developing ways of being together, ways of creating and relating, of expressing and speaking, that are empowering. What is at stake is the understanding that processes of deepening democracy are no less crucial to cultural life than to people's security and empowering development. In cultural life, especially, the line between empowering and disempowering practices is always very thin. Creative impulses are always susceptible to the dead hand of propaganda, commodification, and stereotype.

The recovery of cultural traditions can empower people crushed by the presumption that only modernity and its techniques offer a way forward. The reappropriation of traditions can also provide an opportunity for new forms of mystification by those who claim direct access to the secrets of the past. The search for more holistic forms of knowledge can offer a way out of the atomistic and reductionist instrumentalism through which modern science has treated both people and their environment as objects to be plundered and defiled. This search can also lead to new forms of irrationalism, as well as to still more claims to the possession of the whole Truth and nothing but the Truth. The pursuit of more authentically feminist accounts of the world is undoubtedly crucial, given the extent to which patriarchal assumptions have been passed off as universalist claims about objectivity, reason, and human nature. But feminists, like those attempting to draw on cultural traditions that have been eclipsed by the pretensions of the most powerful, are always in danger of relapsing into claims of privileged access, of reproducing the cultural arrogance they seek to undermine.

Critical social movements may be judged according to conventional measures of political power. They may be identified within the familiar categories as fragmented protest groups, or mass movements, or interest groups, or political parties. Within these categories, cynicism is often appropriate. But cynicism is not realism. It is not enough to measure power against power in order to understand the transformative character of modern life. To take the explorations of critical social movements seriously is to point to the crucial importance not of power as weapons and wealth but of processes that empower people to exercise greater control over the way they live. The transformations in political, economic, and cultural life necessary to do more than treat symptoms of a deeper malaise are usually unspectacular and even invisible to those in the midst of them. If the modern mass media had been around in the late medieval period in Europe, they no doubt would have been reporting on conflicts between the Pope and the emperor, not on the rise of the state or the emergence of capitalism.

FROM POWER TO EMPOWERMENT

Despite the difficulties involved in interpreting the potentials of critical social movements, many activists and observers, like those who have participated in the Committee for a Just World Peace, are convinced that such movements are significant. Yet, in bringing a skeptical optimism to the exploration of this significance, it is possible to be attracted in varying degrees to both more skeptical and more optimistic lines of interpretation. These tensions have made themselves felt in five main dimensions of debate, in five main starting points for discussion about the possibilities that critical social movements may reasonably be expected to encourage. They are visible in the way the promises and problems of critical social movements have been articulated in this book.

First, there is a tension between a sense of outrage and a sense that established political actors are already beginning to get things done. Outrage is directed at particular problems, at the intransigence of particular regimes, at yet another crisis here or there, at still more reports, statistics, or photographs, at yet another election lost, another promising initiative crushed. About forty thousand children will still die today from hunger-related causes. The Strategic Defense Initiative rumbles on. Poisons accumulate. Even so, there are signs of improvement, an opening here, a *glasnost* there, a successful campaign to inoculate children, some restructuring of debt, some negotiations and even agreements about missile reductions, some dictators removed. If political leaders and government agencies can do so much, why not simply encourage movements to put more and more pressure on them?

Second, there is a tension between short-term and long-term time frames. Many problems are urgent. Something needs to be done now. The substantive objectives of movements usually do concern immediate problems. Yet, the explorations in which critical social movements engage while pursuing these immediate concrete objectives seem to respond to the need for long-term social, cultural, and economic transformation. Thus, on the one hand, there are concerns about how to help particular movements in their specific concrete struggles; on the other, there are concerns about how to encourage the kinds of connections among movements that can extend these more wide-reaching explorations still further.

Third, tension arises from the way that critical social movements are now more important in some parts of the world than in others. Living in, say, much of the Middle East, or China, or the Soviet Union, one could ignore such movements almost entirely. In many other places they are part of the fabric of everyday life, even if they do seem marginal.

These three themes of debate combine to form a forth, concerning the relative importance of critical social movements compared with other forces and actors. At times, there is a strong sense of the novelty and significance of critical social movements and of their capacity to transform the situations in which they act. At other times, there is a sense that this is not enough and that in order to get things done it is necessary to do something more: to become a political party, to form a united front with other parties and movements, to develop a common goal or vision.

These themes lead, finally, to a basic tension involving the kind of common goal or vision that is desirable. It is easy enough to agree that prevailing visions and ideologies are not up to the tasks ahead. The practices of critical social movements point in two seemingly contradictory directions with respect to possible alternatives. On the one hand, some claim that a new paradigm is needed, a new vision, a new holistic cosmology; that it is necessary to recognise the priority of our planetary habitat over fragmented national interests. On the other hand, critical social movements often act less out of the search for a common vision than out of a deep suspicion of all common visions. It is certainly the case that One World must also be Many Worlds, but there is deep uncertainty about whether unity or diversity should have priority.

These are all important tensions. They are important tensions because they reflect the practical concerns of critical social movements themselves. They grow out of the contradictory conditions in which such movements act. But, it is clear that it would be a serious mistake to treat them as irreconcilable alternatives. As I have tried to show in this book, the possibilities of creative human activity at the present time depend on making the most of the opportunities to which these tensions and opportunities give rise.

This *is* an age of contradictory possibilities. The scenarios of No World and Two Worlds are plausible. We can easily unleash terminal war. We can accelerate global apartheid. But other directions are also being explored.

Short-term problems *are* urgent. But they can hardly be separated out from the need for long-term transformations.

Critical social movements *are* more important in some places than in others, but they are sufficiently widespread to envisage the possibility of growing networks between movements in different situations. Nor are such movements the only actors offering more hopeful ways forward. It would be absurd to expect them to transform the world on their own. It would be equally absurd to expect them to conform to the expectations or leadership of the dominant political forces of our time.

Visions of planetary integrity, of people's security, of empowering development for all, of deepening democracy everywhere, may be in tension with the fragmented and localized practices of critical social movements. But if One World must also be Many Worlds, then it will be necessary to understand that universalizing visions cannot be formulated in abstraction. They must grow out of an appreciation of the variety of people's experiences, histories, identities, and aspirations.

Critical social movements act in specific circumstances. I have argued that this is not just a consequence of their peripheral location within existing structures of power. On the part of some movements, it is a judgment about the most appropriate places in which to act, about the need to refuse the obvious centers and conventional practices of political life. This judgment leads to a deep skepticism about general solutions and grand strategies. Rather, critical social movements are attracted toward appropriate conjunctions, contingent evaluations, specific projects, and temporary alliances. A pluralism and a diffuseness about the way many movements organize and act are distinctly at odds with prevailing understandings of political practice. There is no principle enemy, no clear goal around which parties or mass movements can be organized, institutions built, or revolutions launched.

These tendencies may be interpreted as signs of weakness. In the judgment of the Committee for a Just World Peace, at least, they are more appropriately understood as indications of the way old images of political change and revolution are fading. Movements of the past have assumed the existence of a principle enemy. They engaged in struggles against imperialism or capitalism, against an easily identified system with a relatively clear determining energy and logic. This conception of an identifiable center that could be challenged and replaced informs many nationalist and socialist projects even now. But this conception is increasingly alien to movements struggling against war, racism, sexism, environmental degradation, or the abuse of human rights. There is less and less conviction that success on any single front will necessarily bring progress on another. There is a greater and greater disparity between what can be achieved by taking the centers of power and what has to be done in order to move toward people's security, toward an empowering development, or toward deepening democracy.

People learn to recognize the multiplicity of power relations embedded in different social practices, relations in which people often participate without knowing it. People learn to recognize not only the authoritarian state "out there"—the identifiable events of armored vehicles and dawn awakenings, of censorship and beatings, of propagandistic images and inaccessible decisions—but also the authoritarian state "in here"—the routines taken for granted, the conveniences of forgetting, the capitulation of apathy.

In this sense, the emphasis on local practices is not appropriately understood in the familiar sense of parochial, of geographical or social backwaters. It is more properly identified as a celebration of the diversity of revolutions to be undertaken. The mix varies from place to place. Each locale has its own diversity of struggles and connections, its own energies and imagination. In some situations, it is possible that some struggles do assume an overriding importance. The struggle against apartheid in South Africa, or against specific oppressive regimes, or on behalf of especially downtrodden peoples all generate tight coalitions, more conventional forms of mass movement, rather than loose networks and shifting alliances. But this precedence is created by local circumstances. It is not preordained.

A celebration of the diversity of revolutions leads to the elaboration of distinct forms of political practice. The grand strategy of the single revolution gives way to tactics of multiple changes. These may be listed but not assigned any necessary priority: lobbying, consciousness-raising, politicizing personal relations, demonstrations, media events, court actions, circulating information, electoral politics, strikes, establishing networks, working with particularly disadvantaged groups, adopting alternative lifestyles, immersion in alternative cultural traditions, explorations of old or new technologies, resistances, reinterpretations, imaginings, rememberings.

The ideal of the grand revolution is graphic and spectacular. It is heroic. It invites *machismo*. And violence. And counterrevolution. The practices of multiple transformations seem tame and unexciting, even evolutionary. They may be seen as diversions from the real goal: radical change. Indeed, very often this may be the case.

In this context, it is interesting to reflect on what "radical change" has so often come to mean. The term carries the implication of radical transcendence, the future denial of all that now is. Yet, even in periods of rapid transformation, everyday life does go on in recognizable ways. Some things change, others are transformed, but familiar patterns continue. The image of change as radical transcendence is in many ways deeply inhibiting. A just world peace calls not for radical transcendence, the wholesale overturning of all that now is. It must begin in a profound transformation of present practices, the infusion of new meanings into familiar habits, and the understanding that this transformation is always being advanced or inhibited by what ordinary individuals, as well as groups and institutions, do on a day-to-day basis.

The transcendent image of revolutionary change glorifies the future. Change will come at some point to come. Because radical change is always construed as imminent, the revolution can be recurrently postponed. For critical social movements, change is always possible in the here and now. A just world peace is not a future event. It is something that is—or is not—already present in the way people act in their immediate circumstances.

A just world peace is not something that can be deferred. It has to inform the everyday practices of people everywhere. The challenge of local practices, in short, is to learn to act upon a double refusal: a refusal to treat politics as a thing "out there" and a refusal to treat peace as a mere future possibility. In taking up this challenge, the practices of critical social movements have the capacity to make a mockery of dominant categories of space and time. This, surely, is not a sign of impotence or infertility.

All human action occurs under constraints. To adapt a formulation of Marx, people make history, though not under conditions of their own choosing. We know that these constraints are changing, are continually being reconstructed. People must necessarily change the ways they make history. They have to change their understanding of what it means to make history. All three of these themes—of structural transformation, of new responses to new determinations, and an emerging intuition of the need to rethink the most basic categories through which we make sense of what is going on and what is possible—are present in the practices of critical social movements.

We live in an age that does seem to be in the midst of epochal transformation. The global structures that constrain what is possible are both very large and very powerful. The immediate problems before us are very dangerous. But to take critical social movements seriously is to celebrate a contradiction that is only apparent. It is to claim that such movements offer a fairly good account of changing structural conditions and of some of the political practices that are appropriate under those conditions. Movements suggest that what counts now is less the existing rigidities of power than the possibility of empowering people in their everyday lives. The struggle for people's security, for empowering development, and for deepening democracy cannot be measured in the same currency as either guns or butter, swords or ploughshares.

This is an age of contradictory possibilities. In the face of scenarios of No World and Two Worlds, existing authorities can achieve a great deal. They can agree about arms control, initiate a nuclear freeze, construct a better law of the sea, eliminate the gross abuse of human rights, end apartheid. Yet such achievements, while urgent, still only amount to a holding operation. They ignore the first principle of political life: everything changes.

This is a time of both immediate struggles and long-term transitions. In an era in which political life has become increasingly concerned with short-term government policies, critical social movements understand that to act in the present is to act in the future. They also understand that although conditions are uneven in different societies, the development of new connections means that the need for new forms of political life everywhere cannot be avoided.

Prevailing images of power and revolution depend upon the image of a center to be taken and held. Unity and the common front, the sovereign state, and the political party: These constitute paradigms of strength. But critical social movements have begun to show that this image is deeply illusory. Movements may be fragile, but they have been able to cut off the roots of excessive state power. They have been able to generate empowering projects, meanings, and practices for people who had seemed helpless.

Prevailing images of peace have assumed that it is necessary to move from fragmentation to unity, from the national interest to the human interest, from the state to the globe. Prevailing images of justice, conversely, have stressed the rights of the downtrodden, the marginalized, the oppressed. They have challenged the presumption that the unity proclaimed by those at the center should hold for everybody. The practices of critical social movements seem to pose a similar contradiction: the need for unity, connection, solidarity, and planetary ecology on the one hand, and localism, specificity, and diversity on the other. But this is less a contradiction than a challenge. It is the challenge of One World/Many Worlds. It is a challenge to rework the principles of inclusion and exclusion that provide the basis for contemporary political, economic, and cultural life.

To explore the opportunities created by profound structural change; to act in the present so as to act on behalf of unborn generations; to act here knowing that all kinds of positive connections can be and are being made with people elsewhere; to understand that struggles to empower people are not marginal or irrelevant, even if they are judged to be so by people reminiscing about old revolutions; to understand how naive it is to pretend that existing forms of solidarity and identity will remain unchanged; to refuse the presumption that One World is inconsistent with Many Worlds: All these are indicative of new openings, new possibilities. They inhibit closure. They encourage a politics of empowerment.

CHALLENGES OF CONNECTION

Critical social movements are already engaged in struggles and practices that enhance the possibilities of a just world peace. Other helpful energies are also visible among state elites, mass movements, political parties, labor movements and trade unions, churches, and individuals. Many of the forces that are driven to participate in No World/Two Worlds policies also have the potential to participate in more encouraging practices. Nothing said in this book should be taken as a claim that critical social movements have a monopoly on ways forward.

Nevertheless, I have argued that the practices of critical social movements are particularly important. They lead to the kind of explorations, interpretations, and empowerment that make it possible to treat the struggle for a just world peace not as a future abstraction but as a process in which to engage wherever one is. In interpreting these practices, I have assumed that questions about what is to be done must be articulated in the context of questions about what is being done. To ask "What is to be done?" in abstraction is to invite the blueprint and the plan, the voice of authority and the manifesto from on high. It is to seek to take power and to plot the revolution. To ask "What is being done?" is to begin to understand how people are learning to empower themselves. It is to become sensitive to the way people are reinventing political life, making new connections, imagining and exploring new possibilities.

The question "What is to be done?" is certainly not irrelevant. Nor is it completely unanswerable. Existing centers of power are capable of generating more prudent policies. Sometimes they do. Critical social movements obviously have to insist that they do so more often. Beyond an insistence on more prudent policies by existing centers of power, however, critical social movements are engaged in broader and less tangible social, economic, and cultural transformations. Ultimately, this is what makes them potentially so important.

Movements engage in highly specific struggles. To offer advice on what should be done in particular situations is not only potentially arrogant but often pointless. The idiosyncrasies of local conditions are likely to make a mockery of generalizations offered from outside. Movements require help to empower themselves, not be told what to do. But struggles of specificity alone do not lead to the creative explorations and solidarities now necessary for the reconstruction of political life. Local can be parochial. Movements can become closed. Processes of empowerment are not easy to sustain.

Movements may begin by reacting to the intolerable in particular situations. They may respond to famine in Africa or communal violence in India, to environmental disaster, nuclear weapons, or dictatorial regimes. But for critical social movements, to realize the potential that lies in their practices, it is also necessary for them to become engaged in struggles of connection and imagination. Struggles of specificity must lead to a conscious awareness that the experiences driving particular struggles occur in a world of emerging connections in an age of axial transformations.

This is not a matter of imposing a common vision; nor of forging a united front capable of storming existing citadels of power; nor of identifying a clear common denominator upon which the interests of all critical social movements can converge. The imposed vision, the manifesto from on high or the conquering hero will not bring about a just world peace. But the forging of connections is crucial. Critical social movements begin in diversity, but they are compelled to recognize that they act in the same world.

Critical social movements must continue to react to the intolerable. They need to react to processes that turn people's lives into a matter of sheer survival, and they must transform those processes through which people are systematically excluded from any say over their lives and destiny. They must protest the irrationality that passes for normal and the mystification that passes for common sense.

This may mean opposing particular weapons systems or challenging the need for aggressive military strategies, such as those involved in the present buildup of superpower naval capabilities or plans for an air-land battle in Europe. But the specific problems of particular weapons and strategies must lead to opposition to the larger forces that make these problems possible. Thus, it is necessary to challenge the way the presumed interests of the superpowers turn into military adventures everywhere. It is necessary to challenge the way economic, social, and cultural life is being swept up into processes of militarization that are now global in scale. And beyond this is the need to challenge the way preparations for war have become normalized. That preparations for SDI have become accepted as normal everyday business, necessary for scientific advance and a booming economy, is as outrageous as the threat to use the final product. That politicians are able to continue to claim the priority of national security in order to justify processes of militarization and strategic postures that threaten No World/Two Worlds signifies an epic failure of the human imagination. That discussions of security can be restricted to matters of military balance when so many people are unable to survive because of a lack of the simplest necessities of life is a moral scandal that no public figure anywhere should ever be allowed to forget.

Reacting to the intolerable means responding directly to the worst cases of poverty and famine. But it also means protesting against the processes that make poverty inevitable: structures of international debt and commodity pricing agreements; the way in which economic growth has become synonymous with the wealth of elites and the only indicator of "development." Above all, it must now mean opposing the cynicism of all Two Worlds solutions that assume the inevitability of poverty for some as the price to be paid for "progress."

Reacting to the intolerable also means opposing torture, disappearances, and the abuse of human rights, particularly the rights to food, shelter, and other subsistence needs. It means challenging any autocratic presumption of the right to rule, whether this presumption is defended with crude force or by appeal to some natural superiority given by gender, race, class, or expertise. It means refusing to treat people as the excluded "other," as the inferior to be condemned as enemy or terrorist, as the universal Palestinian, as the object of either hatred or the shrug of indifference. It means refusing to accept claims to democracy at face value and challenging the reduction of politics to a spectator sport monopolized by professional politicians.

Of course, it is easier to protest than to change things. But one lesson of critical social movements is that people are not always as powerless as they are made to feel. The grand structures that seem so distant and so immovable are clearly identifiable and resistible on an everyday basis. Not to act *is* to act. Everyone can change habits and expectations or refuse to accept that the problems are out there in someone else's backyard—someone else's responsibility. It is possible to challenge apathy and to search for positive energies even in the most oppressive situations. Everyone can say no.

Preparations for war can be resisted. People can refuse to pay taxes supporting militarization—or at least attempt to divert taxes for more productive uses; or at least make a fuss about having to contribute to people's insecurity. They can refuse the absorption of military production and culture into everyday life and economy, into toys, research designs, and dreams. It is especially important to refuse the kinds of propaganda in which war preparations are shrouded: the national chauvinism, the equation of local and regional interests with the interests of superpowers, the fictions of nuclear deterrence theory and claims about civil defense in nuclear war, the claimed need for official secrets, the turning of all politics of difference into the enmity of absolute "otherness," the refusal of toleration and détente in the name of freedom and victory.

The processes that bring maldevelopment can also be resisted. Communities can struggle to prevent their social and environmental structures being ripped apart in order to create more "efficient" production for the world market. They can encourage as much self-reliance as possible in order to resist the dualistic logic of the global division of labor. They can refuse to treat work as simply a way of making commodities to be bought and sold. They can oppose inappropriate technologies, environmentally harmful projects, and the exploitation of more vulnerable social groups. Above all, resistance to maldevelopment means understanding the need to intervene in everyday processes—of work and consumption, of production and distribution, in factories, in fields, in homes and in marketplaces—in order to refuse the determinations of structures that only seem remote.

Everyone can act as critic and conscience of the times. Everyone can remember forgotten promises and lost dreams. Everyone can resist unquestioned authority whether it comes from the iron fist of dictatorship or the velvet glove of the television set.

Critical social movements can show the hypocrisy of power and insist on the accountability of all public officials. They can extend processes of democratization into realms where it has never been tried: into the home, into the workplace, into processes of cultural production. They can act on the insight that knowledge is power in order to establish tribunals and disseminate information. They can refuse to respond in kind to aggression and violence in order to challenge the power of destruction with a creative empowerment that opens up possibilities rather than closes them off.

Critical social movements will continue to refuse the intolerable. They will continue to explore and reinterpret alternative possibilities. And they will continually discover that to act in particular local spaces is necessarily to act on structures that have a global reach. Capital-whizzing between London, Tokyo, and New York may in some sense be untouchable, even unimaginable, but it is tangibly present in the ordinary routines of everyday life. Missile silos may be hidden and guarded, but the processes that make them possible are much too close for comfort. Movements will continue to react to the intolerable in particular places, but the challenge of connections remains.

Part of the potential of such movements lies in their capacity to make connections across time. They resist the myth of History. They have an imaginative capacity to identify with struggles of the past. They can insist on the need to act on behalf of future generations. They can insist that moral concerns can only be serious if they grow out of active participation in continuous struggles against injustice everywhere. To make such connections across time is to underscore the need to always act as if transformation is under way. It is to refuse the revolution postponed.

Although connections across time may require a leap of the imagination, connections with the present can be made with concrete immediacy. If the revolution cannot be postponed, then it is necessary to reclaim the present, to reclaim the potential inherent in existing practices, institutions, and values. Thus, it is not necessary to reject the concept of security in order to think about peace and justice; just the particular understanding of security through which the concept has been more or less turned into its opposite. It is possible to reclaim the relationship between security and defense, a relationship that has been lost in the way national security turns into the accumulation of offensive forces. It is possible to reclaim legitimate regional security needs from the pretensions of superpowers. Respectable military theorists have long argued that military affairs must be treated as an extension of political life. In a world in which this relationship has become dangerously inverted, even a reclamation of some elements of conventional military wisdom would constitute a big step forward.

Nor is it necessary to reject the concept of development, despite the embarrassing quotation marks in which it often appears. Again, it is a term that has come to have less to do with the capacity of people to grow, to express their potential, and to empower themselves than with just the opposite. Maldevelopment must be resisted, but existing aspirations for a properly empowering development can still be recaptured and reinterpreted. Traditions can also be reclaimed, though not in the name of unquestioned authority nor through a simple-minded relapse from the quotation marks of "development" to the quotation marks of "tradition." Tradition can be reclaimed through an openness to the potential vitality of histories, and particularly of the histories of peoples who have been made powerless and marginalized.

Trade unions, labor movements, and working-class parties have undoubtedly been seduced in many societies by the demands of "development." But they too are in crisis as capital becomes increasingly global in mobility while labor remains rooted in particular communities. The explorations of critical social movements are not opposed to the struggles of labor movements, only to one-sided understandings of what it means to labor in the modern world. Connections between feminist or environmental movements and organized labor have already been made in many places, and such connections will undoubtedly have to be extended in the future.

The term "democracy" is certainly in need of reclamation. Every tinpot autocrat invokes the label. But again, more is at stake than just the term. Particular democratic forms have fallen into disrepute because of the way they have become integrated into existing structures. The idea of representative government, for example, has often turned into little more than a periodic plebiscite at election time. Yet, the institutions of representative democracy can often be made to work in ways consistent with the aims of critical social movements. The same is true of bureaucratic institutions or political parties. There are always spaces to be filled, rules to be rediscovered, rights to be reactivated or reinterpreted.

It is always possible to try to reclaim the normative order expressed in law. It is always possible to enter and revitalize the political spaces left open by the dominant institutions. Local government often remains a vacuum waiting to be filled. Everyday life at home or in the workplace offers an immediate opportunity to reclaim basic human decency as both a way of life and as a norm of conduct elsewhere. Women can reclaim the powers feared or repressed as merely feminine. Artists can reclaim meanings and symbols, even undermine the tendency for art itself to turn into a mere commodity to be bought and sold.

Critical social movements make connections across time, connections that draw upon potentials that already exist in established institutions, practices, and values. They also establish connections across both social and geographical spaces. For example, the most striking characteristic of women's movements is their plurality. Although the headlines and the stereotypes have placed the spotlight on a certain kind of Western liberal movement, the struggles of women in different places are remarkable for their diversity. The Argentinian mothers of those who have disappeared have to be understood in terms of highly specific conditions, even though their actions clearly resonate with many other women's struggles elsewhere. Theoretical and ideological disputes are often deeply rooted. Some groups, obviously, provide perfect examples of closed and reactionary movements that are anything but critical. Nevertheless, even more remarkable than the diversity of critical women's movements is the way such groups can connect and share experiences across political, economic, cultural, and linguistic boundaries. The same is true of movements of indigenous peoples and environmentalists or of, for example, movements in Western Europe concerned with nuclear weapons learning to speak to movements in Eastern Europe concerned with human rights and democratization.

Most of these connections are unmapped. They are known mainly by people who have participated in them. But they are crucial to the future of critical social movements everywhere. In fact, one of the most pressing needs of critical social movements is for access to greater information about what movements elsewhere are doing. The dominant sources of information in the modern world find little enough room for news even of smaller states, unless they happen to be the site of tragedy or coup. The activities of critical movements are unsurprisingly invisible. The problems concerning international communication identified in proposals for a New World Information Order also apply to critical social movements. There is a pressing need for alternative media, for alternative sources of information and what is considered to be news.

Perhaps the most helpful immediate project that could be undertaken in this respect would be to establish a regularized source of information about movements on a worldwide basis. Such a bulletin of critical social movements would be able to provide a common focus for the exchange of news, opinions, and inspiration. Such exchanges now occur on an irregular and informal basis. Yet, even people who are deeply committed to movements in one part of the world find it very difficult to find out about what is going on in similar movements elsewhere. It is time for the connections that are being made to become much more visible.

THE CHALLENGES OF ONE WORLD/MANY WORLDS

The scenarios of No World and Two Worlds remain all too plausible. Nothing that has been said here will persuade the convinced cynic that critical social movements will bring release from either fate. The evidence is not auspicious. Guarantees are not helpful.

But cynicism is a retreat from the world, a capitulation to the inevitability of trajectories beyond control. It thrives on action at a distance. The experiences of critical social movements arise from an active engagement with the world, with struggles and practices that respond to the world as it changes in ways that are always unpredictable, never inevitable. Critical social movements may be unlikely candidates for glory, but they may succeed in slowing down the drift to disaster, even in opening up paths to a just world peace.

To open up paths to a just world peace, critical social movements have to act, in the here and now, as if they were already living in One World/Many Worlds. Revolutions cannot be postponed. Transformations are already under way.

Of course, it may be said that we already live in One World/Many Worlds. The state as the primary political category may be claimed to resolve the age-old tension between being a person and being part of a particular culture in a particular territory. But that is an historically specific resolution, one increasingly out of touch with contemporary realities and one badly flawed by the unequal influence of some states in particular as well as by the inherent tendency of the states system to induce war. This is neither the Europe of Napoleon or Bismarck nor even the era of decolonization. Statist nationalism has undoubtedly been a tenacious force, but even it is rooted in historical conditions that now show signs of fading.

In an alternative view, the tension may be resolved by faith in the inevitable spread of the world economy and its accompanying global culture. This was the overt promise of "development," of the necessary progress from barbarism to enlightenment, from tradition to modernity. That dream has been shattered sharply enough. The promise of One World induces Two Worlds. It has already induced the partial obliteration of Many Worlds, the forgetting of histories, and the arrogance of empires. Maldevelopment is no way to resolve anything.

Other resolutions appeal to the rationalist philosophies or the universalist religions. Possibly. But most such traditions either tend to leave the world as it is or are infused with distinctly unhelpful biases of gender, race, class, and culture. The failure of imagination in surviving intellectual, philosophical, ideological, and religious systems is itself, like the failed claims of the states system and world economy, part of the drift toward No World/Two Worlds.

Despite the prevalence of these conventional claims, we do not live in One World/Many Worlds. The reality is unequal development, eversharpening patterns of inclusion and exclusion, brutality and domination coexisting with enclaves of wealth and privilege; a drift toward global conflict; and emerging technologies whose social consequences no one understands.

This is why the apparently contradictory visions that arise from the practices of critical social movements are so important. Many aspire to visions of One World, to ecological holism and planetary harmony. But the practices of such movements insist on the primacy of the local, the particular, the specific. Aspirations for One World are nothing new. Critical social movements, however, temper such aspirations with a deep and often overriding suspicion of all global visions. This is one of the characteristics that distinguishes them from the best-known mass movements of the past.

This apparent contradiction may seem very disturbing indeed. Why, it may be asked, when the problems before us are global in scale and implication, do so many movements insist on small-scale local activities and shy away from offering global vision? The apparent contradiction may seem especially powerful if approached through the intellectual categories that, although associated primarily with the West, have influenced contemporary thinking everywhere. In these categories, One World and Many Worlds are opposites. To struggle for One World is certainly desirable as an ideal, impractical perhaps, but compatible with established standards of truth, good-ness, and beauty, not to mention History. To insist on Many Worlds is to court relativism, anarchy, or simply irrelevance.

Within these categories, especially, the practices and aspirations of criti-cal social movements do appear to be caught in a contradiction. But con-versely, the practices of critical social movements put these very categories into question. They do so both at a very practical level and in a way that poses a range of enormously important questions for thinking about a just world peace.

The practical matter may be stated quite simply, although the implica-tions are very difficult to assess. Critical social movements focus on both the global and the particular simply because this is to recognize the crucial dialectic of the modern age. The major structures and processes that affect us are global—and they affect us where we live and work. The state is no longer the only great mediator between "out there" and "in here," between foreign policy and domestic politics, between capital and labor, between First World and Third World, between self and other. States are by no means irrelevant, but even when they are becoming stronger in some ways, they are beginning to take on the aura of local government. States are becoming too big to respond to the needs of people and too small to respond to the globalization of capital or the challenges of militarization and environ-mental collapse.

To participate effectively in the modern world is necessarily to learn to grapple with the way global structures directly affect particular places and particular groups. Critical social movements celebrate diversity and the local, not only because they understand that it is necessary to become em-powered rather than to seize the state, but also because that is precisely where power has to be challenged. If the simultaneous embrace of both One World and Many Worlds is a contradiction, then it is a contradiction that is inherent in the way the world is becoming. Categories that try to resolve the contradiction at the level of the state, or by insisting on the necessity of moving toward universal development and global culture, simply fail to grasp what is going on.

At a practical level, movements respond to the intolerable in particular places and discover that they must and do connect. At this point in time, the challenge of connection is especially urgent. But to act as if we are already living in One World/Many Worlds is to face many additional challenges. These are not the challenges of particular problems. They do not call forth better policies or manifestos. They do demand that, whatever the immediate urgencies to which particular movements respond in specific places, critical social movements will have to become more and more concerned with what it means to struggle for a just world peace everywhere. Conversely, they pose the problem of how to live on one earth without surrendering to the arrogance that there is only one key to the universe.

Over and above the demand for practical policies, for solutions to particular problems, eight challenges are now crucial. Tentative responses to these challenges are visible in the way critical social movements now act. These challenges are less a matter of finding policy solutions to be carried out either by movements or by more established actors than of clarifying the questions to which all political actors must now respond.

There is, first, the *challenge of difference,* of learning to see Many Worlds not as the negation of One World but as the condition for its possibility. This challenge may be more difficult for movements in the West and for all those who have absorbed the philosophies, ideologies, and theologies that insist that all difference must be resolved into unity. It means learning to act locally and immediately while refusing to be parochial, learning to be movements of specificity but also of connection and imagination. It means learning to draw on local experiences without being romantic or reactionary. Cultures and traditions die when they have to be simply defended rather than created and recreated.

There is, second, the *challenge of tactics.* Critical social movements necessarily walk a fine line. On one side is the potential arrogance of surveying the whole, and on the other is the potential timidity and cooptation of the parochial. Movements have to refuse the escalation of tactics into grand strategy and also the degeneration of tactics into the logistics of particulars.

There is, third, the *challenge of otherness.* To celebrate diversity is necessarily to refuse to treat others as "other." It is to be aware of a moral duty to be obligated to others. Yet movements act in a world in which the creation of an "other" has become a condition of everyday life. Even struggles for peace and justice can seem easier if they are focused against a common foe, a "them" to be blamed and overturned. The cold war, like holy war, takes otherness to extremes. Struggles against racism and patriarchy involve learning to speak from positions long cast as the mere shadow of dominant groups. National identity, like the modern idea of individual identity, celebrates the necessity, indeed the "freedom" that comes from historically constituted structures of exclusion and alienation.

In One World/Many Worlds, others cannot be "other." They may be different—but not cast as exclusion and inferiority. Critical social movements have to struggle toward new solidarities, new identities, and new communities that refuse to submit all differences to the tyrannical logic of same or other, us or them, friend and foe, me or you. The challenge of One World/ Many Worlds is a challenge not only to make connections. It is also a challenge to work with the necessary reciprocity of connections between peoples able to speak on equal terms.

This leads, fourth, to the *challenge of obligation.* All states presume, indeed insist upon, obedience on the part of their citizens. But the grounds for this presumption are very slim indeed. Histories of political theory are full of ways in which the necessity of obedience has been justified in the past: tradition, the wisdom of the elders, natural law, divine right, efficiency, father knows best. In practice, the arguments of the philosophers are often of less weight than simple force and propaganda. Whatever the holders of power may think, all claims to political obligation are in serious trouble. If existing authorities are inducing No World/Two Worlds, contemporary obligations point less to obedience than to resistance.

Yet, it is no less important to sustain the viability of decent and humanely concerned values within the societies people belong to and, thus, to justify allegiances to groups and leaders who act effectively on behalf of those values. To work for new connections and solidarities is necessarily to generate a moral need for political creativity and invention. It is to create a political ethics of mutual understanding and human solidarity rather than the greed and violence that is the contemporary substitute. It is to act as a citizen of One World/Many Worlds while knowing that there is currently no global polity of which to be a citizen.

The challenge of obligation is inseparable from, fifth, the *challenge of human identity*. To live in a world of histories is to be aware of the multiplicity of the range of identities through which people find meaning and express themselves. It is also to be aware that the primary structures of the modern world have reduced the ways in which meaning and identity may be expressed. At one extreme, identity occurs as individuality. At another extreme, identity occurs in the form of citizenship, as participation in the community of state. Yet, as an extreme, the modern notion of individuality, the individual as free from the constraint of others, implies a loss of participation in community. And as citizens of particular states, people may well be admitted to the most powerful and encompassing of all political communities, but they are then necessarily cut off from any broader community of humankind. The modern ideals of both individualism and citizenship depend upon a sense of identity generated by the severest of exclusions. As extremes, they offer scope for endless oscillations between seemingly incompatible claims to ultimate political identity. Such has been the fate of so much modern ideological dispute about individualism and socialism, nationalism and cosmopolitanism. In a world of histories and global structures, these oscillations seem terminal and the exclusions bankrupt.

Critical social movements also focus on two key moments of political identity, but they are different moments, and they are not exclusive. From one direction comes the demand for the grounding of meaning, expression, belonging, and aspiration in particular places within particular groups. There is a demand for autonomy, including the autonomy of individuals. There is a celebration of self-assertion, but not the self-aggrandizement of separation. Yet, from the other direction, comes the demand for human identity, for the expression of a consciously shared heritage. This demand may draw on traditional philosophies and religions, and especially on cultures that have not been so deeply implicated in the oscillations of modernity. It increasingly draws on a sense of common ancestry, on a sense of common emergence from the same earth. There is a growing recognition of the objective structures that link us together in bizarre and unexpected ways and of the technical gadgets that turn us all into missile fodder. The expression of a consciously shared heritage generates a sense of responsibility for the planet and all who live on it.

Contemporary political debate is dominated by the identities of individual and state. Concepts of rights and freedoms, for example, are inevitably held within their gravity. Where modernity has not swept aside all else, of course, other identities are expressed with great force. This is what the contemporary proliferation of histories is all about. Yet, although the identities of modernity dominate debate, and many other identities join the conversation with great vigor, critical social movements focus on the autonomous identities of particular communities and on a sense of the common human identity shared by people living on the same planet. It seems increasingly rooted in the primary contradictions of a world still coming into being.

This is why the notion of human identity seems so inevitable, yet so impossible: so necessary, yet also undesirable. It invites the kind of closure that has marred the oscillations of modernity. It invites the equation of human identity with one world, forgetting that human identity can only be realized in the plural. It invites the premature claim of discovery when it is something that can only be achieved.

To speak of obligations or human identities is to enter into seeming abstractions. It is to grasp at energies that may well already exist but do not yet take a clearly tangible form. But it is to raise similar issues to those posed by the sixth major challenge that has to be taken up by critical social movements, the *challenge of humane governance*.

Critical social movements are suspicious of institutionalization. In this they share in a wider suspicion of the bureaucratization and rigid hierarchies that have become characteristic of political life in most societies. But movements also recognize that some kinds of formal organization is essential. They learn to work with institutions that already exist and to challenge them in ways that make them more democratic and responsive to the needs of people. The problem is less the existence of institutions as such than the form that particular institutions take.

For example, it has been fashionable recently to criticize the United Nations, particularly since it has slipped out of the firm grasp of the most powerful Western states. It is especially noticeable that the most strident critiques have been aimed at UNESCO and UNCTAD rather than at, say, the World Intellectual Property Organization or the IMF. International organizations may have serious problems as a result of excessive bureaucratization and the proliferation of agencies, reports, meetings, and costs, but these organizations have made enormous contributions to peacekeeping, decolonization, information gathering, human rights, and international law, as well as to the programs of the sectoral agencies concerned with food, health, and so on. Indeed, there is an ever more pressing need for a United Nations that has the resources and energies to be open to new realities and aspirations. There is no reason, for example, why anyone should be satisfied with the way people are represented only through the formal sovereign equality of the General Assembly or the overtly hierarchical order of the Security Council and the World Bank. There is more and more justification for creating a third forum open to people rather than only to political and economic elites.

Whether through the networks among the estimated eighteen thousand international nongovernmental organizations or among critical social movements themselves, there is a growing sense of the need to rethink the way political life can be institutionalized. In the tension between bureaucracy and democracy, bureaucracy has come out ahead far too often. Movements have to take seriously the project of creating more democratic institutional forms. They have to show how it is possible to resist hierarchies from the top down and to insist that problems be solved as far as possible through the participation of the people most directly involved. Some problems have to be solved at a global level, but even here it is necessary to ensure effective accountability.

There is, seventh, the *challenge of cultural creativity.* Critical social movements often reject utopian visioning, but the problem is less the relevance of visions or utopianism as such than the way in which our understanding of visions has relied on the image of a model of future perfection. The challenge of cultural creativity is not only a matter of creating visions of a better world but of reconstructing the conditions under which the future may be imagined. Cultural creativity does not occur in abstraction. It arises from concrete everyday practices, from people able to make connections with each other and engaging in dialogue about the meaning of their experiences.

Finally, there is *the challenge of uncertainty.* In this book I have constantly drawn attention to the sense of uncertainty that permeates the practices of critical social movements. However much this sense of uncertainty is resisted, it is an undeniable characteristic of contemporary political consciousness and action. But it is resisted: by those who stress the need for a clear vision of the way ahead; by those who understand the need for persuasive messages that will mobilize millions; by those who have absorbed the expectations of History and have learned to equate local differences and plural histories with weakness, parochialism, and relativism. It is also resisted by those who equate success with short-term achievements. When, for example, the Western European peace movements were unable to prevent the deployment of cruise and Pershing II missiles, this was widely interpreted as a sign of failure, even though challenging the presence of these weapons had a powerful impact on the climate of expectations about national security in a nuclear age. The theme of uncertainty as a guiding star often makes even activists within critical social movements feel very uncomfortable.

In fact, the challenge of uncertainty is not so much an indication of weakness as a crucial element of the way thinking about and struggling to achieve a just world peace must lead to a challenge to what it now means to be certain. For the appeal to certainty cannot be separated from the structures and traditions against which critical social movements are struggling. It is especially important to understand that the search for certainty has been an especially important characteristic of modernity. It underlies the characteristic appeal to science or the need for firm philosophical foundations as a prerequisite for legitimate knowledge.

Yet, if scientific and philosophical speculation over most of the twentieth century tells us anything at all, then it is that the search for absolute certainty is illusory. And if the challenge to History is taken as seriously as it must now be, then the certainties—of "progress" and "development," of peace and justice as the necessary move toward One World—must be put into question.

Critical social movements, like many of the most powerful intellectual currents of our time, are engaged in a rethinking of what it means to live in a world in which the certainties of modernity have been shattered. Under these conditions, cynicism, parochialism, relativism, and self-righteousness are possible and dangerous options. But certainty is also dangerous. It can give rise to cynicism, to the parochialism and relativism of those able to insist on the priority of their interpretations, and to the self-righteousness of uncontested power. It can also tranquilize.

The most pressing need is to reconstruct the conditions under which we have been persuaded that without a single light to guide us, we are lost. Again this is the challenge of One World/Many Worlds. Critical social movements are not the only actors taking up this challenge, but they, more than most, have the capacity to show where it might lead.

None of these challenges are easy. Nor are they likely to be among the immediate concerns of movements struggling in particularly oppressive situations. Yet, if critical social movements must necessarily be open to the emerging connections of a world of rapid transformation, then creative responses to these challenges are now unavoidable.

Selected Bibliography

A full bibliographic guide to material covered in this book would be much longer than the book itself. The following list is therefore restricted to recent literature that elaborates on the primary theme of the book, namely, the relationship between global structural transformations and the emerging practices and aspirations of critical social movements. Two sources have been especially helpful. One is the journal *Alternatives: Social Transformation and Humane Governance,* published by Butterworth Scientific, Westbury House, Bury Street, Guildford GU2 5BH, England. The other is the *IFDA Dossier* published by the International Foundation for Development Alternatives, 4, Place du Marché, 1260 Nyon, Switzerland.

Arato, Andrew, and Jean L. Cohen. "Social Movements, Civil Society and the Problem of Sovereignty," *Praxis International* 4, October 1984, 266-283.

Arrighi, Giovanni, Terence K. Hopkins, and Immanuel Wallerstein. "Dilemmas of Antisystemic Movements," *Social Research* 53, Spring 1986, 185-206.

Bernard, Jessie. *The Female World from a Global Perspective* (Bloomington and Indianapolis: Indiana University Press, 1987).

Blomström, Magnus, and Björne Hettne. *Development Theory in Transition: The Dependency Debate and Beyond* (London: Zed, 1984).

Boff, Leonardo. *Church, Charisma and Power: Liberation Theology and the Institutional Church* (New York: Crossroads, 1985).

Boggs, Carl. *Social Movements and Political Power: Emerging Forms of Radicalism in the West* (Philadelphia: Temple University Press, 1986).

Bookman, Ann, and Sandra Morgan. *Women and the Politics of Empowerment* (Philadelphia: University of Pennsylvania Press, 1988).

Borda, Orlando Fals, ed. *The Challenge of Social Change* (Delhi: Sage, 1985).

Bourdieu, Pierre. "The Social Space and the Genesis of Groups," *Theory and Society* 14, 1985, 723-744.

Boyte, Harry C., and Frank Riessman. *The New Populism: The Politics of Empowerment* (Philadelphia: Temple University Press, 1986).

Boyte, Harry C. *Community is Possible: Repairing America's Roots* (New York: Harper and Row, 1984).

Cagatay, Nilufer, *et. al.* "The Nairobi Women's Conference: Towards a Global Feminism?," *Feminist Studies* 12, 1986, 401-412.

Campbell, Beatrix. *Wigan Pier Revisited: Poverty and Politics in the 80's* (London: Virago, 1984).

Carino, Feliciano. *Theology, Politics and Struggle* (Manila: National Council of Churches in the Philippines, 1986).

Castells, Manuel. *The City and the Grassroots: A Cross Cultural Theory of Urban Social Movements* (Berkeley and Los Angeles: University of California Press, 1983).

Chatterjee, Partha. *Nationalist Thought and the Colonial World: A Derivative Discourse?* (London: Zed, for the United Nations University, 1986).

Cohen, Jean L. "Strategy or Identity: New Theoretical Paradigms and Contemporary Social Movements," *Social Research* 52, Winter 1986, 663-716.

Dahlerup, Drude, ed. *The New Women's Movement: Feminism and Political Power in Europe and the USA* (Beverly Hills: Sage, 1986).

Dunn, John. *Western Political Theory in the Face of the Future* (Cambridge: Cambridge University Press, 1979).

————"Political Obligations and Political Possibilities," in Dunn, *Political Obligation in Historical Context* (Cambridge: Cambridge University Press, 1980), 243-299.

Eder, Klaus. "The New Social Movements: Moral Crusades, Political Pressure Groups, or Social Movements?" *Social Research* 52, Winter 1985.

Eide, Asbjörn. "The Human Rights Movement and the Transformation of the International Order," *Alternatives* XI, July 1986, 367-402.

Eisenstein, Hester. *Contemporary Feminist Thought* (London and Sydney: Unwin, 1984).

Falk, Richard. *The Promise of World Order* (Philadelphia: Temple University Press, 1988).

Falk, Richard, S. S., Kim and S. H. Mendlovitz, eds. *Towards a Just World Order* (Boulder: Westview Press, 1982).

Falk, Richard, for the Committee for a Just World Peace. "Openings for Peace and Justice in a World of Danger and Struggle," *IFDA Dossier* 62, November-December 1987, 17-35.

Feher, Ferenc. "Redemptive and Democratic Paradigms in Radical Politics," *Telos* 63, Spring 1985, 147-156.

Foucault, Michel. *Power/Knowledge: Selected Interviews and Other Writings,* edited by Colin Gordon (New York: Pantheon, 1980).

Frankel, Boris. *The Post-Industrial Utopians* (Oxford: Polity Press, 1987).

Gilbert, Alan, and Peter Ward. "Community Action by the Urban Poor: Democratic Involvement, Community Self-help or a Means of Social Control," *World Development* 12, 1987, 769-782.

————"Community Participation in Upgrading Irregular Settlements: The Community Response," *World Development* 12, 1984, 913-922.

Gran, Guy. *Development by People: Citizen Construction of a Just World* (New York: Praeger, 1983).

————"Beyond African Famines: Whose Knowledge Matters?" *Alternatives* XI, 1986, 275-296.

Green, Philip. *Retrieving Democracy* (Totowa, N.J.: Rowman and Allenheld, 1985).

Hanninen, Sakari, and Leena Paldan, eds. *Rethinking Marx* (New York: International General/IMMRC, 1984).

Hamilton, Roberta, and Michele Barrett. *The Politics of Diversity* (London: Verso, 1986).

Hawthorn, Geoffrey. *Enlightenment and Despair,* 2nd edition (Cambridge: Cambridge University Press, 1987).

Held, David. *Models of Democracy* (Oxford: Polity, 1987).

Held, David, and Christopher Pollitt, eds. *New Forms of Democracy* (London: Sage, 1986).

Hirsch, Joachim. "The Fordist Security State and New Social Movements," *Kapitalistate* 10-11, 1983, 75-87.

Hutchful, Eboe. "The Peace Movement and the Third World," *Alternatives* IX, Spring 1984, 593-603.

International Foundation for Development Alternatives. "Alternatives for Survivors: A Report from the Third System Project," *Development Dialogue,* 1981:1, 67-101.

Jayawardena, Kumari. *Feminism and Nationalism in the Third World* (London: Zed, 1986).

Kaldor, Mary. *The Baroque Arsenal* (London: Andrew Deutsch, 1982).

Kaldor, Mary, and Richard Falk, eds. *Dealignment for Western Europe* (Oxford: Basil Blackwell, 1987).

Katzenstein, Mary F., and Carol M. Mueller, eds. *The Women's Movement in the United States and Western Europe* (Philadelphia: Temple University Press, 1987).

Kim, Samuel S. *The Quest for a Just World Order* (Boulder: Westview, 1984).

Konrad, Gyorgy. *Antipolitics: An Essay,* trans. Richard E. Allen (London: New Left Books, 1984).

Kothari, Rajni. "On Humane Governance," *Alternatives* XII, July 1987, 277-290.

————"On the Non-Party Political Process: The NGO's, The State and World Capitalism," *Lokayan Bulletin,* 4, 1986, 6-26.

————"Party and State in Our Times: The Rise of Non-Party Political Formations," *Alternatives* IX, Spring 1984, 541-564.

Kumar, Krishan. *Utopia and Anti-Utopia in Modern Times* (Oxford: Blackwell, 1987).

Laclau, Ernesto, and Chantal Mouffe. *Hegemony and Socialist Strategy: Toward a Radical-Democratic Politics* (London: Verso, 1985).

Lefort, Claude. *The Political Forms of Modern Society: Bureaucracy, Democracy, Totalitarianism,* ed. J.B. Thompson (Oxford: Polity Press, 1986).

Liddle, Joanna, and Rama Joshi. *Daughters of Independence: Gender, Caste and Class in India* (London: Zed, 1986).

Love, Janice. *The U.S. Anti-Apartheid Movement: Local Activism in Global Politics* (New York: Praeger, 1985).

Magnusson, Warren, C. Doyle, J. DeMarco, and R.B.J. Walker, eds. *After Bennett: A New Politics for British Columbia* (Vancouver: New Star Books, 1986).

Melucci, Alberto. "The Symbolic Challenge of Contemporary Movements," *Social Research* 52, Winter 1985.

Mendlovitz, Saul, and R.B.J. Walker, eds. *Towards a Just World Peace: Perspectives From Social Movements* (London: Butterworths, 1987).

Michnik, Adam. *Letters from Prison and Other Essays,* trans. Maya Letynski (Berkeley and Los Angeles: University of California Press, 1985).

Mies, Maria. *Patriarchy and Accumulation on a World Scale* (London: Zed, 1986).

Miliband, Ralph, J. Saville, M. Liebman, and L. Panitch, eds. Special Issue on "Social Democracy and After," *Socialist Register,* 1985/86 (London: Merlin Press, 1986).

Miller, Lynn H. *Global Order: Values and Power in International Politics* (Boulder: Westview, 1985).

Mitchell, Juliet, and Ann Oakley. *What is Feminism?* (New York: Pantheon, 1986).

Mouffe, Chantal. *Gramsci and Marxist Theory* (London: Routledge and Kegan Paul, 1979).

Nandy, Ashis. "Cultural Frames for Social Transformation: A Credo," *Alternatives* XII, January 1987, 113-124.

Nerfin, Marc. "Neither Prince Nor Merchant: Citizen—An Introduction to the Third System," *IFDA Dossier* 56, November-December, 1986, 3-28.

————"The Future of the United Nations System: Some Questions on the Occasion of an Anniversary," *Development Dialogue,* 1985:1, 1-25.

Offe, Claus. "New Social Movements: Challenging the Boundaries of Institutional

Politics," *Social Research* 52, Winter 1986, 817-868.

Paggi, Leonardo, and Piero Pinzauto. "Peace and Security," *Telos* 63, Spring 1985, 3-40.

Pasquinelli, Carla. "Power Without the State," *Telos* 68, Summer 1986, 79-92.

Pietila, Hikka. "Tomorrow Begins Today: Elements for a Feminine Alternative in the North," *IFDA Dossier* 57/58, January-April, 1987, 37-50.

Poggi, Gianfranco. *The Development of the Modern State* (London: Hutchinson, 1978).

Polan, A.J. *Lenin and the End of Politics* (Berkeley and Los Angeles: University of California Press, 1984).

Rahnema, Majid. "The Grassroots of the Future," *IFDA Dossier* 43, September/October 1984, 49-53.

Resnick, Philip. *Parliament vs. People* (Vancouver: New Star Books, 1984).

Roy, Ramashray, and R.K. Srivastava. *Dialogues on Development* (New Delhi: Sage, 1986).

Sampson, Steven. "The Informal Sector in Eastern Europe," *Telos* 65, Fall 1985, 44-66.

Sarkar, Saral. "The Green Movement in West Germany," *Alternatives* XI, 1986, 219-254.

Seager, Joni, and Ann Olson. *Women in the World: An International Atlas* (London: Pan Books, 1986).

Sethi, Harsh, and Smitu Kothari. "Lokayan (1980-85)," *Lokayan Bulletin* 3, 1985, 3-37.

Sharp, Gene. *The Politics of Non-violent Action,* 3 vols. (Boston: Porter Sargent, 1973).

Sheth, D.L. "Grass-roots Stirrings and the Future of Politics," *Alternatives* IX, Summer 1983, 1-24.

Sivard, Ruth Leger. *World Military and Social Expenditures, 1985* (Washington, D.C.: World Priorities, 1985).

Smith, Dan, and E.P. Thompson, eds. *Prospects for a Habitable Planet* (London: Penguin, 1987).

Thompson, E.P. *et. al. Exterminism and Cold War* (London: Verso, 1982).

Tickner, J. Ann. "Local Self-Reliance Versus Power Politics: Conflicting Priorities of National Development, *Alternatives* XI, October 1986, 461-484.

Tilly, Charles. "Models and Realities of Popular Collective Action," *Social Research* 52, Winter 1985, 717-748.

Touraine, Alain. "An Introduction to the Study of Social Movements," *Social Research* 52, Winter 1985, 749-788.

————"Social Movements, Revolution and Democracy," *Graduate Faculty of Philosophy Journal* 10, 1986, 129-146.

————*The Voice and the Eye: An Analysis of Social Movements* (Cambridge: Cambridge University Press, 1981).

Verhagen, Koenraad. *Self-Help Promotion: a Challenge to the NGO Community* (Amsterdam: Royal Tropical Institute, 1987).

Visvanathan, Shiv. "Bhopal: The Imagination of a Disaster," *Alternatives* XI, January 1986, 147-165.

————"From the Annals of the Laboratory State," *Alternatives* XII, January 1987, 37-60.

Walker, R.B.J., ed. *Culture, Ideology and World Order* (Boulder: Westview Press, 1984).

Wells, Troth, and Foo Gaik Sim. *Till They Have Faces: Women and Consumers* (Penang: International Organization of Consumers Unions, 1987).

Williams, Raymond. *The Year 2000* (New York: Pantheon, 1983).

————"Toward Many Socialisms," *Socialist Review 85,* January-February 1986, 46-49.

Wolf, Eric. *Europe and the People Without History* (Berkeley: University of California Press, 1982).

World Commission on Environment and Development. *Our Common Future* (Oxford: Oxford University Press, 1987).

World Resources Institute. *World Resources 1987: An Assessment of the Resource Base that Supports the Global Economy* (New York: Basic Books, 1987).

Worsley, Peter. *The Three Worlds: Culture and Development* (Chicago: University of Chicago Press, 1984).

Zielonka, Jan. "Popular Movements in Poland: The Case of the Committee for Social Self-Defence (KSS-KOR), *Alternatives* IX, Spring 1984, 565-579.